S0-ECN-260

Net-Working

Teaching, Learning
& Professional Development
with the Internet

LB
1044.87
.N47
1999
west

edited by Kwok-Wing Lai

UNIVERSITY OF OTAGO PRESS

Published by University of Otago Press
PO Box 56/56 Union St, Dunedin, New Zealand
Fax: 03 479 8385, e-mail: university.press@otago.ac.nz

First published 1999
© Kwok-Wing Lai and individual authors 1999
ISBN 1 877133 68 X

Cover image by Ashleigh Taylor (5), Randwick Park School, Manurewa.
Runner-up in the 1998 *Computers in New Zealand Schools*
Computer Graphics Competition, 5-9 years category.

Text design by Jenny Cooper
Printed by Otago University Print

Contents

Preface

Since our last book *Words have Wings: Teaching and Learning with Computer Networks* was published three years ago, there have been a lot of new developments in the use of the Internet and the World Wide Web in schools. As expected, there are now models of faster and more powerful computers, more user-friendly systems and application software, as well as more advanced browser technology to make Internet surfing more appealing to novice users. More schools have been connected to the Internet and have established their presence by hosting their own websites on the Net. As well, new ideas and practices about Web use in the classroom have been developed and tried out, and more teachers have become computer literate or what some have called 'network literate'. With all these developments, however, there is one thing that has not changed: information and communication technology (ICT) is far from well integrated into the school curriculum because there is a lack of professional development.

One of the major reasons for the lack of professional development is the lack of resources. This book is written specifically to assist teachers and educators to meet this need. We believe that the use of computer-mediated communications (CMC) in education has the potential to create new learning environments and opportunities for both teachers and students. To realise this potential, however, there is a need for teachers to be well-informed not only about the nature of this new medium of communication, but also about the psychological, social, cultural, and curricular implications related to its implementations in the classroom. We have to make the technology work for us. Thus, the title of this book: the NET should be WORKing for teachers, not the other way round.

This book has ten chapters. The introductory chapter outlines some of the misconceptions surrounding the use of computer-mediated communication in the classroom and highlights the importance of the teacher in a CMC learning environment. Chapter 2 explores issues related to the use of ICT in the New Zealand school curriculum. As well, it proposes a conceptual framework to reflect on the possibilities of Internet Mediated Learning (IML) across the curriculum. Chapters 3–6 focus more on the practical aspects of Web use in the classroom. Chapter 3 discusses ways of handling and evaluating information gathered from the Internet; Chapter 4 is an Internet and Web resource guide that documents useful curriculum materials for both primary and secondary teachers; Chapter 5 outlines the process of designing and implementing CMC projects in schools; and Chapter 6 discusses issues related to designing school websites. Chapters 7–10 discuss several pertinent issues in the use of CMC in education. Chapter 7 focuses on rural education; Chapter 8 on networking and professional development; Chapter 9 on ethical and legal issues involved in the use of the Internet in the classroom, including the controversial issue of censorship. The focus of the last chapter is on women's participation in online communication.

I believe in collaboration, and many people have worked closely with me in producing this book. I am particularly grateful for the support of the contributors. It has been a joy to work with this committed and talented group of people. The publication schedule has been exceptionally tight but they were very willing and able to meet the deadline. I also wish to thank Wendy Harrex, the managing editor of the University of Otago Press, and her team, for their unfailing support. It is their professional skills and hard work that have enabled this book to be published on schedule. The support of my colleagues at the University of Otago, during a most unsettling time, is also gratefully acknowledged.

Finally, I must thank my wife, Sook-Han, for her encouragement, patience, and love. It would not be possible for me to spend so many late hours at work without knowing that she was behind me wholeheartedly. I also wish to thank my children, Shang-Chin and Keng-Yin, for their understanding and smiles. Without their support, this book would not have materialised. I am pleased to dedicate this book to them.

KWOK-WING LAI
School of Education, University of Otago

1 Teaching, Learning, and Professional Development: The Teacher Matters Most

Kwok-Wing Lai

According to a survey conducted by the *Business Week* (1997), the number of Web users in the United States alone has doubled from 20 million in 1996 to 40 million in 1997, showing a tremendous increase of interest in using the Internet in recent years. No doubt this trend will continue into the next millennium. In terms of Internet connectivity in schools, access in the USA also has skyrocketed with 85 per cent of public schools having Internet connections in 1998, an increase of 21 per cent over the previous year (Market Data Retrieval, 1998). Further increase is expected, as President Clinton has set a goal of having every classroom and library connected to the Internet by the year 2000 (Benton Foundation, 1997). In New Zealand, there has recently been a huge increase in Internet connectivity in schools as well. For example, World Wide Web access has increased in primary schools from 6 per cent in 1995 to 37 per cent in 1996, and in secondary schools from 19 per cent to 63 per cent in the same period (Telecom Education Foundation, 1996). One indication of the widespread use of the World Wide Web in New Zealand schools in late 1998 is that over 300 school websites (out of a total of about 2,800) were registered with the *CWA Education Web*'s registry (http://www.cwa.co.nz/eduweb/edu/nzschool.html). No doubt many more school websites not registering with this database are around and are currently using the Web for a variety of teaching and learning purposes.

While there is an obvious increase in the access to information technology, and particularly to the Internet and the World Wide Web, information and communication technology (ICT) is far from fully integrated into the school curriculum or universally used by teachers in their classrooms (Abdal-Haqq, 1995). Even in the USA, for example, according to one survey (Market Data Retrieval, 1998), 22 per cent of public schools reported that none of their teachers used computers daily in 1998. When computers are used, they are either used informally or are employed as an alternative or an add-on to the existing curriculum. No wonder research in ICT use in education, while documenting exemplary case studies, has so far reported little major impact in the classroom (Brownell, 1997).

Whether and how the Internet and the World Wide Web will be integrated into the school curriculum depends mainly on the understanding and knowledge of the teachers, as well as their beliefs and practice in teaching and learning. Teachers need to be clear in their minds about the educational values of using the Internet and the World Wide Web before they adopt the technology in their classrooms. Just putting computers into the classroom and connecting them to the Internet cannot guarantee that students will learn more, faster, and better (Chavez, 1998). The aim of this introductory chapter is to outline some misconceptions and illusions about the use of computer-mediated communication (CMC) in the classroom, and to highlight the important role of the teacher in a computer-supported learning environment as well as the need for further professional development.

Misconception 1: More Information the Better

With the advent of ICT, we can easily have the world's information right at our fingertips. Hailed as the world's largest library, one can virtually get every last bit of information from the Internet. It is suggested that going to the Web will give a traditional 'information-poor' classroom valuable and useful resources, as online information is current, comprehensive, readily accessible, represented in various formats, and comes from primary sources. As well, information can be gathered first-hand when students engage in dialogues with online experts (Alloway *et al.*, 1996). Traditional approaches to learning are normally content-driven, and based on printed materials such as the textbook. With the use of the World Wide Web, students can organise their own learning in a more goal-driven manner.

Information overload and chaos

To gather information from the Web, however, requires a whole new set of information accessing and processing skills previously not available to teachers and students. The library is very often used as a metaphor for the Internet but, unlike a library system, information on the Internet is distributed in a disconnected fashion; it is not situated in a context, and anyone who has access to a Web server can publish personal information publicly. The return from a Web search is almost instant, but what you get is a list of totally unrelated site addresses. In a library where books are organised in a particular system (e.g. the Dewey decimal system) each book is placed in a wider context and in a sense they are all connected to each other. Getting information from the Internet is quick if you have a fast connection but sifting through screens and screens of information and digging out the useful ones requires time and skills, even if you have a specific topic of search in mind. Users are faced with the problem of knowing what to attend to when they are bombarded with multiple streams of information as well as how to integrate them perceptually, cognitively and physically (Marchionini & Maurer, 1995). Current browser technology does not offer adequate assistance as limited search history is kept (by bookmarking or checking the history files). Also, record-keeping becomes a major issue when information is searched in multiple settings (Alloway *et al.*, 1996).

At present, it seems that teachers and parents are more concerned with speeding up their Internet connections in order to gather more information in a shorter time. To these users, it is important not to miss out any information. They seldom reflect on the question of why they needed the information in the first place. As well, the quality of the information retrieved and whether it serves educational purposes are largely ignored. Postman (1992) maintains that it is more important for learners to pay attention to what problems can be solved by additional information and to reflect on the implications and consequences of the process of information gathering, than simply to acquire skills to generate, retrieve, gather, and distribute more information, in easier and faster ways. As we are driven to access unneeded information, not only will we reach information overload, but we will also experience what Postman (1992) called 'information chaos'. There is a danger that 'an excess of information may actually crowd out ideas, leaving the young mind distracted by sterile, disconnected facts, lost among shapeless heaps of data' (Roszak, 1986, p.88). Students may have to be taught that they do not need that much information.

Information overload does not occur only when one retrieves information from the Web. When participating in computer-mediated conferencing, such as a USENET newsgroup discussion, users may also experience information overload or chaos as they are overwhelmed by conference postings and lose track of the discussion threads.

The Internet has transformed the way we approach knowledge and the source of expertise. Very often when we encounter a problem, instead of going to a human expert, or searching the library catalogues systematically for information, we now type a keyword into our search engine and see what we can get from the Web. As well, we may post our questions to a discussion list, hoping to return some expert answers. This gives us an illusion that we now have more control and freedom in our learning. It is in fact a paradox. The Web, as an interactive medium of communication, should be a user-control medium. However, just like using any other interactive media, the user 'expects to have control, and yet … does not know enough to be given full control' (Laurillard, 1995, p. 185). The lack of control is particularly evident for beginner users as they seldom have the skills to search or evaluate information successfully by themselves. Web search exercises become chaotic and confusing for students who do not have proper guidance and support. As a result, they may 'over-generalise from instances, remain unaware of incompleteness, fail to recognise inconsistencies' (Laurillard, 1995, p. 186) and cannot meet their goals. Some learners may even be misled into believing that conducting research on the Web simply means collecting as much information as possible.

From information to personal knowledge
In dealing with the problem of information overload, software engineers hope to develop more intelligent search agents that are more responsive to the needs of the user. It is hoped that by constructing a better user profile, Web searches will be more focused and more appropriate information will be returned by the search engines. This could perhaps reduce the amount of information retrieved in each search exercise but cannot solve the more basic problem of how to convert disconnected facts (information) into usable personal knowledge. To make information useful and accessible at a later stage, students have to be able to select the information needed, organise it into a structure, and link it to their existing knowledge structure so that it can be used to solve problems in other settings, thereby producing new ideas. There are therefore different depths (or levels) in communicating with information, from simple communication (i.e. gathering information) to production of knowledge. More information does not mean more knowledge. Connecting information into a structure and giving it personal meaning is an individual as well as a social process that requires a lot of reflection. Reflecting on the information selected is essential to create ideas

and knowledge. The Web in itself provides no structure to assist such a process. To use the Web as a tool for reflective thinking, a supportive learning environment has to be designed. Without critical reflection, the information retrieved is merely a collection of fragmented textual, graphical and audio elements without personal meaning for the learner (Reeves, 1993).

Reflective inquiry

As we need more reflection rather than more information, it is essential to design Web-based activities and tasks that encourage and engage students in a process of reflective inquiry. A reflective process involves learners querying the implications of the information, comparing it with their own experience and creating links to their existing knowledge structures so that new conceptual knowledge is formed and can be applied in different settings (Laurillard, 1995). It takes time and effort for learners to reflect on their experience. Time spent in gathering information reduces the time much needed for reflection. Whenever the learning process forces the pace, it disadvantages students' reflective inquiry. Recently it has become popular to use project-based work in schools. Project-based work is best supported in a Web environment. It allows learners to work with the teacher and other students, and to work at their own pace and set their own goals, thus giving them the opportunity to integrate their experiential and conceptual knowledge (Laurillard, 1995).

Misconception 2: CMC is Student-Centred Education

Apart from gathering information from the Web, teachers and students increasingly use the Internet for communicative purposes. Although the Internet is championed as a huge information archive, I believe its potential lies in its capability to help users reach out to other people. There are software tools that support different modes of communication, from synchronous to asynchronous, and from one-to-one and one-to-many, to many-to-many interaction. Computer conferencing software can be used to support a shared discussion by a group of people. The software allows participants to access a central host computer and discussion is facilitated by posting messages to this computer. It has been suggested that, because it is independent from time and place, text-based computer-mediated conferencing can connect students to a collaborative, interactive and democratic environment, thus breaking down some of the traditional barriers in education (McCabe, 1998).

Computer-mediated communication (CMC) indeed has the potential to support a learner-centred environment. The following quote, referred to in a previous book edited by the author (Lai, 1996), is still relevant today:

> If effective teaching and learning call for a way and a place to express and explore interests, to raise and respond to questions, to discover, practise and experiment with ideas and cognitive skills, to identify and examine relevant information and ideas, and to broaden and deepen individual ways of thinking about the world by providing the opportunity to consider and evaluate alternative views both privately and through interactive 'live' discussions, then certainly CMC more than qualifies (Marantz & England, 1993, p. 74).

CMC is more than a solution to spatial and temporal limitations of traditional classroom communication. In computer conferencing, as participants respond more specifically to the contents of the messages rather than to the attributes of the authors (such as their age or status), learners have more time and space to reflect on the message contents (Henri, 1995; Lai, 1997). Time is needed to organise and express thoughts. In the process the learner has to articulate and edit his or her thoughts and make them explicit for other people to understand. The learner thus is forced into a reflective mode that may result in thoughtful and well-constructed contributions. Conference transcripts also provide a useful record for reflection at a later stage. As well, as students in an online discussion environment can maintain an online personality because of the delayed nature of communication, they can manage the presentation of their identity in more thoughtful ways (Feenberg, 1989). Reflective inquiry is facilitated in a supportive group discussion as attitudes and thinking can be safely challenged (Thorpe, 1995).

However, it should be noted that students might have difficulties in publishing their thoughts publicly on the Web if they lack guidance or are inadequately supported. Online communication is a mixture of spoken dialogue and written interaction and participants can become too selfconscious about their online messages. Davie (1989) made the following observations a long while ago:

> I think that for graduate students, the problem seems to lie in the perception that leaving a note in the conference is an act of publishing, rather than an act of speech. As a student confronts the issue for the first time (or maybe at any time) life scripts relating to significant other's reactions to one's written work are activated. We become overly concerned about how others will view our writing (Davie, 1989, p. 80).

Students participating in my online classes have occasionally expressed such fear. For example, one of the students posted the following message to a class discussion (Lai, 1997):

> I didn't actively participate in any of the discussion topics, not through lack of interest or desire. I did find the conference discussions interesting; however, I was not quite confident enough to contribute my own ideas. Seeing my thoughts and opinions on the computer screen in the knowledge that others would be reading and judging my very emerging ideas seemed just too frightening (Participant M).

The permanence of the written word was too threatening for this student. Without being given adequate reassurance and support, she might have become a 'lurker' who was unwilling to take part in a critical reflective process at the social level. Fortunately, she became an active participant once she had been reassured about the nature of the conference and her role as an interlocutor.

CMC and interactivity
The Web as a medium of communication can support a high level of interactivity. However, we have to be careful when we talk about interactivity in a Web-based learning environment. There are several levels of interaction in such an environment as the learner may interact with the browser or the conferencing software, the information

gathered, or other participants in the conferencing environment. According to Bretz (1983, cited in Henri, 1995), a genuine interactive behaviour requires the presence of both a transmitter and a receiver of information, the two expressing themselves in turn and exchanging roles with each new transmission; there is no prepared scenario to control their communication. As suggested by Plowman (1996), there is not necessarily a correlation between the sophistication of the technology and the level of interactivity. For example, a very sophisticated conferencing software such as Lotus's *Learning Space* may not result in a higher level of interactivity between the participants than would a simple mailing software. This is because interactivity has more to do with the design of the learning environment and the relationship of the participants than with the technology used.

CMC and participation

Some researchers argue that because of the lack of social cues, communication on the Internet is inherently more democratic and participatory than in traditional face-to-face classroom settings. Communications and interactions in an Internet environment are distributed horizontally rather than vertically, as is commonly found in traditional classrooms. Horizontal communication is said to help break down the hierarchical relationship of the participants. Traditionally, the teacher has been viewed as the controller and distributer of information, and thus the source of power in the classroom. Now that every participant can produce and validate information, this learning environment has become more democratic and learners have more control of their learning. However, whether communication in a computer-mediated environment can be truly horizontal again depends very much on the role of the teacher. Although communication technology reduces some social and status cues, these cues are by no means totally absent. For example, a participant can achieve status by posting more messages and it is not uncommon to find discussion being dominated by a small group of participants (Lai, 1996).

The teacher matters

When examining the educational technologies used by teachers since 1920, Cuban (1986) concluded that each of the machine technologies (film, radio, instructional television and computers) went through a cycle of expectations, rhetoric, policies and limited use. I suspect CMC is at present going through its rhetoric cycle, as studies in the field overwhelmingly assert its importance in helping create a learner-centred environment. There is no doubt that we can identify a score of benefits from using CMC in the classroom in supporting interactive, collaborative, and active learning (Lai, 1996). However, we should be reminded that CMC as a medium of communication in itself does not make for a learner-centred education. In fact, research (e.g. see McCabe, 1998) has shown that CMC can support a variety of learning environments, from teacher-led lecturing to student-centred seminars or workshops. It is teachers' attitudes towards technology, their beliefs in teaching and learning, and their styles of teaching that determine how students use the Web and what sort of learning experience will be acquired. For example, teachers who do not believe in exploratory learning may structure a Web search exercise in such a way as to explore the Internet by bookmarking websites or by providing prescribed worksheets for students to follow. In this case, although CMC is used, limited control is given to the learner and the learning process is rather passive. Similarly, when the Web is used to deliver a course, it can be designed in a variety of ways, reflecting the teaching styles and the beliefs of the teachers. The Web can be used to archive course materials such as lecture notes or examination questions in such a way that it is used primarily as an electronic page-turner. The Web thus can easily be used to replicate a traditional classroom setting where the student speaks, and the teacher responds by confirming, approving, and reinforcing (Henri, 1995).

Using the Internet does not only let teachers and students do things faster but requires a shift of paradigms in teaching and learning. It provides an opportunity to develop a totally new relationship between the teacher and the learner, where teachers take up the role of a facilitator or mentor in a learner-centred environment with non-deterministic learning outcomes. Here the role of the teacher, rather than the technology, is crucial.

Misconception 3: Lack of Social and Interpersonal Communication

Too much attention has been placed on the cognitive aspect of computer-mediated communication. It is perhaps time for teachers to look at the social and interpersonal implications of using the Internet or the Web in the learning process. As has been well documented, learning is best supported in a social environment (for example, refer Scott, Cole, & Engel, 1992). As observed by Shneiderman (1993),

> I see more clearly than before that the path to motivating students is that joy of creation, exploration, and discovery. I see also that these processes are social in nature and that shared experience in class and through teamwork projects are vital.

Earlier research on computer-mediated discussion has criticised the lack of contextual and social cues of this mode of communication and maintained that interaction and discussion in this environment by and large occurs in a social vacuum (Baym, 1995). Because body language and facial expression cannot be conveyed, it is argued that there is little room to exchange personal, interpersonal and social information, which results in a negative social climate. CMC is therefore not considered as a medium for socialising and interpersonal exchange. More recent studies, however, dispute this 'cues filtered out' approach and downplay the influence of the computer in the communication process. For example, a number of studies (e.g. Riel & Levin,1990; Baym, 1995; and Gunawardena,1995) have reported factors other than the computer as contributing to the formation of social context and climate as well as in the development of learning communities. Empirical studies have found a great deal of social interaction in both formal (e.g. see Lai, 1998) and informal computer conferencing (e.g. see Baym, 1995). In these studies, it is noted that the lack of social cues can usually be compensated for and that factors such as group characteristics, purpose of interaction, and infrastructure support will impact on the nature of the communication and determine whether a social community can be cultivated

(Gunawardena, 1995; Baym, 1995). In a formal university course designed by the author and delivered on the Web, students shared personal stories and socialised extensively in the learning environment (Lai, 1997, 1998). One striking example came from a computer conference about Internet censorship, where strong feelings were communicated. One of the students who migrated to New Zealand from a former Eastern European communist country related his personal experience on censorship under the communist rule and vowed that he would never ever live in a country where anything could be censored by any authority.

His posting triggered a stream of responses. Within just three hours, there were two responses (altogether his posting was cited ten times). The sharing of personal feelings actually helped stimulate the participants' thinking and provided insights in examining issues related to Internet censorship in this particular conference. The following comment is an example of how emotions interact with the cognitive aspect of learning:

> B, I agree with E, do not apologize for an emotional or personal comment on this topic, it has taken me two days to feel comfortable in making a contribution to this conference after reading your message. For me this is the first time that a conference has 'come alive', prior to this, conferences have been stimulating and a steep but enjoyable learning curve, however, your message stopped me dead and forced me to re-evaluate my thinking on censorship. (Student I)

As suggested by Walther (1996), computer-mediated communication is rarely impersonal. On the contrary, it can support hyperpersonal communication, which is more socially desirable than the experience of face-to-face interaction. According to Walther,

> CMC liberates by transmitting information across distance in almost no time and keeps it there until needed. It limits the kinds of communication cues at our disposal ... and allows us selectively to minimize or maximize our interpersonal effects ... CMC affords opportunities, however, to communicate as desired; an impulse that seems to be inherently human yet may be more easily enacted via technology (Walther, 1996, p.33).

The role of the teacher is again crucial in enhancing social and interpersonal communication in a Web-based learning environment. For example, in the online courses offered by the author (refer to Chapter 6 of this book for more information), a rich social context is provided to encourage interpersonal exchanges. Features such as a coffee lounge, synchronous chat rooms, photos of the participants and their biographies were included to create some social presence. Collaborative tasks were designed so that students could work together and this provided yet another opportunity for interaction (Lai, 1998).

The Need for Professional Development

It is important to reiterate that no matter how much technology a school has and how sophisticated it is, it is the teacher that matters most to the student's learning. The importance of the teacher in the learning process is underlined in a report titled *What Matters Most: Teaching for America's Future,* commissioned by the National

Commission on Teaching and American's Future (NCTAF, 1996), which concludes:

> What teachers know and can do is the most important influence on what students learn. Educators and policy makers can talk about things like governance structures, instructional methods, curricula, and standards – all crucial elements in making school more effective for children – but that connection between student and teacher is something we can get passionate about ... Teaching is what matters most (Available at http://www.tc.columbia.edu/ ~teachcomm/What.htm).

This report maintains that one of the major barriers to providing students with access to caring, competent, and qualified teaching in schools is the lack of professional development for teachers. This seems to be a worldwide problem. For example, in New Zealand, the Education Review Office (1997) reported that between 1992 and 1996, only 7,000 (14 per cent) of the approximately 50,000 full- and part-time teachers received training in information technology through Ministry of Education funded professional development contracts. In the USA, it was reported that in 1994 only 15 per cent of teachers had nine hours or more of training in educational technology and fewer than 10 per cent of recent teacher graduates felt that they were competent to use electronic network collaboration capabilities (Office of Technology Assessment, 1995).

The lack of training is definitely not due to the lack of demand. Teachers clearly perceive a need for continuing professional development. For example, in New Zealand, a recent study conducted in Otago and Southland with a sample of 475 secondary and area school teachers (36 per cent of the population) and 23 principals (53 per cent of the population) reports that teachers valued professional development highly, with 81 per cent ranking it as very important to their work (Cowan & Diorio, 1998). An earlier report also confirms that teachers were keen to participate in professional development activities in the use of computers in the curriculum if these programmes were available to them (Renwick, 1994).

Barriers to professional development

So why is there a lack of professional development for teachers? There are a number of reasons but the most pertinent barriers, according to several reports (e.g. see Renwick, 1994), are the lack of funding and relevant programmes.

It is indeed surprising to know that so little money has been spent in providing professional development for technology-using teachers, compared to the funds spent on computer hardware and software. For example, it is reported that in the USA, school districts only spent 1–3 per cent of their resources on teacher development (NCTAF, 1996). That is why, according to this report, most elementary school teachers had only 8.3 minutes of preparatory time for every hour they taught, while high school teachers had just 13 minutes per class hour. In the educational technology area, another report shows that only about 15 per cent of the typical educational technology budget was devoted to professional development and it is recommended that this figure should be increased to at least 30 per cent (President's Committee of Advisors on Science and Technology Panel on Educational Technology, 1997). The study conducted by Cowan and Diorio (1998), mentioned previously, reports that schools in Otago and

Southland spent on average 5.3 per cent of their annual budgets on professional development in 1997, already higher than the 4 per cent reported in an earlier report published by the Education Review Office (1995).

Professional development activities may not be relevant to the needs of the teachers because they are very often piecemeal activities organised in response to some new development of software applications. There is no long-term planning. The following quote represents how some teachers feel about professional development:

> 'If I told you how many courses I've taken in computers, you would roll on the floor,' says Bonnie Bracey, a teacher who was appointed by President Clinton to a federal panel on information technology from 1993 to 1995. The problem is, those courses had 'no connection to what I teach,' she adds. 'It took us a long time to figure that out.' (Zehr, 1998).

Providing Relevant Professional Development for Teachers

In implementing ICT in schools, teachers face issues such as how to use ICT as pedagogical tools, how to integrate ICT into their existing school curriculum, how to plan and organise resources for students to use, and how to assess students in an information technology-rich learning environment (Dillon, 1998). A relevant professional development programme is more than skill training. It involves changes in attitudes, values and beliefs. To develop appropriate ICT professional development programmes, teachers, course designers, and policy-makers need to have an understanding of the process and stages of development in implementing an innovation in schools. As well, they need to foster the conditions which will lead to successful implementation.

Understanding the process and stages of development

Like any other innovation, it takes time for teachers to adopt ICT in their practice, as it involves changes in the ways of doing things. According to Somekh (1998), teachers need to have an understanding of the situational nature of innovation and there is no blueprint to manage this complex and non-mechanical process effectively. Teachers also need to develop a belief that they can make a positive contribution to change in the classroom. As well, a critical mass is needed to provide collegial support, and the key players should form a partnership with the community and industry. Teachers should also understand the importance of professional development and that conducting research into their own practice is a form of professional development.

Innovation goes through stages of development. In designing professional development programmes for ICT, Somekh (1998) suggests a six-stage model:

- *Orientation* is the stage when participants seek out information about the innovation.
- *Preparation* comes next when participants are getting ready to begin.
- *Routine* is the first stage of implementation, when participants establish low-level, routine use.

- *Refinement* is the stage when participants seek to refine and improve their use of the innovation.
- *Integration* is the stage when participants take steps to integrate their use of the innovation fully into their practice.
- *Creative integration* is the stage when participants seek more effective ways of using the innovation, going beyond what has been achieved by others. (p. 17).

In providing professional development in ICT, it is therefore important to identify the needs of the teachers and the stage of development they have reached, and then design a programme to meet their needs, with the aim of scaffolding as well as extending their knowledge and skills to get to the next stage. According to Somekh's model (1998), in the first three stages the focus is more on developing the teachers' personal and professional skills in using ICT (for example, using specific educational software or Internet access software). In the next three stages, the focus will be more on how ICT can be integrated into the existing curriculum as well as enhancing it. In these latter stages, it involves changes in the teachers' values and beliefs as well as their practices. The roles of the teachers will also be re-examined in relation to the underpinning theories of learning (McDougall & Squires, 1997).

Considering standards

In recent years, frameworks or standards of ICT competencies for teachers have begun to emerge as a core of information technology skills have been developed in the school curriculum. These standards may provide some guidelines as to what could be included in an ICT professional development programme. In the UK, the National Council for Educational Technology, in conjunction with two other professional organisations, has developed a framework of competence for pre-service student teachers. In this framework, a teacher is expected to have 'a holistic understanding of the ways in which IT contributes to teaching and learning, an understanding of the developing nature of IT capability, and an awareness that it is integral to the whole structure and purpose of the curriculum' (Dillon, 1998, p. 39). In implementing ICT, a proficient teacher is expected to 'use the computer to support everyday classroom or field work activities at an appropriate curriculum level, assess the learning which takes place and ensure progression, and bring to this an evaluative framework that enables critical reflection on how IT changes the teaching and learning processes' (p. 40).

In the USA, the International Society of Technology in Education (ISTE) has developed a set of foundation standards adopted by the National Council on Accreditation of Teacher Education (NCATE). Teachers seeking initial certification are expected to meet these standards. In the ISTE standards, teachers are expected to acquire skills and knowledge in three areas. First, they are expected to know some basic computer/technology concepts and demonstrate knowledge of the uses of computers and technology in business, industry, and society. They are also expected to use multimedia computer systems to run software and to access, generate and manipulate data; and to publish results. They will also evaluate performance of hardware and software components of computer systems and apply basic troubleshooting strategies as needed. The second area concerns personal and professional use of technology by applying these tools to enhance their own professional growth and productivity. They will use technology in communicating, collaborating, conducting research and solving problems. In addition, they will plan and participate in activities that encourage lifelong learning and will promote equitable, ethical, and legal use of computer/technology resources. In the third area, teachers need to apply technology in instruction in their grade level and subject areas. They must plan and deliver instructional units that integrate a variety of software, applications, and learning tools. Lessons developed must reflect effective grouping and assessment strategies for diverse populations (the full document is available at http://www.iste.org).

New Zealand has no such standards. There are some very general guidelines, however, that teachers may follow. For example, *The Capable Teacher*, a document recently published by the New Zealand Education Review Office (1998), suggested that a capable teacher should demonstrate informed professional knowledge of appropriate technology and resources and should (a) use a range of resources and technology that demonstrates informed knowledge of what is available in the school and the wider community; (b) use resources and technology in a planned and relevant way to contribute to the achievement of learning objectives; and (c) demonstrate willingness to extend skills in using information technology.

Providing role models

Pre-service teacher education has been widely criticised in the literature for failing to develop relevant programmes for student teachers because teacher educators do not provide a good model of appropriate use of ICT in their own teaching or research. Very often these teacher educators do not have sufficient understanding of the new demands on classroom teachers to use ICT in their teaching. After reviewing models of using technology in teacher education programmes, Brownell (1997) concluded that it is important for teacher educators to serve as role models, as their attitudes and uses of technology in their classrooms will greatly influence their students. This underlines the need to provide role models for teachers, not only in formal teacher education but in school-based professional development programmes as well. For example, a small group of teachers in a school can be trained initially to provide models of teaching and then a critical mass of ICT users can be created. To be effective, a whole-school approach, aiming at infusing ICT across the school curriculum and involving every teacher rather than offering a single course for a selected few, should be adopted. Teachers also need to be exposed to technology-rich classrooms and be shown what can be done in such environments. If teachers do not see effective practices in other schools, it is unlikely that they will use them in their own school. Collegial support therefore is essential for change to occur in an educational setting.

Providing vision and leadership

There is a need to provide leadership at the school, community, and national level. The aim is to transform the culture of the school to one in which ICT is seen as an agent of changing relationships between students and teachers and between learners and knowledge construction. Leadership is essential in generating a vision for the school regarding the use of ICT. Once a vision is formed, an ICT plan should be developed. This is not just a plan for purchasing computer hardware or software. Rather, it is a plan for integrating information and communication technologies across the curriculum, for professional development of both teachers and supporting staff, and for building a support structure to sustain the innovation. The plan should also include specific outcomes for both teachers and students and the associated costs. The information technology plan will serve as a road map for ICT activities. It will be used to justify future expenditures, set priorities, define needs, and provide a timetable for future development.

Providing resources

Resources in professional development programmes for technology-using teachers include not only computer hardware and software but time as well. Time is the single scarcest resource of teachers. Lack of time is almost universally considered as the most important barrier to teachers participating in professional development activities (Little, 1993). Teachers have to be shown that using ICT is worth the time and effort. Unfortunately, at present very few teachers see that ICT is beneficial to the student's learning. For example, a survey in 1998 reports that only 13.4 per cent of the teachers in the USA believed Internet access has helped students to achieve better results (Market Data Retrieval, 1998). It is time-consuming to use ICT in the classroom. For a technology-using teacher, the convenience of showing a *PowerPoint* presentation in class comes dearly, with hours of time spending in preparation. Teachers simply do not have the time to experiment with this innovation. No wonder data in the Cowan and Diorio study (1998) showed that almost four-fifths of the respondents indicated that time was a major obstacle for their professional development. How to give teachers more free time for further professional development is an issue that has to be considered and resolved if professional development in ICT is to be effective.

Ownership of professional development programmes

Many professional development programmes have been criticised by teachers because of the lack of ownership. Programmes would be more effective if teachers themselves were involved in planning them, as there is always a tension between meeting the needs of individual teachers and the need to advance the organisational goals of their schools and the funding authorities such as the Ministry of Education. Traditional professional development activities, such as the one-day conference and seminar, usually adopt a top-down model in terms of organisation, and teachers have little input into the design. This provides limited channels for participants to own the programmes or to collaborate and communicate with each other. The emerging consensus is that teachers should be involved in planning their own learning experience rather than being passive recipients of knowledge. School-based professional development activities designed by teachers for small clusters of schools should be encouraged to provide a sense of ownership.

Building online communities

The isolation of teachers is a worldwide phenomenon. For example, New Zealand statistics show that 52 per cent of all primary teachers (full primary and contributing) are in schools with fewer than seven teachers and 36 per cent of them are in schools with fewer than two teachers (Ministry of Education, 1998). Physical isolation also implies emotional and intellectual isolation. Encouragement to develop or participate in professional communities would help alleviate the problem. According to Kozma (1996),

> Typical summer institutes (how about one day workshop) for teachers do little to alter the isolated and isolating character of classroom teaching. Too often, teachers returning from these experiences have little opportunity to implement what they have learned and make significant changes in established practices in their home schools. Ongoing, collaborative approaches to professional development help establish a professional culture that creates self-expectations among teachers that they will be studying some aspect of practice, comparing notes on implementation, seeking new ideas, and help each other out. (Kozma, cited in NCTAF, 1996)

A community is defined here as a group of people with shared interests who interact with each other either face-to-face or virtually (Thayer-Bacon, 1996). In an online community, membership can be fleeting and temporary, or it can last for a lifetime. Unlike a physical community where sharing the same space is essential to keep the community going, in a virtual community a common interest or a common experience is the key factor. As has been reported previously (Lai, 1996), an online community is flexible and democratic,

- providing validation for pedagogical method of teaching;
- fostering intellectual stimulation and creating multiple perspectives;
- enhancing proximate community;
- facilitating peer-peer collaboration by sharing exemplary practices and course materials, and by co-constructing, reviewing, and publishing resources;
- broadening teachers' learning horizons by discussing new beliefs and teaching practices.

There has been a growing interest in the educational community about using the Web as an interactive communication-rich environment to enhance collaboration and shared construction of knowledge (Ravitz, 1997; Blanton, Moorman, & Trathen, 1998). To use the Internet for professional development, it is important to conceptualise it not as a knowledge presentation medium but as one that supports collaborative learning through the building of learning communities. (For a more detailed discussion on online professional development networks, refer to Chapter 8.)

Concluding Remarks

This chapter began by outlining some common misconceptions about the use of CMC in the classroom. It is hoped that raising these issues will encourage teachers to reflect on their own experience and so become more caring, competent, and qualified in the use of ICT in the school curriculum. It is the belief of the author that the teacher matters most in a computer-supported learning environment and professional development is essential if the potential for the use of ICT to support learning is to be realised. To provide a relevant professional development programme for teachers, this chapter highlighted the importance of understanding the stages the teachers are at in their ability to use the new technologies, as well as creating favourable conditions such as resourcing, role modelling, collegial support and leadership, so that its implementation is successful.

References

Abdal-Haqq, I. (1995). *Teacher Use of Instructional Technologies: Demands & Obstacles.* Available at <http://www.ed.gov/database/ERIC_Digests/ed389699.html>.

Alloway, G., et. al. (1996). Creating an inquiry-learning environment using the World Wide Web. In D. Edelson & E. Domeshek (Eds.) *Proceedings of International Conference on the Learning Science* (pp. 1-8). Charlottesville, VA: AACE.

Baym, N. (1995). The emergence of community in computer-mediated communication. In S. Jones (ed.) *Cybersociety: Computer-Mediated Communication and Community* (pp. 138-163). U.K.: Sage.

Benton Foundation (1997). *The Learning Connection: Schools in the Information Age.* Available at <http://www.benton.org/Library/Schools/connection.html>.

Blanton, W., Moorman, G., & Trathen, W. (1998). Telecommunications and teacher education: A social constructivist review. In P. Pearson & A. Iran-Nejad (eds.). *Review of Research in Education* (pp. 235-276). Washington DC: AERA.

Brownell, K. (1997). Technology in teacher education: Where are we and where do we go from here? *Journal of Technology and Teacher Education*, 5 (2/3), 117-138.

Business Week (1997, May 5). *Special Report on Internet Communities.*

Chavez, P. (1998, June 2). Do students really learn on the net? Available at <http://www.msnbc.com/news/105763.asp>.

Cowan, B. & Diorio, J. (1998). *Using Computers in the Professional Development of Teachers: An Otago/Southland Survey.* Unpublished manuscript.

Cuban, L. (1986). *Teachers and machines: The classroom use of technology since 1920.* N.Y.: Teachers College Press.

Davie (1989). Facilitation techniques for ther online tutor. In R. Mason & A. Kaye (Eds.). *Mindweave: Communication, Computers and Distance Education.* Oxford: Pergamon Press.

Dillon, P. (1998). Teaching and learning with telematics: An overview of the literature. *Journal of Information Technology for Teacher Education*, 7 (1), 33-50.

Education Review Office (1995). *In-service Training of Teachers: The Responsibility of Board of Trustees.* Wellington: Education Evaluation Reports.

Education Review Office (1997). *The Use of Information Technology in Schools.* Wellington: Education Evaluation Reports.

Education Review Office (1998). *The Capable Teacher.* Wellington: Education Evaluation Reports.

Gunawardena, C. (1995). Social presence theory and implications for interaction and collaborative learning in computer conferences. *International Journal of Educational Telecommunications*, 1 (2/3), 147-166.

Henri, F. (1995). Distance learning and computer-mediated communication: Interactive, quasi-interactive or monologue? In C. O'Malley (ed.). *Computer Supported Collaborative Learning*, (pp. 145-161). Berlin: Springer-Verlag.

Lai, K. W. (1998). Social interaction and communication in a Web-based tertiary course: Some observations. In T. Chan, A. Collins, & J. Lin (Eds.) *Global Education on the Net: Proceedings of ICCE '98* (Vol. 1, pp. 79-85). Bejing: China Higher Education Press & Berlin: Springer-Verlag.

Lai, K. W. (1997). Interactivity in Web-based learning: Some observations based on a Web-based course about CMC in education. In B. Collis & G. Knezek (eds). *Teaching and Learning in th Digital Age:*

Research into practice with Telecommunications in Educational Settings. (pp. 211-230). TCET & ISTE.

Lai, K. W. (1996). Computer-mediated communication: A new learning context. in K. W. Lai (ed.) *Words have Wings: Teaching and Learning in Computer Networks* (pp. 1-18). Dunedin: University of Otago Press.

Little, J. (1993). Teachers' professional development in a climate of educational reform. Educational Evaluation and Policy Analysis, 15(c), 129-151.

Laurillard, D. (1995). Multimedia and the changing experience of the learner. *British Journal of Educational Technology*, 26 (3), 179-189.

Marantz, B., & England, R. (1993). Can CMC teach teachers training? *Educational Media International*, *30*(2), 74-77.

Marchionini, G. & Maurer, H. (1995). The role of digital libraries in teaching and learning. *Communication of the ACM*, 38(4), 67-75.

Market Data Retrieval (1998). Technology in Education, 1998. Available at <http://www.schooldata.com/publications3.html>.

McCabe, M. (1998). Lessons from the field: Computer conferencing in higher education. *Journal of Information Technology for Teacher Education*, 7 (1), 71-87.

McDougall, A., & Squires, D. (1997). A framework for reviewing teacher professional development programmes in information technology. *Journal of Information Technology for Teacher Education*, 6 (2), 115-126.

Ministry of Education. (1998). *Education Statistics of New Zealand.* Wellington: Ministry of Education.

National Commission on Teaching and America's Future. (1996). *What Matters Most: Teaching For America's Future.* Available at <http://www.tc.columbia.edu/~teachcomm/What.htm>.

Office of Technology Assessment. U.S. Congress. (1995). *Teachers & Technology: Making the Connection.* Washington, DC: Government Printing Office.

Plowman, L. (1996). Designing interactive media for schools: A review based on contextual observation. *Information Design Journal*, 8 (3), 258-266.

Postman, N. (1992). *Technopoly: The Surrender of Culture to Technology*. New York: Alfred A. Knopf.

President's Committee of Advisors on Science and Technology Panel on Educational Technology (1997). *Report to the President on the Use of Technology to Strengthen K-12 Education in the United States.* Available at <http://www.whitehouse.gov/WH/EOP/OSTP/NSTC/PCAST/k-12ed.html#exec>.

Ravitz, J. (1997). *An ISD Model for Building Online Communities: Furthering the Dialogue*. ERIC Document ED 409 863.

Reeves, T. (1993). Research support for interactive multimedia: Existing foundations & new directions. In C. Latchem, J. Williamson & L. Henderson (Eds.). Interactive Multimedia: Practicer & Promise (pp. 79-96). London: Kogan Page.

Renwick, M. (1994). *Teacher Development in State Secondary Schools: A Pilot Study*. Wellington: New Zealand Council for Educational Research.

Riel, M. & Levin, J. (1990). Building electronic communities: Success and failure in computer networking. *Instructional Science*, 19, 145-169.

Roszak, T. (1986). *The Cult of Information*. New York: Pantheon Books.

Scott, T., Cole, M., & Engel, M. (1992). Computers and education: A cultural constructivist perspective. In G. Grant (Eds.). *Review of Research in Education* (pp. 191-251). Washington DC: AERA.

Shneiderman, B. (1993). *Education by engagement and construction: Experiences in the AT& T Teaching Theater.* Paper presented at the ED-MEDIA 93. Orlando, FL.

Somekh, B. (1998). Supporting information and communication technology innovations in higher education. *Journal of Information Technology for Teacher Education*, 7 (1), 11-32.

Telecom Education Foundation. (1996). *How Wired Are Our Schools? Telecommunications in New Zealand Schools, 1993-1996.* Wellington: Business Research Centre.

Thayer-Bacon, B. (1996). Democratic Classroom Communities. *Studies in Philisophy and Education*, 15 (4), 333-351.

Thorpe, M. (1995). Reflective learning in distance education. *European Journal of Psychology of*

Education, 10 (2), 153-167.

Walther, J. (1996). Computer-Mediated Communication: Impersonal, interpersonal, and hyperpersonal interaction. *Communication Research*, 23 (1), 3-43.

Zehr, M. (1998). Education Week, Sept 28, 1998. Available at <http://www.edweek.org/>.

2   The Wired Curriculum:
A Choice of Content, Connectivity or Community?

Mark E. Brown

Why are schools rushing to get wired? Why are so many teachers learning to surf the Internet? Why has the Internet renewed interest in the use of information and communication technologies (ICT) within the curriculum? These are important questions. This chapter critically addresses such questions before the curriculum is wired and teachers are swept away in the current tide for technology in New Zealand schools.

There is no doubt that the Internet is a major force in reshaping the nature of school. The Internet is more than just a technology; it is an evolving human phenomenon which defies simple explanation. Therefore, a deeper understanding of the Internet is required and the chapter embarks on an educational journey in search of new meanings. It challenges teachers to look past the horizon of the technology itself and venture beyond technical understandings of the Internet. Accordingly, teachers are asked to cast aside their initial enthusiasm for the first wave of Internet implementation in schools. The intention is to offer teachers a critical and enduring conceptual framework to better understand the raft of possibilities for Internet Mediated Learning (IML) across the curriculum.

In recent years, most New Zealand schools have acquired access to the Internet (Owens, 1996). The hype associated with IML, however, makes it very difficult for teachers to fully understand the technology's potential. Although most teachers have some basic knowledge of hardware and software, relatively few understand the ocean of opportunities the Internet provides for active and meaningful learning (Grabe & Grabe, 1998). For many teachers, the Internet remains a solution in search of an educational problem (Brown & Ryba, 1996). It is a large sea in which teachers are lost vessels floating with no clear direction. The point of this analogy is to demonstrate that better access to the technology does not guarantee teachers will successfully integrate the Internet within the curriculum. Such integration is dependent upon teachers with a sound conceptualisation of IML, which is linked to a contemporary understanding of the learning and teaching process. Without this understanding, there is a danger that the Internet will become merely another passing wave in the history of educational technology in the school (Collis, 1996). The need for teachers to take charge of the technology and anchor their understandings within an educational framework is the central message of this chapter.

The chapter begins by discussing the nature of ICT and IML in terms of the *New Zealand Curriculum Framework* (Ministry of Education, 1993). It argues that the Internet should be used for knowledge construction as opposed to knowledge instruction. This dichotomy is further developed by a brief account of Constructivist and Socio-cultural learning theory. These theoretical perspectives are used to contend that students must use computers to learn, rather than spending their time learning to use the Internet. Hitherto, the chapter rejects technocentric definitions of the Internet and outlines a powerful conceptual framework for the use of IML in school. Although this framework requires further refinement, it emphasises the integration of the Internet based on contemporary learning theory. The role of the teacher, nonetheless, is shown to be crucial in translating the framework into good classroom practice. Such practice is not synonymous with the Internet; it requires good teachers. Finally, a number of guidelines are provided for teachers who want to steer a new course with ICT into the uncharted waters of IML in future schools.

ICT and the New Zealand Curriculum

The role of ICT has been problematic for a number of years in the New Zealand Curriculum. There is much confusion over the term and still no generally accepted definition (Brown, 1995). It is only recently that some direction has been given as to the meaning of ICT in the New Zealand educational context. One of the interesting features of *Interactive Education: An Information and Communication Technologies Strategy for Schools* (Ministry of Education, 1998a) is the choice of terminology and the definition provided. However, the definition of ICT within this document does little to clarify widespread confusion. It further muddies the water!

The latest definition of ICT is based on a description of hardware and software. Teachers should be wary of statements that define ICT in such a restrictive way. This definition is directly at odds with a more enlightened understanding of technology and technology education. It is generally understood that technology is a process by which society identifies human problems and seeks solutions to solve them; such as, an artefact, environment or system (Burns, 1997). Hence, even the classroom as an environment is a type of ICT designed for the problem of human learning. By ignoring a broader definition of technology, the Ministry of Education does not walk its own talk! For example, the document *Technology in the New Zealand Curriculum* (Ministry of Education, 1995) is based on a more enlightened understanding of technology in school. The point is that the current definition of ICT does not provide a solid foundation upon which to build a national strategy for computers in education.

In New Zealand, the term ICT already refers to a distinctive Technological Area within the technology curriculum. In addition, it is now being identified as an important theme across all essential learning areas. According to Brown (1997), there are essentially three main dimensions to ICT within the curriculum. The figure below shows a tripartite relationship between: (a) learning specific technological knowledge and capability *in* this technological area; (b) learning *about* the relationship between this area of technology and society; and (c) learning *with* ICT across the curriculum (see Figure 1). The latter dimension transcends all the essential learning areas, whereas the other two are located within the technology curriculum.

While these three dimensions are not mutually exclusive, it is very important for teachers to understand the key differences. A recent guide on *Implementing Technology in New Zealand Schools* helps in this regard, by stating:

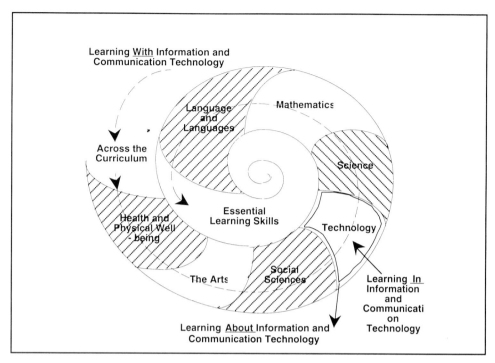

Figure 1: The dimensions of ICT in the curriculum

> It is important to make a clear distinction between technology education – the development of students' technological knowledge, capability, and understanding of the relationship between technology and society – and the use in education of learning technologies such as internet, CD-ROM ... (Ministry of Education, 1998b, p.7).

The term *Learning Technologies* is particularly significant. It signals that the main emphasis is on the learning process. In other words, learning with ICT is not an end in itself, but rather a means of helping students to become more effective learners – within and across the curriculum. In many ways, confusion over the three dimensions of ICT education could be overcome by the adoption of the term *Learning Technologies*. This term, arguably, better acknowledges the fact that ICT is not always designed for learning. Alternatively, at the expense of being pedantic, the more traditional phrase *Educational Technologies (ET)* is a preferred description as it encompasses both learning and teaching processes within a broader educational context.

The problem of nomenclature is not the main focus of this chapter. It is important, nevertheless, to locate the Internet within the context of the New Zealand Curriculum. Accordingly, the aforementioned discussion serves to demonstrate that ET is a subset of ICT and that IML is a subset of both (see Figure 2). There is little agreement, however, on the best term for describing the use of telecommunications in education, and IML is used only as it clearly signals the partnership between people and technology in the process of learning. With the terminology established, the remainder of the chapter is devoted to the Internet in the learning and teaching process.

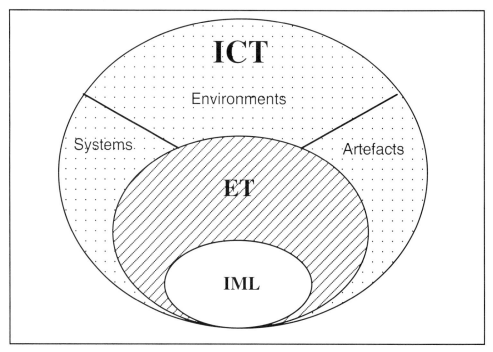

Figure 2: Locating ICT within New Zealand education

IML and Contemporary Learning Theory

The Internet provides a number of opportunities for better learning. It has the potential to support individualised instruction and at the same time make the learning experience more social. The social nature of learning is a unifying theme of contemporary learning theory (Roblyer, Edwards & Havriluk, 1997). Well-planned IML experiences, informed by educational theory, allow students to engage in challenging higher-order intellectual activities where they work with others to actively construct their own knowledge. The idea that effective learning and teaching is based on knowledge transmission is rather antiquated. There has been a cognitive revolution that Dwyer (1996) describes as a shift from knowledge instruction to knowledge construction (see Table 1). Two dominant cognitive perspectives currently influence thinking about knowledge construction and the promotion of meaningful learning: (a) Constructivist and (b) Socio-cultural theories.

Constructivism views learning as an active process of making sense of experiences in terms of prior knowledge (Duffy & Jonassen, 1991). Implicit in constructivist theory is the view that new understandings are built on existing knowledge structures and these are derived from previous experience. The basic tenet is that people learn by processing information they encounter on the basis of what they already know, and thus construct their own knowledge (Jones & Mercer, 1993). However, constructivism is often misunderstood by teachers as there are many blends of contructivist theory (Phillips, 1995). Although originally a personal theory of cognition emphasising the

Knowledge Instruction	Knowledge Construction
Teacher Centred	Student Centred
Product Driven	Process Driven
Passive Engagement	Active Engagement
Extrinsic Motivation	Intrinsic Motivation
Surface Learning	Meaningful Learning
Individualised Learning	Collaborative Learning

Table 1: Knowledge instruction vs. knowledge construction

processes that occur within the individual, recent developments in social constructivism now acknowledge that learning occurs in a definite social context. There is a wider appreciation that learning does not take place in a vacuum and that social interaction is a prerequisite for active and meaningful learning.

In like manner, socio-cultural perspectives argue that human learning is socially grounded within culture. Learning is profoundly defined as a social phenomenon; that is, conceptualised as something distributed within culture, rather than as just a set of cognitive processes thought to exist in the head (Crook, 1994). Implicit within this perspective is the idea that the environment is not just a mediator of learning. All learning is deeply embedded in social and physical contexts. There are three main themes that encompass a social-cultural view of learning: (a) the importance of culture; (b) the central role of language; and, (c) the Zone of Proximal Development (ZPD).

A basic tenet is that cognitive attributes of the individual are the outcome of engagement with culture. Vygotsky (1978) claims that a learner's experiences are initially encountered on an inter-psychological plane and only understood at the intra-psychological plane once they have been socially mediated through culture. Thus, individual accounts of cognition must incorporate a dimension of culture with a strong contextual flavour (Crook, 1994).

In contrast to earlier views of the learning process, language is thought to be an organiser of thinking and a cognitive tool that helps people think in new ways (Jones & Mercer, 1993). This assumption implies that speech and action are directly related; language is central to the development of higher-order thinking processes. Consequently, student-student communication is vital for effective learning, and teachers must create environments that promote an increasing mastery of language.

The importance of language and culturally-mediated learning is expressed through a concept known as the ZPD. The ZPD refers to the distance between actual development, as determined by independent problem solving, and the level of potential development as determined through problem-solving under adult guidance or in collaboration with more capable peers (Vygotsky, 1978). It is through shared understandings and collaborative interactions in this zone that students are scaffolded to gradually take control of their own thinking processes; they show evidence of metacognition.

Metacognitive skills are a set of higher-order thinking processes that students use to regulate their own learning. A basic premise is that 'metacognitive awareness and self-regulatory activity has its root in social interactions with others' (Reeve & Brown, 1985, p. 347). The significance of these skills is that they are attributed toward the ability to learn how to learn. In recent years, the New Zealand Curriculum has placed increasing emphasis on metacognitive and self-management skills in the development of more reflective thinkers and self-directed learners.

In sum, the duality between Constructivist and Socio-cultural theories suggest that students learn best through social interactions; where thinking processes are distributed in collaborative and reflective learning environments. A strong emphasis is placed on meaningful learning where students acquire knowledge and skills in the social and functional contexts of their use. Hence, learning should be embedded in contexts that are representative of the problems to which students will have to apply their knowledge and skills in the future. Ideally, learning experiences should 'situate cognition' in authentic problems that are relevant to the real world of students (Young, 1997). This contrasts with traditional classroom activities, where learning is often divorced from the world outside of school. The ultimate goal of situated cognition is to help students learn to think within a specific domain, and encourage the transfer of new knowledge into the ability to learn how to learn.

IML and the New Zealand Curriculum

The Internet can help transform the curriculum, but only if the technology is used to support models of learning that are known to be based on sound teaching practice. In other words, the Internet can only amplify an already sound curriculum; it cannot supplant a deficient one. Too often in the past teachers have attempted to graft new technology on to out-of-date approaches to learning (e.g. early experiences with computer-assisted instruction). Prior experience has taught us that mere exposure to vast expanses of information will not promote effective learning. It is the analysis, interpretation and evaluation of information in ways that are personally meaningful that 'adds value' to the educative process (Brown & Ryba, 1996). We now understand that it is insufficient for students to be passive recipients of large volumes of information. Using the Internet as a large diameter pipeline through which to pump increasing amounts of information will only lead to 1950s style curricula on twenty-first century networks. The lesson is that advanced technologies must be linked to advanced teaching practices.

It is generally recognised that an integrated and multi-disciplinary approach is required in order to translate the theory of knowledge construction into practice. While construction can take many different forms, the essential point is that active engagement, learner control and student collaboration are vital. An integrated curriculum designed for collaborative, cross curricular, projects and problem-based learning can result in a great deal of positive transfer across different subject areas (Perkins, 1994). Such an approach to learning requires students to use a range of problem-solving strategies and work effectively with other people. The people effects, as Ryba (1991) points out, are far more important than the machine effects when learning with new educational technologies.

Figure 3: The Internet learning dichotomy

Access to technology and the Internet, in particular, should be viewed as a starting point – not as an end in itself (Dede; cited in O'Neil, 1995). Accordingly, there is a clear dichotomy in terms of the integration of IML within the New Zealand Curriculum. Students can either learn to use the Internet, or use the Internet to learn (see Figure 3). The point of this dichotomy is to show that little will be gained from merely training students to use the Internet. Arguably, monkeys can be taught to click a mouse and thereby navigate the Web. Furthermore, the technology rapidly changes, such that newly acquired Internet skills will quickly become obsolete. In this regard, IML needs to shift from training memories to educating minds (Perkins, 1994). An emphasis on active and meaningful learning is the only defendable rationale for using the Internet within and across the curriculum.

IML and Classroom Practice

How do teachers integrate the Internet into their classroom programmes in a meaningful way? Before this question can be addressed it is important to define the Internet. The search for a simple definition, however, is no easy task. There are various dimensions to the Internet and the language associated with the different technologies can be very intimidating. Typically, the Internet is described as a 'network of networks' (Wiggins, 1994). It is a communication network that provides access to thousands of other computer networks all around the world. All you need in order to gain access to these networks is a computer, modem, telecommunications software and telephone line. It is fair to say that the telephone system is the backbone of Internet. Thus, the Internet with its labyrinth of interconnecting networks is not even a physical entity. It is merely a bunch of wires that allow access to a myriad of information.

The problem with the aforementioned definition is this description of Internet focuses on technical features of the technology. It is technocentric! The definition ignores the educational context in which Internet is used in the classroom. A technical understanding of the Internet and its various dimensions – chat, e-mail, newsgroups, and the Web – does not bestow on teachers any new insights into the wealth of opportunities for curriculum integration and meaningful learning. Although teachers need to know some technical aspects of networking, it is quite possible to learn how to sail without learning about the history of sailing and the different types of rigging. This knowledge does not automatically help one to become a better sailor. The analogy demonstrates that a technical understanding of the Internet is an inadequate definition for teachers. It is time to seek new understandings of the technology that locate Internet within the context of classroom practice.

Taylor (1980) classifies educational computing into a framework comprising of three main modes – tutor, tutee and tool. The '3Ts' provide one of the more enduring frameworks for the use of computers in school. Moreover, the framework clearly locates IML within the tool mode. As tool, the computer is used to complete tasks faster and solve problems more efficiently than would otherwise be possible. A tools approach assumes that the Internet has general-purpose use and that it can be flexibly applied by students to various topics (Grabe & Grabe, 1998). The emphasis shifts from what students can learn from the computer, to what they can do with the computer (Ryba, 1991). However, despite its utility this framework remains flawed; it defines the educational potential of computers based on features of the technology itself. In other words, it does not take into account the context in which specific applications are being used. The main message to emerge from educational research in recent years is that the context of classroom technology strongly mediates learning outcomes (Miller & Olsen, 1994). There is still a need for a conceptual framework that takes into account the differing contexts of using computers in the classroom.

Crook (1994) offers a more contemporary framework for understanding the role of computers in learning and teaching. In this framework, the focus is not on the computer, but on the types of collaboration between the computer, students and the teacher. There are four configurations of collaboration described within this framework: (a) interactions with computers; (b) interactions in relation to computers; (c) interactions at the computer; and, (d) interactions around and through computers (Crook, 1994). Using computers to learn has a different meaning under each category and the framework reveals how a definition of technology anchored in contemporary learning theory, and the context of classroom practice, leads to very different understandings.

The challenge is to develop a framework for the different uses of the Internet that retains a strong contextual quality and similar explanatory power. Such a conceptual framework would help teachers, and teacher educators, to better understand the Internet and help to potentially realise the opportunities for curriculum integration and meaningful learning in New Zealand classrooms.

IML and the Sea of Opportunities

This section outlines a powerful conceptual framework for thinking about the use of Internet in school. The framework is still at an embryonic stage, but it provides a useful taxonomy of teaching that highlights the potential differences between IML activities. These activities are situated around three different contexts of Internet use: (a) Content, (b) Connectivity and (c) Community (see Figure 4). A real strength of these '3Cs' is that each context is informed by, and embodies, the main elements of learning theory, as outlined earlier in this chapter. Furthermore, the model is equally applicable to both students and teachers. It shows how the Internet can be a powerful learning tool for students in the curriculum and for teachers beyond the regular classroom.

The Internet is content

The Internet is, arguably, the best resource that students and teachers have at their disposal for up-to-date information in any content area. It is like a huge ocean with few constraints and many rich resources – some yet undiscovered! Part of the attraction of the Web is the thrill and excitement people get as they discover new resources by sheer chance (Brown, 1995). However, the Web is so huge that it is easy to flounder while surfing and get lost in the vast ocean of information. Too often, the Internet is used to drown students in information but starve them of knowledge (Brown & Ryba, 1996). The key point is that there is more to the Internet than just a 'giant CD-ROM in the sky' (Williams, 1997, p. 44). In other words, learning is not just about the acquisition of subject content.

The amount of information now available through electronic and other means requires that students become effective processors of information; and, furthermore, that students (and teachers) become navigators of knowledge. This requires a deeper understanding of the learning process and involves using Internet content for more than tele-access activities (Schrum & Berefeld, 1997). After all, the Internet provides an ideal context for authentic and collaborative learning activities, where students are actively involved in the problem-solving process (Harris, 1998a). For example, students can work in groups to research genuine problems and in the process reflect on which strategies are best for getting specific information. These strategies can be refined in activities like an 'Internet Investigation' where students must locate information from around the world in relation to a particular theme (Riley & Brown, 1998). There are many such tele-research activities that provide opportunities to directly teach thinking skills by requiring students to wonder, wiggle and weave through a systematic investigative process (Lamb, Smith & Johnson, 1997).

The point is that the added value of the Internet is not simply viewing someone else's creation, but rather the type of learning processes students engage in as they investigate meaningful problems, debate and reflect upon the results, and eventually publish and share their findings with a wider audience. Of course, the Internet provides an excellent audience and publication medium for student·creations and the construction of Web pages is a logical extension of the 'cyber cycle' (Brown & Riley,

1997). This cycle is consistent with recent curriculum developments and the emphasis on team investigations allows the Internet to be easily integrated within most classroom programmes. Although access to the Internet is important, this approach does not automatically privilege Web-based resources over traditional materials. The point is that Internet can be readily grafted on to already sound educational practice.

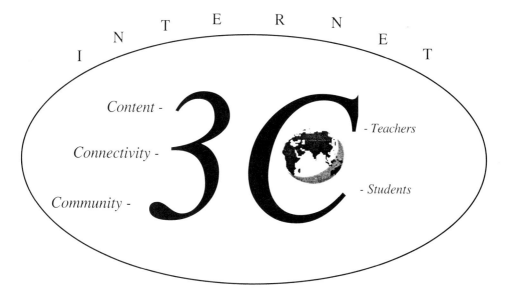

Figure 4: The 3Cs of IML

The advantage of the Web, however, is that it enables students to reflectively follow an authentic line of inquiry using time-sensitive data. Hitherto, knowledge is seen as dynamic and constantly changing, rather than fixed at a point in time (Brown & Ryba, 1996). Conflicting information from a variety of sources require both students and teachers to determine which ones are not only factual, but also trustworthy and honest. Accordingly, students are more likely to make sense of the information they have gathered by distinguishing between inert knowledge – that which is factual but does not make much difference to their life – and generative knowledge which has the potential to change their whole perspective of the world (Dede; cited in O'Neil, 1995). An essential aim of using the Internet to gather content should be to foster the development of generative knowledge by opening students' thinking to wider scrutiny. It is these uses of the Internet that provide opportunities for students to become teacher-independent thinkers.

The Internet is connectivity

The Internet is a tool for communication and its various technologies open up a whole new world of connectivity. This connectivity affords opportunities for 'intellectual partnerships' where people can learn from one another, without the limitation of geographical constraints. When people interact in these virtual relationships, they learn to see how others think and potentially start to reflect on their own thought processes. The privacy and relative safety of electronic communications – chat, e-mail and newsgroups – provides an excellent way for students to articulate their thinking processes and gradually share their personal beliefs with a wider audience. In an online environment, social interaction takes on a new meaning and virtual exchanges are often a rich source of 'cognitive conflict', which aids in the development of higher-order thinking skills.

The connectivity of the Internet also allows for students and teachers to expand their ZPD and, thereby, develop skills and knowledge not possible in other contexts. It creates a partnership between people and the technology that is similar to one with a more capable peer (Salomon, Perkins & Globerson, 1991). In other words, keypal and tele-learning experiences provide a chance for people to engage in thinking processes that are of a higher order than the ones they would develop without this connectivity. The point is that the Internet, or at least its connectivity, has the potential to amplify cognition.

There are many opportunities for 'ask an expert' and tele-mentorship type online relationships (see for example, Serim & Koch, 1996). These relationships allow teaching to be scaffolded by an expert where students learn as 'apprentices' working alongside a more experienced old-timer. As a consequence, learning becomes more authentic as it models the type of relationships that occur in environments outside of the classroom. After all, there is nothing better than asking an expert for assistance when you need help. In this way, the Internet can imitate situations in the real world which are difficult to create in traditional classrooms, and thus support greater transfer of learning to actual life situations.

Whatever the form of communication, best practice will encourage a greater sense of intimacy between people and connectivity of understandings. The Internet makes it possible to talk with people from different backgrounds and to hear first-hand about their difficulties; a near impossible learning experience under normal circumstances. It enables students to compare and contrast other cultures with their own and reflect on similarities and differences – metacognition in action! Moreover, students can join 'cyber journeys', where they become active participants in voyages of discovery. Such voyages or tele-presences provide a clear transformational advantage over conventional classroom activities (Grabe & Grabe, 1998). The pivotal message is that connectivity should be used for educational activities that nurture rich forms of collaboration not possible by alternative and more conventional means (Robinson, 1993).

The Internet is community

The most promising use of Internet is where the buoyant partnership of people and technology creates powerful new learning communities. A community is loosely defined as a basic form of social organisation consisting of people who share common interests, values and goals (Schrum & Berefeld, 1997). The view advanced here is that communities of learning are far more powerful than connectivity alone – there is more to learning under the metaphor of community than just communication. This metaphor builds on the connectivity of the Internet and acknowledges that learning is a mediated process where human cognition is distributed across time and space. However, it also recognises that learning is a complex process which frequently takes place unintentionally within informal and non formal communities. The Internet can nurture these communities and give birth to new 'cognitive clusters' that are conducive to better learning.

When learners become members of a virtual community they acquire new insights and understandings that reshape their values and beliefs. At the outset, learners start on the outside of the community and slowly progress toward deeper understandings as they identify the culture and become more active within its social milieu. The progression is similar to the difference between learning about another country, from someone who lives in that country, to actually visiting the country itself. Then, after a period, moving from being a visitor with a tourist's gaze, to a resident with all the tacit knowledge that comes from membership of a local community (Williams, 1998). Hence, learning in a virtual community is a process of gaining increasing wisdom overtime – it can be thought of as a work in progress!

Bear in mind, people are normally members of more than one community and each Internet, or Intranet, community can be thought of as a separate ZPD. The Internet makes it possible for the learner to have multiple zones in different contexts, that often intersect and overlap. Consequently, the union between the ZPD and the Internet as community provides a three-dimensional model for tele-learning. With this model teachers should not underestimate the power of traditional Internet technologies such as listservs and chat. These technologies can support new virtual communities during tele-sharing and tele-collaborative projects (Schrum & Berefeld, 1997) where ideas are debated, risks are taken, and mistakes are seen as steps in learning – necessary features of 'guided apprenticeship' from novice to expert. It is these virtual apprenticeships in online communities that help students and teachers to construct new knowledge with the potential to result in educational transformations.

IML and the Learning Continuum

The different contexts of Internet use can be seen on a learning continuum (see Figure 5). At one end, the Internet is used for the acquisition of content knowledge. Whereas, at the other end of the continuum knowledge is actively constructed 'with' the Internet. When students learn 'from' the Internet there is no guarantee the content offers a transformational advantage over more conventional classroom materials. The reality is that most schools use the Internet to merely access and disseminate information (Barron & Ivers, 1998). While there are a range of activities for online student projects (see for example, Harris, 1998b), without mindful and strategic navigation, the Internet as content does not necessarily lead to knowledge construction.

When the Internet is used to connect people there is greater potential for the construction of knowledge in a socially meaningful context. New intellectual partnerships can arise from online relationships leading to increased curiosity, inquisitiveness and social interaction. The Internet as connectivity allows for deeper levels of thinking and a stronger sense of efficacy as a thinker. The acquisition of higher-order thinking skills is, however, tightly intertwined with domain-specific knowledge and it is only in communities of practice that much of this tacit knowledge can be acquired. Thus, Internet is part of a larger social system of learning where the construction of knowledge is a process of induction within a wider social community. The key point is that a rich Internet learning culture is likely to develop when learners actively participate in these extended classroom communities, especially with guidance from an expert or master teacher.

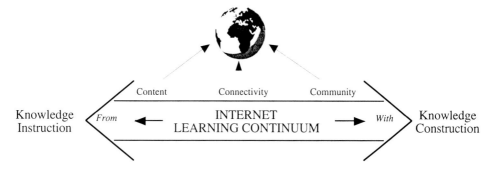

Figure 5: The Internet learning continuum

IML and the Teacher's Role

The increasing availability of information has required a change in the teacher's role from provider-of-information to facilitator-of-learning (Brown & Ryba, 1996). As facilitator, the teacher acts as a co-learner and works alongside students in jointly constructing knowledge. This can be achieved by novice students and master teachers becoming partners in the learning enterprise. However, it requires teachers to feel confident and comfortable about using the Internet in the classroom. Accordingly, teachers need to have some basic technical knowledge as well as an understanding of how IML can be used to develop the Essential Skills identified in the *New Zealand Curriculum Framework* (Ministry of Education, 1993). Particular attention should be given to teaching practices that improve the conditions of learning. After all, it is up to teachers to help transform data into information, and information into knowledge that empowers students to become more autonomous and self-directed learners.

But technology does not change teaching practice, good teachers do! As Fullan (1993) points out, the success of any educational innovation is dependant on the beliefs and values of the teacher. So, good teachers are vital to exploiting the potential of the Internet in school (Owston, 1997). Obviously, teachers need a good conceptualisation of what is possible, but technical know-how on its own will not alter their classroom practice. While it is easy for most teachers to learn how to use the Internet, learning to harness its educational potential is quite another matter (Trentin, 1996). Instead of teacher education focusing on the Internet *per se,* it should address the existing pedagogical beliefs of teachers and link these to ways of using new educational technologies to create conditions for meaningful learning. In other words, there is a real need for professional development that challenges teachers' existing practice through a better understanding of contemporary learning theory. The role of theory is that it provides teachers with the conceptual tools to better critique and transform their classroom practice.

Good teaching, with or without the latest technology, depends on the wisdom of the teacher. Giving mediocre teachers the best technology is not a recipe for better teaching (Abi-Raad, 1997). On the other hand, if you want to create good teachers then you have to provide the right tools for the job. The message is that for lasting educational transformations to occur, beliefs about teaching and technology must change together. As Cuban (1998) points out, high-tech schools need high-tech teachers! In sum, there is a crucial need to ensure that advanced technologies are accompanied by sound educational principles such as those outlined in this chapter.

Conclusion

Teachers should be cautious. Prior experience tells us that many people have unrealistic expectations about the effects educational technology have on learning (Noble, 1996). The Internet is no Holy Grail and beyond the first wave of implememtation the problems of learning are still much the same as ever; this is why there is a need for further research (Windschitl, 1998). However, in the hands of a wise teacher the Internet is likely to offer many possibilities for active and meaningful learning. This type of learning, nevertheless, does not happen by chance. Like every learning opportunity in the classroom, the Internet needs to be thoroughly integrated into the curriculum. Such integration requires careful planning and timely intervention by teachers who are knowledgeable about the learning process. Accordingly, if schools are going to make the most out of the Internet they should be mindful of the following points:

1. *Develop a clear rationale for the use of Internet in your school.* Consult widely with interest groups but ensure the rationale is based on existing educational goals and sound principles of learning and teaching.
2. *Help teachers link the Internet to contemporary learning theory.* Do not see the Internet as end in itself, but rather as a catalyst for helping to design more active and meaningful learning environments.
3. *Plan activities that utilise the Internet carefully.* Activities should have a specific focus and be fully integrated within the curriculum. The Internet should be used for information as well as communication that is linked to other classroom activities.
4. *Teacher education is essential.* Ask teachers to identify their own individual needs and link these to theoretically informed professional development activities. Spend as much money on teacher education as you spend on the costs of getting wired.
5. *Avoid and actively discourage technocentric thinking.* Look beyond technological solutions and only support the use of Internet in your school when it offers a clear transformational advantage over other methods of teaching.

Finally, teachers must be critical of the wired curriculum. You only get waves when the ocean has no depth! It is easy to be seduced by the attraction of the surf, but history shows that technology waves in school are potentially quite dangerous. The real potential of the Internet is highly dependant on teachers who can look beyond the horizon of the techn·¹ogy itself. This chapter has provided teachers with a theoretical lens to better see the raft of opportunities for building strong new learning communities with the Internet. The challenge is for teachers to cast aside pre-existing conceptions of technology that harbour old models of learning, and embark on a fulfilling voyage of discovery on an expansive virtual ocean. Anchors away!

References

Abi-Raad, M. (1997). Rethinking approaches to teaching with telecommunication technologies. *Journal of Information Technology for Teacher Education*, 6 (2), 205-214.

Barron, A., & Ivers, K. (1998). Who's doing what on the Internet? *Learning and Leading with Technology*, 26 (2), 37-42.

Brown, M.E. (1997). Information and communication technology: More than just computers! In J. Burns (Ed.), *Technology in the New Zealand curriculum* (pp. 248-268). Palmerston North: Dunmore Press.

Brown, M.E. (1995). What is the role of information and communication technology in the New Zealand curriculum? *Computers in New Zealand Schools*, 7 (2), 7-15.

Brown, M., & Riley, T. (1997). Creations in cyberspace: Challenging clever kids with computers. *Australian Journal of Educational Computing*, 12 (1), 32-35.

Brown, M., & Ryba, K. (1996). The information superhighway: A teacher's guide to the Internet. In K.W Lai (Ed.), *Words have wings: Teaching and learning with computer networks* (pp. 19-34). Dunedin: Otago University Press.

Burns, J. (1997). Technology – Intervening in the world. In J. Burns (Ed.), *Technology in the New Zealand curriculum* (pp. 15-30). Palmerston North: Dunmore Press.

Collis, B. (1996). The Internet as an educational innovation: Lessons from experience with computer implementation. *Journal of Educational Technology*, 26 (6), 21-30.

Crook, C. (1994). *Computers and the collaborative experience of learning*. London: Routledge.

Cuban, L. (1998). High-tech schools and low-tech teaching. *Journal of Computing in Teacher Education*, 14 (2), 6-7.

Duffy, T.M., & Jonassen, D.H. (1991). Constructivism: New implications for instructional technology. *Educational Technology*, 31 (5), 7-11.

Dwyer, D. (1996). The imperative to change our schools. In C. Fisher, D. Dwyer & K. Yocam (Eds.), *Education and technology: Reflections on computing in classrooms* (pp. 15-33). San Francisco: Jossey Bass Publishers.

Fullan, M. (1993). Why teachers must become change agents. *Educational Leadership*, 50 (6), 12-17.

Grabe, M., & Grabe, C. (1998). *Learning with Internet tools*: A primer. New York: Houghton Mifflin.

Harris, J. (1998a). Educational teleresearch a means, not an end. *Learning and Leading with Technology*, 26 (3), 42-46.

Harris, J. (1998b). Curriculum-based telecollaboration. *Learning and Leading with Technology*, 26 (1), 6-15.

Jones, A., & Mercer, N. (1993). Theories of learning and information technology. In P. Scrimshaw (ed.), *Language, classrooms and computers* (pp. 11-26). London: Routledge.

Lamb, A., Smith, N., & Johnson, L. (1997). Wondering, wiggling, and weaving: A new model for project and community-based learning on the Web. *Learning and Leading with Technology*, 24 (7), 6-13.

Miller, L., & Olsen, J. (1994). Putting the computer in its place: A study of teaching with technology. *Journal of Curriculum Studies*, 26 (2), 121-141.

Ministry of Education. (1998a). *Interactive Education: An Information and Communication Technologies Strategy for Schools*. Wellington: Ministry of Education.

Ministry of Education. (1998b). *Implementing technology in New Zealand schools*. Wellington: Learning Media.

Ministry of Education, (1995). *Technology in the New Zealand Curriculum.* Wellington: Learning Media.

Ministry of Education, (1993). *New Zealand Curriculum Framework.* Wellington: Learning Media.

Noble, D. (1996). Mad rushes into the future: The overselling of educational technology. *Educational Leadership*, 54 (3), 18-23.

O'Neil, J. (1995). Technology in schools: A conversation with Chris Dede. *Educational Leadership*, 53 (2), 6-12.

Owens, J. (1996). A survey of computer use in New Zealand schools. *The Research Bulletin*, 7 1-9.

Owston, R. (1997). The World Wide Web: A technology to enhance teaching and learning? *Educational Researcher*, 26 (2), 27-33.

Perkins, D. (1994). *Smart Schools: from training memories to educating minds.* New York: The Free Press.

Phillips, D. (1995). The good, the bad, and the ugly: The many faces of constructivism. *Educational Researcher*, 24 (7), 5-12.

Reeve, R.A., & Brown, A.L. (1985). Metacognition reconsidered: Implications for intervention research. *Journal of Abnormal Child Psychology*, 13 (3), 343-356.

Riley, T., & Brown, M. (1998). Internet investigations: Solving mysteries on the information superhighway. *Gifted Child Today, 21* (1), 28-33.

Robinson, B. (1993). Communicating through computers in the classroom. In P. Scrimshaw (ed.), *Language, classrooms and computers* (pp. 111-129). London: Routledge.

Roblyer, M., Edwards, J., & Havriluk, M. (1997). *Integrating educational technology into teaching.* New Jersey: Prentice Hall.

Ryba, K. (1991). What we've got – is it right? *Computers in New Zealand Schools*, 3 (3), 12-16.

Salomon, G., Perkins, D.N., & Globerson, T. (1991). Partners in cognition: Extending human intelligence with intelligent technologies. *Educational Researcher*, 20 (3), 2-9.

Schrum, L., & Berefeld, B. (1997). *Teaching and learning in the information age.* Boston: Allyn and Bacon.

Serim, F., & Koch, M. (1996). *NetLearning: Why teachers use the Internet.* Sebastopol, CA: Songline Studios Inc.

Taylor, R. (1980). Introduction. In R.P. Taylor (Ed.), *The computer in the school: Tutor, tool, tutee* (pp. 1-10). New York: Teachers College.

Trentin, G. (1996). Internet: Does it really bring added value to education? *International Journal of Educational Telecommunications*, 2 (2/3), 97-106.

Vygotsky, L. S. (1978). *Mind in society.* Cambridge, MA: Harvard University Press.

Wiggins, R.W. (1994). *The Internet for everyone: A guide for users and providers.* New York: McGraw-Hill.

Williams, M. (1998, August). *Don't tell lies about the Internet to our students and teaching colleagues.* Keynote address presented at Teaching for Effective Learning: Using IT in the Classroom. Auckland.

Williams, M. (1997). Professional associations: Supporting teacher communities. *Computers in New Zealand Schools*, 9 (3), 42-47.

Windschitl, M. (1998). The WWW and classroom research: What path should we take? *Educational Researcher*, 27 (1), 28-33.

Young, A. (1997). Higher-order learning and thinking: What is it and how is it taught? *Educational Technology*, 37 (4), 38-41.

3 Handling Information on the Internet

Elizabeth Probert

The Internet can be a wonderful way to open up the world to students and staff at school. We can use it to find information on the World Wide Web, to share information by publishing Web pages, to communicate information or ideas using electronic mail. More recently in schools there has been a growing movement to use the Internet to link student communities of various kinds around the world.

However, while there are many rewards, there are also many pitfalls that can seem worrying and alarming. The issues that rise up to meet us sometimes seem overwhelming. What's more, many of these issues don't become apparent until we have been involved in helping students to use the Internet for some time.

The first part of this chapter, therefore, is a case study based on our experiences with the Internet at Pakuranga College. The second part addresses the processes involved in searching for and evaluating information found on the Internet.

Using the Internet with Students: A Case Study Based on the Experiences of Pakuranga College

Pakuranga College is a large co-educational high school about 16 km east of downtown Auckland. The school had a roll of 1,850 students in 1998, over 1,900 expected in 1999 and 2,000 or more in 2000. There are 43 nationalities represented in the student body, 48 per cent of whom were not born in New Zealand.

The school is in the forefront of some aspects of information and communications technologies. We have our own UHF channel, and media studies students are involved in producing daily television programmes which are beamed around the school during morning roll call. There is also a lunch time radio station, Munch Music, and 100.4 FM Information Radio, broadcasting to the local community. Media studies also has a 3.7-metre satellite dish specialising in digital transmissions from Asia Sat2. This allows us to broadcast programmes from Deutch Welle and other European and Asian broadcasts into the school.

During 1992 library staff started to investigate telecommunications in the shape of the K12Net Bulletin Board which uses Fidonet, an amateur network, to send and receive electronic mail (Beath & Probert, 1996). K12Net bulletin boards are similar to the listservs and newsgroups many of us use today and allow teachers and students to communicate easily and cheaply. We had a fair amount of success using K12Net, although we needed to have it available through more computers. Students used to queue at lunchtime to send messages and staff used some of the subject oriented discussion groups.

In 1993 we joined SchoolsNet, but staff found it difficult and not user friendly (there were no graphical user interfaces then – everything was text based) so in 1994 we took out a subscription with ICONZ (Internet Company of New Zealand) and started some tentative 'surfing' using Mosaic as our browser. It became obvious that the use of the Internet was going to grow enormously and, as there was already an increasing demand for access from students and staff, in 1995 we took the big step of installing an ISDN line, obtaining a domain name, pakuranga.school.nz, installing Web and mail servers and setting up our own site. With the help of some funding from Telecom and our Community Education Department we began to provide classes to the public and to our own school in using the World Wide Web and electronic mail.

What follows is a discussion of some of the major issues we have faced during this time of development.

Getting connected

We started off with a single modem linked to a single computer using the single phone line into the school library. This is the simplest type of connection and the one many of us have at home. I would still very strongly recommend this as a very good way for schools to start venturing onto the Internet. We had this type of access for a year or so and it worked well. It allows teachers and students to get to know their way around gradually and it also allows for the slower revelation of the pricklier problems like control of the access, students getting hold of unsuitable material, printing setbacks and so on. If we had started off with a whole lot of computers all able to access the Internet at the same time we would soon have found ourselves in strife trying to manage multiple-user access at the same time as learning the necessary skills ourselves.

Costs

One immediate issue is the cost. Which budget pays for the school Internet access? If you are in a big school, how is the cost divided up among departments? Does Administration pay for the phone line and call charges and another department pay for data charges? Who is in charge of monitoring these costs or can anyone use the Internet whenever they like?

In our school, Administration pays the line and call charges and the library pays the data and router charges. The Internet is seen as another source of information like the other resources in the library. Trying to work out which department to charge for what amount of usage has so far been put in to the too-hard basket. Library staff do record and monitor the usage figures, however.

Training

We hold training sessions in the library for staff, who need to show they are competent users of the WWW before they allow their classes access. If not, they need to make sure a member of the library staff is available to help them. Teachers really need to be familiar with the WWW if they are expecting their students to gain anything from the experience – otherwise there is little point in having their students use this resource. We train students by issuing Internet Licences once they have completed and passed the two online tutorials on our website. All Form Three students do these at the moment, when taking the ICT module in the Technology Curriculum, and other forms also go through the process. Gradually we are hoping that the majority of our students will develop good searching and evaluation skills. Go to http://

pakuranga.school.nz and click on Tutorials lifebelt to find our school tutorial sessions.

Control of access

No student can use the WWW or e-mail until they have returned their Internet Use Contracts (see http://pakuranga.school.nz/IRC/policies.html) signed both by themselves and their parents. As these are returned, students' names are checked off a central roll kept in the library. At the start of the year 1,800 AUP forms were issued to all students via tutor group rolls, so that next year only the new intake of Form 3 students and new students entering other forms will have to sign. Senior students with signed contracts and Internet licences may apply for a permit card which will allow them to use the Internet unsupervised during study periods. However, we also run a proxy server, which means that all traffic on the WWW goes in and out through one server, allowing us to read the logs of all traffic. We keep these logs onscreen in the workroom all day and so can easily check to see who is going where, if necessary.

This issue of access control changes as school access grows. When we first started using the WWW we had only one computer and one modem. We were therefore more easily able to monitor the access and to supervise and instruct. Once we had twenty computers all able to go online at the same time, and thirty or so students all on the WWW or e-mail we found we needed to have policies for use and supervision in place. Now there is Internet access from about sixty computers around the school and we are about to revisit our procedures yet again.

A school with a large whole-school network may have individual logons for each student and Internet access can therefore be controlled in this way.

Equity of access

This can be a big issue as although a significant percentage of our students have Internet access at home, many do not and we must allow these students to have access when necessary – before and after school, lunchtimes and so on.

Using the printer

Issues associated with printing need to be discussed in schools. It is much faster to allow students to print Web pages, rather than have them sitting there for ages taking notes, but this raises the problem of printing costs. Trying to charge students for printing can be a problem when so many are clustered around the network printer. We decided to allow five pages to be printed, but of course we then had to make sure students knew how to go to 'Print Preview' to check the number of pages on a site, and then how to either request that only certain pages be printed or highlight and paste material into a wordprocessing program. Some form of a Smartcard that could be used as an ID card, a library card, and also for printing and photocopying would be a real boon in schools.

Use of diskettes

Many schools do not allow student to download material onto their own diskettes for fear of spreading viruses. This problem can be solved by adopting a whole-school policy. At Pakuranga College students are not able to access A-drive in most computers, apart from those in one room where they use only disks provided by the teacher, who counts in the disks at the end of each lesson. Not being able to use disks is a nuisance for those wanting to bring work from home to use at school, though. One solution is for students to e-mail material to themselves at school, continue working on it during the day and then e-mail it back to themselves at home.

Using electronic mail

Schools which have e-mail addresses for students may allow them to use e-mail quite freely, provided they do not break the Internet contract (AUP) they have signed. However, some schools have reported problems with students, particularly junior students, sending abusive or stupid mail to other students and have decided to limit e-mail to senior students only. Other schools use one of the free Web based e-mail systems, such as Hotmail, so that while every student and staff member can have an e-mail address, the school does not have to run its own mail server and does not have to administer the system.

I am wary of this solution. The school has no control at all over the content or destination of any of this e-mail, all of which is generated by students and staff, and which is coming and going using school equipment. It may seem a simple and wonderful solution if no one at school knows much about running a mail server or if the local ISP can't help in this area, but in the long run it could lead to problems. When students start joining projects such as book raps (which are discussion groups centred around various books or other projects), the school may find they are glad to have direct control over the content of e-mail. After all, electronic mail is never guaranteed to be totally private anyway, as some in high places have discovered. The systems administrators of any mail system can always look at any mail they want to. However, such people are appointed to those positions because they are responsible and mature, and would not go ferreting around in the mail without cause. Nevertheless, no one should ever assume their mail is totally secure. This applies to school systems and to systems such as Hotmail. Allowing school administration details to be e-mailed using Hotmail does not seem a very good idea. We believe that setting up our own system is much preferable and allows us greater security.

We found we did not need to have individual student addresses to start using e-mail in classes. A classroom or school address can work well and students can add their contributions to either a single piece of mail or can identify themselves in the subject line when sending individual mail.

Using e-mail with students

E-mail is great to use with students. It is cheap and there aren't all the problems that abound when using the WWW in school. Most students have no problems learning to operate an account and become really involved when taking part in e-mail projects such as the discussion groups set up to allow students from other schools, perhaps in other countries, to discuss issues in various subjects or exchange views about books that they are reading in class.

Many students find it really interesting to e-mail students in other countries using another language. We have students taking German, for example, who correspond with classes in German schools who are learning English. The German students try out their English on our students and ours try out their German. There is often hilarity in the room when corrected versions arrive back. Last year a form five class at Pakuranga College who were studying *Z for Zachariah* corresponded, in English, with a class of students at a school in Germany who were also reading the same book in a German translation.

Book raps are a particularly good e-mail activity for students. A book rap is a book discussion conducted via electronic mail. Individuals or groups of students from across the country or around the world can discuss the scheduled books. OzTeacherNet (http://rite.ed.qut.edu.au/oz-teachernet/projects/book-rap/calendar.html) has the current Australian Book Rap Calendar. It is a good place to go if you want to find out about how book raps work and how to participate. Morris Gleitzman's *Misery Guts* was a recent book under discussion. English OnLine (http://english.unitecnology.ac.nz/) is currently establishing a Book BackChat which will operate along similar lines to the Australian Book Rap but which will focus on New Zealand books. Go to http://english.unitecnology.ac.nz/bookchat/schedule.html to see the books scheduled for Term 1, 1999 and to find out how to join in.

Teachers and e-mail

All teachers if possible should subscribe to some of the many listservs or e-mail discussion groups. There are lists for English teachers, Maths teachers, library staff, IT teachers, ESOL teachers and so on but the best way to find a useful list to join is to ask your local curriculum association. Someone will know. You can go to somewhere like http://falcon.jmu.edu/~ramseyil/listserv.htm or http://tile.net/listserv/ to get a list of listservs but it can be hard to tell which ones may be really useful. Some discussion groups generate enormous amounts of e-mail, so you do need to be selective and to ask around for recommendations.

Technical support

This is a very big issue in many schools. Often the person who looks after the computers is not very knowledgeable about the Internet, and so the Internet expertise will come from another area of the school. Under the current system, where schools are all separate and independent entities, there is no provision for centrally provided expertise and support. This means that each school has a different method of providing telecommunications. Many schools, too, have not yet realised that technical support is not cheap, often costing more than a teacher's salary, and that as their systems grow and expand they need to make realistic budget provision for this support.

At Pakuranga College we have faced – and are still facing – these issues. More and more staff are becoming familiar with available resources on the the WWW and are wanting to use these with their students. These demands are putting pressure on the school to provide more computers and other equipment, and to provide a satisfactory solution to the issue of technical support.

Finding and Evaluating WWW Information

While we often hear about the wonders of the World Wide Web, we also often hear about how much rubbish can be found there and how hard it is to find anything useful. We also hear teachers blaming the growth of information technology for poor assignment work, complaining that it makes it too easy and tempting for students to copy material from Web pages, paste it into their assignments, change it around a little and pass it off as their own work.

Many of these complaints about student use of Web-based information only serve to underline just how important it is to make sure all students develop good information skills.

Students have always copied material, either by hand from books or with the help of the ubiquitous photocopier. Some have always tried to get away with inserting this copied material into assignments. The widespread use of wordprocessors and the Internet have only made this easier to do, and harder for teachers to recognise.

Underpinning the use of all sources of information is the need to develop good information handling skills and this is even *more* crucial when using the Internet. Students with poor information skills are going to flounder when using the WWW. No amount of use of the WWW or material from the WWW or any other type of information technology will compensate for the lack of information skills. Therefore it is important to place the issues involved in searching and using material from the WWW firmly within the framework of information skills development across the curriculum. It is very encouraging that so many educators now are realising the importance of the planned development of information skills in student learning, and that changes need to be made in order to improve that learning. As Carol Gordon says: 'What's wrong with the research assignment? [It] has become analgous to: "Take two aspirins and call me in the morning." (Gordon, 1998, p.45).

One successful method is Gwen Gawith's six stages of Action Learning. 'Action Learning breaks the process of finding, using, analysing and producing information into segments and stages ... Action Learning sets the key information finding and using techniques and strategies into a six-stage framework.' (Gawith, 1991, p. 14.) This method fits well with the description of information skills in the list of essential skills 'to be developed by all students across the whole curriculum' where students will 'identify, locate, gather, store, retrieve and process information from a range of sources; will organise, analyse, synthesize, evaluate and use information; will present information clearly ...' (Ministry of Education, 1993, p.18).

In the six-stage system, students first need to define what it is they are looking for – i.e. they need to have formed some questions to answer. These need to be *good* questions, preferably including some they have formed themselves. Good questions cannot be answered by copying material and pasting it into an assignment, perhaps with a little switching of words here and there to make it seem their own work. Good questions require making comparisons, considering possibilities, weighing up points – in other words they require students to *think*. When we as teachers give our students assignments, we need to think about where they are going to find the necessary material. Too often I come across students trying to find material that is really impossible to get hold of, often because the teacher involved did not check possible resources first or did not allow enough time. We have some examples on our website of questions at http://pakuranga.school.nz/questions.html. Another very useful discussion on this questioning/thinking stage is found on Jamie McKenzie's *From Now On Education Technology Journal* (March 1998), available at http://www.fromnowon.org/mar98/flotilla2.html.

Once students have formed some questions, they need to think about finding answers. Contrary to the opinion of many students, the WWW is not the only source of information in the world. There are many other resources as well, such as books and periodicals, which are often more appropriate sources. One student who was doing an assignment on the game of cricket found he just couldn't cope with the variety of material he found on WWW and was more successful when he started with *World Book Encyclopedia* and other books. From there he began to sort out what he actually needed find out and only later did he use WWW for more unusual information. Another popular resource in New Zealand is *INNZ* or *Index New Zealand*, the periodical and newspaper index from the National Library. Students use this to find possible articles and they can then send off for photocopies of them. There are also numerous CD-ROMs which are excellent sources of information.

Students also need to be able to skim and scan material to see that the information they have found is indeed suitable. If so they may need to take notes from the various sources, which they then combine to form thoughtful answers. It can be a good idea to adopt a school-wide notetaking method, such as the Dot-Jot style, which is common to all students (see http://pakuranga.school.nz/notes.html).

Students who have found a lot of what seems like appropriate information now have to *use* it to answer their questions. Then they need to start putting together their presentation, which could be in the form of an essay, a chart, a report, a speech or it could be computer generated. (They were of course told the form of the presentation right at the start of the assignment.) They should also correctly acknowledge all their sources of information so that they cannot be said to have plagiarised material. Again it is helpful to have a school-wide model such as that based on the APA (American Psychological Association) styles. An example is available at http://pakuranga.school.nz/citing.html.

There are thus a great number of skills involved in the information process. Learning to use the WWW efficiently requires even more skills, some of which are very sophisticated indeed.

Finding information on the World Wide Web

In a regular library all the information is organised using the Dewey Decimal system, with every book or periodical classified according to its content, and assigned a number somewhere between 000 and 999.999. When we want information on a certain topic we use the catalogue, find the Dewey number of a particular book or subject and go to the appropriate shelves.

However, as the National Library observes, 'The Internet, with its diverse and limitless range of material available for instant transfer, has taken information outside the boundaries of library systems.' (National Library of New Zealand, 1998, p.3.) The document goes on to point out that the 100 million users in 1998 will rise to a projected one billion by 2005.

It is also worth thinking about the differences between the information found in a school library and that found on the Internet. Any book we use in the school library, for example, has been through a careful selection process – first by the publisher, then the bookseller, and then the library staff who decide to buy it, then classify and catalogue it ready for use.

But the information on Web pages can be written by anyone, published immediately and usually no one ever checks it. Web pages are certainly never classified or catalogued using the Dewey Decimal system, so finding anything can be a real gamble. We either need to know the URL (address of a page) or we have to use a search engine or directory.

Search engines

Search engines are the main method of finding information on the Internet. They are computer programs, sometimes also called 'robots' or 'spiders' or 'crawlers', which constantly wander around through Web pages. Each search engine has built up indexes of website contents and these robots roam around looking for material and links which can be added to the indexes to keep them up to date. For example, when we look at who has visited our own school site at Pakuranga College we often notice something called 'Scooter' has been into almost every page on our site. 'Scooter' is the spider for AltaVista Search Engine and it is combing our site for new material to update the AltaVista indexes. If you have published material on a Web page and you want it included in search engine indexes, you notify various engines which will eventually send out spiders or robots to go over your pages and add the contents to their various indexes.

How do they work?

When we ask a search engine to look for pages containing a certain keyword/s (also called a search string), it will search all its indexes looking for pages containing those word/s. However we have to be careful about the keywords/ search string we use. A search engine is a computer program, not a person, and it has no idea what we really want. If a word has two meanings, it will find sites with both meanings. If we use 'cricket' as a keyword, we will get pages about the sport cricket and the insect cricket. If we put two or three words (search string) in the search box, many engines will find all the pages they can which contain all or any of those words. You may therefore end up with over a million pages in the 'hit' list, few of which will be of much use.

Directories

Directories are sometimes called subject trees because searchers start with broad searches (the trunk) which then gradually get more specific (into the branches). The information in these directories is grouped in subject headings, not keywords. We can search for categories such as mammals and from there get lists of sites of various mammals. We can then look for pages on the mammal/s we want. Directories look like search engines but they are put together by humans, not computer programs. Yahoo is probably the best known directory. Each site added to its directories is reviewed by human workers and this often seems to give us better search results. Yahoo therefore is an excellent place to start if we are looking for information on broad topics or on themes, whereas it can be better to use a search engine (e.g. Infoseek or AltaVista) when searching for specific topics.

The key to finding anything is to use one of the many search engines or directories. But remember that the people who started these search engines and who run them are not librarians and so have not organised the indexes and pages their engines search in the same way that librarians would.

Each search engine has a pool of different websites it searches. Some will search the same pages, some have other pages. Some search engines seem very large because they automatically index every word on a Web page.

A search engine will return a list of possible pages for you to check. Usually there is an abstract (summary) for each site telling you what to expect on that page. However, with some engines this is done automatically and the first twenty-five words on a page are used as the abstract. AltaVista summaries for example consist of the first twenty-five words of a page's contents. This can be very misleading. Other engines such as Excite have abstracts written by humans who review each site.

Techniques for Successful Searching
Boolean operators

Many search engines mention that they support Boolean operators or Boolean searching. This is something everyone really needs to become familiar with if they want to be a successful searcher of the WWW. Boolean searching is named after George Boole, a famous mathematician who lived in the time of Queen Victoria. For more information about George Boole, please check http://www.cohums.ohio-state.edu/philo/boole.html.

Boolean operators are the words AND, NOT, OR and NEAR which are used to narrow or expand a search. Many search engines will search for pages containing every word or some of the words entered in the search box. This is annoying as searchers may get thousands of pages containing just one of the search words used.

Example: When I entered Pakuranga College Library I got 32,300 pages because AltaVista also returned every page it could find with College or Pakuranga or Library or any combination of those words. I therefore got many pages about college libraries which were no use at all.

It seems strange that using AND will actually narrow a search rather than widening it, but it's true. Putting Pakuranga AND College AND Library means the engine should be searching for pages containing all three words. There should be far fewer pages containing Pakuranga and/or College and/or Library. It is important to understand that all search engines will allow the use of either the operator words AND NOT OR or the signs + - . Users need to get into the habit of thinking carefully about the keywords they want to use, and then using them with operator words or signs.

However, if all the words needed should be in a certain order in the pages that come up then use '...' at either end of the search words (string). That way the engine should find only those pages that contain those words in that order.

Examples: I want to find pages about the Pakuranga College Library.

If I enter those words in a search engine I get thousands of pages. Some pages contain all three words, some only college and library, and some only Pakuranga.

If I enter Pakuranga AND College AND Library or Pakuranga +College +Library I should only get pages which contain those three words somewhere in the text. I have actually *narrowed* the searched by using AND.

If I enter 'Pakuranga College Library' I should only get pages containing those three words in that order.

Search results

Excite, Hotbot and *Infoseek* did well – especially with 'Pakuranga College Library' where only two or three sites were returned. (Excite for example returned 2,784,325 pages with all three words and only twenty when I used 'Pakuranga College Library').

Webcrawler for some reason refused to accept the AND or the sign + or the '...'. The first search with all three words, though, was efficient and not too many pages were returned.

AltaVista did badly, returning over 32,000 pages when searching with all three words and not many fewer when using AND and + or '...'. It says that it accepts Boolean searching but it doesn't seem to carry it out very successfully.

Of course I could also have put Pakuranga AND Library NOT College to get information about the Pakuranga Library (the public library) down the road and not the college library.

The importance of developing perseverance

All of the above means that searchers have to be prepared to try a variety of methods to find useful information. If using two or more keywords *always* use AND or NOT or OR (users need to think about what they want to find) or enclose the words with '...'.

As mentioned before, search engines are not organised like the library catalogue and so searchers must learn to be flexible – if getting nowhere one way or with one engine, try another method or another engine. In other words ... *persevere*.

It is also a good idea to read the Help pages that each engine has. These often provide very clear instructions about advanced searching and how to get better results. However, because every engine is different, it can be muddling to try and remember each engine's methods. Most accept Boolean operators or the + and – signs and also '...'

Students need a lot of practice with searching. They need to be able to think of keywords and search strings to use. *The students who have the most difficulty are those who have not mastered the school library catalogue.* Often a frustrated student who complains about not being able to find anything is actually entering whole sentences instead of keywords. While there are a few search engines which support that kind of 'natural language searching' (Infoseek), students need to learn to become proficient keyword searchers.

Another problem crops up if students think that the place to enter their search string is in the location bar of the browser – where the URL goes. They then wonder why they get nowhere. Some students put the keywords in that same slot only as a sort of URL – www.monkeys.com or www.tallest.mountain.co.nz. Yet others use .com.nz or .co.ca and wonder why they get error messages. The process of searching and finding material on the WWW is very complicated and requires many skills. It can take years of practice to become a proficient searcher.

Suggested exercise

Give students a short assignment where they help write the questions. Discuss possible keywords that could be used and divide the class into small groups. Have each group use a different search engine. After fifteen minutes or so, get feedback from the class to see what the groups discovered about the engines they were using. Put the results on a whiteboard for comparison. This exercise always works very well and leads students into discussions about search engines and the way they work.

The list below identifies some of the useful search engines.

Webcrawler (http://www.webcrawler.com). This has a small database but humans review the pages and write the abstracts. It has excellent searching facilities, including Boolean and natural language (it can deal with a sentence entered in the search bar).

Excite (http:// www.excite.com). Another excellent but small engine. Again there are very good search facilities and it allows the use of Boolean operators AND, NOT, OR.

HotBot (http:// www.hotbot.com). This engine offers many search options – eg geographic areas, Proper Names, dates, images, sounds, media types, file extensions, Internet Domains, programming languages.

Infoseek (http:// www.infoseek.com). Not very large and it doesn't support Boolean searching although it does allow '+' and '-' It does cope with natural language e.g. 'Why is the sea blue?' It is very fast and if users know exactly what they are looking for, Infoseek can return good results.

AltaVista (http:// www.altavista.com). Often said to be the most comprehensive but that's mainly because it is so big. It indexes every word on a site electronically and the abstracts for each site are not necessarily useful as they are the first twenty-five words on those pages. It employs few staff as most of its operations are automated. It can return excellent results BUT users must think carefully about the search terms they enter, otherwise they can end up with lots of 'noise' (rubbish). It uses a spider called Scooter to roam sites and update the enormous indexes.

Meta Engines

These search engines search many other search engines at the same time and then return a list of findings for the user to examine.

Metacrawler (http://www.go2net.com/search.html). A powerful search engine which searches many other engines.

Dogpile (http://www.dogpile.com). This is a meta engine, which means it searches more than twenty search engines using the search terms entered. If Boolean operators are used with the search terms, it will search those engines which support Boolean searching first.

Searching for people on the Internet

Yahoo (http:// www.yahoo.com). This is a *Directory* and one of the most popular starting places for seaches on the Web. Humans review the sites and write extracts and it is an excellent place to start, especially if you are not sure where to go. You can search by category (e.g. mammals), which will lead you to lists of mammals. You can also use Boolean operators in Yahoo.

Another directory which lists the e-mail addresses of people all over the world is available at http://www.whowhere.lycos.com/. It can be disconcerting to find your own e-mail address appears so quickly.

New Zealand search engines

Often it can be very useful to search for New Zealand sites only.

SearchNZ (http://www.searchnz.co.nz) A rapidly expanding search engine catering for New Zealand sites.

Anzwers (http://www.anzwers.com.au) A search engine for Australian and New Zealand users.

News Groups searches

Deja News (http://www.dejanews.com/) Searches newsgroups for various topics.

Useful search engines for students

Ask Jeeves (http://www.aj.com/). This is a question and answer service where students can use 'natural language' to ask their questions such as 'What time is it in London?'

AskA Locator (http://www.vrd.org/locator/subject.html).

This service is organised by librarians at the Virtual Reference Desk. Students can ask questions in a variety of subject areas and the VRD will provide resources and links to experts who will answer such questions.

Kidsclick! (http://sunsite.berkeley.edu/KidsClick!/). Another excellent site for student searching and again run by librarians.

Teachers @ work (http://www.work.co.nz). Mark Treadwell's excellent site for curriculum information.

Yahooligans (http://www.yahooligans.com). Yahoo's site especially tailored for student use.

Evaluating the Information on the Internet

It is very, very important to get into the habit of checking up on the value of the information found on WWW sites. This is not something many are used to doing. Teachers may check books, periodicals and CD-ROMs to see they contain appropriate and useful information, but don't usually check out the author or the publisher as they tend to take it for granted that material found in the school library has been checked beforehand by the library staff.

It is therefore a very useful exercise to consider again the difference between many of the print and CD-ROM sources and the material found on the WWW. Consider, for example, the steps that occur before students get to use a book on North American Indians in the school library. First the book was researched and written and accepted by a publisher who thinks that the contents are accurate and won't harm the firm's reputation and that people will buy it. It is edited, printed and distributed to booksellers, who take it because they too think people will buy it, and then it is chosen by school library staff after they have examined it to see if it will be useful. Often heads of departments are also asked for an opinion on this purchase. Only then is the book processed and put on the shelves where students can borrow and use it. Students can be pretty certain, therefore, that the information in that book is accurate and up to date and could be helpful, depending on their needs.

Now consider material on Web pages. Who checks these pages for accuracy, keeps them up to date, edits them and examines them before we get to read them? Often no one. It has to be remembered that anyone can publish *anything* at *anytime, anywhere* on the WWW. Anyone could put up a page about American Indians on a personal Geocities site, for example, and no one checks the contents for accuracy. It might be a very well-designed page with fancy buttons and images but it could be full of absolute rubbish. All staff and students must be aware of this and get into the habit of looking for the clues that indicate worthwhile content or rubbish.

Evaluation guide

1. Check the URL – the address or Uniform Resource Locator, e.g. http://www.pakuranga.school.nz is the URL for the Pakuranga College site.
   (a) Look at the two letter country code at the very end of the URL. If the URL does not end in a two letter country code then it is from the USA, as most USA URLs do not have '.us'. It can be important to know where the material is published. Lots of pages about Maori culture published on a site in Switzerland might make one wonder about the authenticity of the material.
   (b) Check what type of organisation carries the site –
   .govt in New Zealand or **.gov** in North America indicates that it is a government site and so the information should be reliable.
   .org indicates the site is maintained by a non-profit organisation and is not a business site. However watch out for the point of view of the writer. Are students being persuaded to believe something? That's okay as long as they recognise what's going on.
   .co in New Zealand or **.com** in North America and Australia indicates a

commercial or business site – there to make money in some way. Beware of these sites and get students to ask themselves what are they being asked to buy or advertise.

.milt in New Zealand or **.mil** in North America are military sites. Again the information should be accurate and up-to-date, but may be there to persuade viewers.

.ac (tertiary level), or **.school** (secondary or primary) in New Zealand, or **.edu** in North America and Australia indicate an educational institute, usually a university, and so students should be able to rely on the information.

2. A 'sound' site should have a link to the organisation that supports it or to information about the author that can be checked. Students need to know what background and expertise the writer has.

3. The site should have been updated recently, not two years ago.

4. Can the writer be contacted? There should be an e-mail address or some way to contact the writer or publisher. A surprising number of sites have no facility for further contact.

5. Check that references to information from other sources have been cited.

6. The language should be at a suitable level for the students wanting to use the site.

7. There should actually be some useful information on the page or on linked pages, and not too many fancy 'bells and whistles'.

8. Watch out for personal pages everywhere. Personal pages can be identified by the /~ in the URL. This comes after the main part of the URL and is usually followed by the name of the person who wrote the page/s. For example, www.argyle.com/~tsmith is Tom Smith's personal page which lives on the server at the Argyle Company.

   • Always beware of the contents of personal pages, no matter what the URL is. NO ONE checks them. Even though some universities allow students to have personal sites held on the main university server, there is no guarantee that the contents of those personal pages have been checked. In fact most universities carry a disclaimer announcing that they have no responsibility for the contents of personal pages. The URL www.mdu.edu/~bsmith might look trustworthy coming from Mary Deane University, but Barbara Smith could still be publishing rubbish on her personal pages.

   • Personal pages may look wonderful, with excellent graphics and good layout giving the general impression of authority, but be wary. Good layout does not always mean good content.

   • Always try and check out the author of personal pages. There should at least be an e-mail address.

   • Check to see that there are references given for factual statements. There are a few personal pages with excellent content, backed up by accurate references to the sources used by the author.

Web-based evaluation

There are some very helpful websites concerned with the evaluation of Web material

such as *Evaluating Internet Sources* (http://members.aol.com/xxmindyxx/evaluate/question.html) which has a useful summary telling students to look at:
- Authorship
- Source
- Point of view
- Documentation
- Intended audience
- Currency
- Hyperlinks
- Structure
  Other excellent sites for discussion and help in evaluating Web material are:
- Ann Scholz's work at Purdue University Libraries found at http://thorplus.lib.purdue.edu/research/classes/gs175/3gs175/evaluation.html;
- John Henderson's work at Ithaca College Library http://www.ithaca.edu/Library/Training/hott.html;
- The work of Jan Alexander and Marsha Tate at Widener State University, *The Web as a Research Tool: Evaluation Techniques* http://www.science.widener.edu/~withers/evalout.htm;
- Kathy Schrock's *Guide for Educators* http://www.capecod.net/schrockguide/;
- Dr Jamie McKenzie's work at http://fromnowon.org.

Web-based Services

Many information services are now available through the World Wide Web and provide a safer, more focused environment for students, although they still need to develop good searching skills to get the most from these services:

- **Reuters** is now offering its news service to New Zealand schools. For an annual amount, schools can have access to the Reuters News Service, finding up-to-date full-text news stories from every country in the world, photographs, foreign exchange rates, share market information and more. For an online demonstration see http://www.bizinfo.reuters.com/search.html

- **EBSCO World Magazine Bank.** Students can search for relevant full-text articles from various countries and covering a wide range of subject headings. http://www.epnet.com/ehost/login.html

- **SIRS** (Social Issues Resources) contains articles on a wide variety of social issues, although a large percentage is US-based. There is an annual subscription but it can be well worth the cost. (It can be a good idea to sign up for the free 60-day trial.) http://researcher.sirs.com/

- **Encyclopedia Britannica Online** You can get a seven-day trial and they will tell you the cost of subscribing which depends on how many computers will access it. http://www.ebo.com

- **Electric Library** This service, while USA-based, contains full-text articles from many newspapers, periodicals, books, pictures, etc and could be well worth joining (http://www.elibrary.com/).

- **Index New Zealand**, a CD-ROM subject index of over 300 magazine and newspaper articles. Students choose the articles they want and the request is mailed or faxed to the National Library, Wellington, which sends back photocopies of the articles they need within the week.

- **PCInfos** on disk is put out by Statistics New Zealand in both Mac and Windows formats and contains an enormous amount of statistical information in various forms for students to work with.

It can also be helpful to develop a school website and have a curriculum page containing links to useful sites under subject headings. Students can then be directed to these sites first, although they can go out searching later themselves. This method at least provides some early satisfaction for students, who can then build up their confidence more gradually as they develop the searching skills they need in order to find appropriate information for themselves. Senior biology students, for example, can look under 'Biology' on the school 'Curriculum Links' page and find links to Department of Conservation, New Zealand Government, Ministry of Agriculture and Fisheries, Landcare, the *New Scientist* Search Page and other relevant sites.

Helping students learn to make good use of the Internet requires time, purposeful planning, knowledge, time (again) and determination on the part of teachers, but the results of all this effort are enormously rewarding.

References

Gawith, G. (1991). *Ripping into Research.* London: Longman Paul Ltd.

Gordon, C. (1998). Students as authentic researchers. *Scan,*17 (4), 45-49.

Ministry of Education (1993). *The New Zealand Curriculum Framework.* Wellington: Learning Media.

National Library of New Zealand (1998). *Towards the 21st century: Strategic Plan of the National Library of New Zealand.* p. 3.

Probert, E. & Bruce, B. (1996). K12Net in New Zealand schools. In K. W. Lai. (ed.) *Words have Wings: Teaching and Learning with Computer Networks* (pp. 119-128). Dunedin: University of Otago Press.

4 Using Internet Resources in the Classroom

Ann Trewern

The Internet is the best single archive of information available today. The volume of information is not only extensive but is expanding at a significant pace and the variety of that information is as diverse as the many millions who contribute to the knowledge structures of this archive. Any individual can now access a larger body of information than is available from any traditional source such as a library – and all without having to leave a computer terminal. Textual information, high resolution pictures, video clips, audio clips or software can be easily read, viewed, listened to and even downloaded and stored in your own computer or on disk.

Attempting to understand what the Internet is all about can be an overwhelming experience for the newcomer. Simply grasping a basic understanding of what is available is daunting enough, but trying to use the Internet as an effective classroom resource can be intimidating. The purpose of this chapter is to provide teachers in particular with some insights into its use in the classroom, with emphasis on what resources are most useful to classroom teachers and what they can be used for.

Within the vast array of resources available through an Internet connection there are basically two ways that information can be shared 'online':

- **Among people** – the interpersonal resources, of which the communications tools such an e-mail, Internet chat-rooms, Internet phone, and text and audio conferencing, are a part.
- **Between people and remotely located computers** – the informational resources, of which the publicly accessible databases, file archives and hypertext pages of the World Wide Web are a part (Harris, 1995).

Both the interpersonal and informational resources can provide new and interesting ways for teachers and students to explore curriculum-related topics. New and different resources are available to the teacher and the student without their having to leave the school or perhaps even the classroom. The range of resources can expand the teacher's repertoire of ideas and subtly alter the way content is delivered and knowledge is imparted.

Internet Communication Resources For Teachers

Most communication activities use e-mail. It is easy to access and relatively cheap in that much of the process of planning, composing, and typing can be done when the computer is not directly connected to the Internet provider. Because e-mail communication is asynchronous, teachers find this a useful way of being involved in exchanges of information and ideas. This can occur when convenient time slots are available to the classroom teacher between instruction periods and other school demands.

Increasingly, teachers are expanding classroom communications activities by combining video conferencing, real-time chat sessions and other possibilities with e-mail communications. Scheduling real-time interactive sessions can be problematical for the busy classroom teacher. Synchronising online time between a distant group and one's own students is often difficult for teachers, given inflexible teaching timetables, room organisation and the diverse activities of students. A knowledge of protocols that work well can aid the educational value of the exchanges. Good preparation is the key to success. Structured sessions provide more educationally valuable interchanges than unstructured sessions.

The types of exchanges listed below can be used at any level of the primary or secondary school, and are frequently integrated across curricular areas. There are a variety of ways that communications exchanges can occur. Among the first that most newly connected teachers become involved in are:

1. **Keypal exchanges**, or letter writing between individuals or groups. Most interconnected classes probably maintain one or two good class key-pal links over a school year. A good class-to-class link can be a very worthwhile experience for students. There is so much about the daily school life of others, such as important school events, an ordinary school day for the students or an interesting field trip to a place of local interest that can be shared.
2. **Global classrooms**, where two or more classrooms can study a common topic and collaborate to produce some form of publication of the experience.
3. **Electronic appearances**, where special guests can be invited or students can send questions to conference areas or involve themselves in real-time meetings for a specific event.
4. **Electronic mentoring**, where students ask an adult expert for information, such as ask Dr Math at the Maths forum, or where older or more expert students may mentor younger or less expert students.
5. **Impersonations**, where an individual or team investigates and plays the role of a famous or historical character in an interview or simulated event.

There are other types of communications projects available, too. Data gathering in various forms appears in many Internet projects. These include:

1. **Information exchanges** – students and teachers get together to share information about certain events such as a celebration.
2. **Collecting information** – often organised to build a database. Examples are collecting recipes from around the world for the electronic publication of an ethnic cookbook, or collecting information about national holidays and celebrations for the multicultural calendar project.
3. **Telefield trips** – an extremely popular Internet activity. These are often expeditions undertaken by adults who share reports about their experiences through the Internet. In New Zealand the Telecom Foundation and LEARNZ organise telefield trips each year and international organisations such as Global Schoolhouse (Where on the Globe is Roger?) and Classroom Connect (Africa Quest, Galapagos Quest) also run a number of telefield trips.

Problem-solving projects are popular communications projects:

1. **Information searches** are activities where students use clues and reference material to assist in solving a problem. Geogame is a popular information search, in which participating classes provide information about themselves and a number of interesting facts about where they live. The project moderators separate school and country from the remaining clues and participants use maps and atlases and attempt to rematch the information correctly for about 20 schools participating in each section.

2. **Parallel problem-solving** activities are also quite a common Internet activity. Students participating in a project called SS Central America Shipwreck project were all involved in a science investigation called Shipwreck in a Bottle. Each class group performed the same experiment, immersing a number of specific items in seawater in a plastic drink bottle. The bottle were sealed and refrigerated and when they were opened six months later participants discussed their results by e-mail and chat facilities.

3. **Electronic process** writing is often a real-time activity where classes may get together on a moderated chat facility to create a combined story about a specific topic. Serial creations can occur where groups of students may pass a story or poem between two groups or around a larger group to add the next line or the next paragraph.

4. **Social action projects** are cross-curricular in nature and support the 'think globally and act locally' ethos. There are a number of such projects currently available from the I*EARN group. Some examples are discussed a little more fully in the Social Studies section of this chapter.

5. **Simulations** are staged events that are intended to recreate an actual situation. Academy One has sponsored an event called the Simulated Space Shuttle Program for older students on several occasions. Schools around the world took part in simulated space shuttle missions, with each school taking a separate role in the simulation.

Finding People for Communications Links

Once teachers have their computer connected to the Internet, they can find schools to link to. Table 1 on the next page lists some of the websites where teachers can locate other teachers and classes to link with.

Internet projects are distance learning activities which create unique learning environments that are stimulating for both students and teachers. They incorporate the technology into a real-time learning experience. Curriculum Connections – Keypals and Telecollaborative Projects at <http://www.ala.org/ICONN/cur_key.html> provides examples of projects, how to create your own and examples of successful projects. Judi Harris also describes many examples of Network-Based Educational Activity Structures which can be found at <http://www.gsn.org/web/_lib/_harris/ Harris-A.htm>.

Table 2 (page 61) lists some of the major sites which sponsor online interactive projects. Communications activities in different curriculum areas are covered in later parts of this chapter.

Information Resources Available for Teachers

An enormous amount and variety of information is available. Text, pictures, video files, audio files and software can be shared and accessed from remotely located computers by using the World Wide Web, file transfer methods (FTP), directly accessing a remote computer database (Telnet), and e-mail.

• **CWA Education Web** – **http://www.cwa.co.nz/eduweb/edu/e-mail.html**
An extensive list of New Zealand schools' e-mail addresses is available here.

• **Web 66** – **http://web66.coled.umn.edu/**
This is an international directory of schools with e-mail addresses.

• **KeyPals Club** – **http://www.mightymedia.com/Keypals/**
The service provides a database of registered teachers and students and a search tool to quickly locate and contact a student or a class from around the world. There are 25,000 registered users from over 76 countries.

• **Rigby Heinemann Keypals**
http://www.reedbooks.com.au/heinemann/global/keypalt.html
Teachers electronically post a message about the class and a little about themselves which is added to a lengthy list. Mailto options are provided.

• **ePALS Classroom Exchange projects**
http://www.epals.com/cgi-bin/search.cgi?cat=New
A searchable database of registered participants interested in e-mail contacts.

The following sites allow for more interaction to occur before links may be established around a project or a shared activity:

• **The Global Schoolhouse** – **http://www.gsn.org/teach/list/hilites.html**
The HILITES mailing list contains information about the Global schoolhouse e-mail projects. An archive of past e-mail projects can be found at http://archives.gsn.org/hilites/index.shtml

• **E-Mail Around the World** – **http://www.siec.k12.in.us/~west/proj/mail/index.html**
A number of activities are available at this site, including contacting individuals or classes, joining and starting your own e-mail projects, participant lists, and message boards.

• **Kidlink** – **http://www.kidlink.org/**
Kidlink is a grassroots organisation aimed at getting youth through to the age of 15 involved in a GLOBAL dialogue and works through a system of mailing lists.

• **Intercultural E-Mail Classroom Connections** – **http://www.stolaf.edu/network/iecc/**
In operation since 1992, the IECC has distributed over 19,000 requests for e-mail partnerships. There are more than 7300 teachers in approximately 73 countries participating in IECC lists.

Table 1: Finding people for communication links

A wide variety of previously different application programs are increasingly becoming integrated into a system with a single users' interface appearance. Netscape and Internet Explorer are the predominant softwares which help users to 'browse' text and images simultaneously, and to print, copy, download, store and manipulate text information as easily as one might from a wordprocessor. They allow for the viewing of video clips, streaming of audio broadcasts in a similar way to radio and for listening to archived audio files, such as historically significant speeches. As well, these softwares have integrated e-mail and Telnet functions. New softwares are available to allow users to directly contribute resources and ideas to the WWW and to communicate via the Web with others. There are also softwares which allow for direct manipulation of components that users see on the screen.

Many different kinds of sites are of value to educators and to secondary and primary students. Sites now have such a range of different functions and distinct purposes that it is almost impossible to briefly describe the variety. For teachers, there is a wealth of material to be accessed and this includes teaching plans and teaching ideas, interactive games, puzzles and challenges, images, interactive stories, magazines and newspapers, as well as up-to-the-minute information such as weather maps and software. Used well in the school situation, the Internet has the potential to enhance student education by expanding learning opportunities and offering greater and more readily accessible

---

- **Global Schoolhouse projects and programmes main page**
  http://www.gsn.org/project/index.html
An extensive list of projects is available, which includes Where on the Globe is Roger, Global Zoo, Travel-buddy Project, Cyberschoolbus, and many more.

- **Classroom Connect – http://www.classroom.com/**
High-quality e-mail projects are available from this website, including Galapagos quest and Africa Quest.
To join the Classroom connect mailing list send an e-mail message to:
crc-request@listserv.classroom.net
Leave the subject line of your message blank.
In the body of your message type:
  Subscribe Digest crc

- **Houghton Mifflin Project Center – http://www.eduplace.com/projects/**
This is a collection of current projects gathered from a wide variety of sources listed under curriculum areas. This is an excellent resource for the teacher looking for a curriculum specific topic and is updated weekly.

- **TEAMS Distance Learning**
  http://teams.lacoe.edu/documentation/projects/projects.html
These are Internet projects across the curriculum which are designed to involve students in collaborative activities that extend and enhance student understanding of the concepts they are learning.

Table 2: Finding e-mail projects and online projects

resources for students and teachers without requiring them to leave the school. Nevertheless, the effectiveness of the Internet depends very much on how teachers go about integrating it into their curriculum delivery.

How can teachers make use of informational resources?

Teachers have two driving needs for informational materials. The first is the need to expand their resource base for classroom use, and the second need is to develop and grow professionally. The Internet can be a very effective medium for meeting both needs.

Teachers are usually on the lookout for new ideas and resources for the classroom. This is an ongoing task of core importance to teachers (Collis, 1996). Teachers appreciate finding out about new ideas that other teachers have already tried out and found useful, or ideas that can be used in a relatively direct way without too much need for reorganisation of the material to fit into the individual teacher's style of delivery or established learning environment. Online lesson plans can provide some great teaching ideas. There are large databases of these stored with ERIC, Big Sky and Explorer (Maths and Science). Units of work also provide extensive and useful teaching resources. Some of the best of these are provided in an online format by museums and science centres, NASA and other organisations – such as the National Geographic Society – and many have been listed in the curriculum areas section of this chapter.

While many of these resources are designed to be used directly online with groups of children, the teacher with only one classroom computer or the school with limited connections can use the materials in other ways. Online teaching units can be copied onto a hard drive with software capture programmes such as WebWhacker or parts or portions can printed out and used in a variety of interesting ways for group activities. Some teaching units also provide printable worksheets in PFD file format to accompany online pictorial information. Downloading a free copy of Adobe Acrobat Reader from <http://www.adobe.com> from the Internet is very worthwhile to obtain these well formatted and interesting worksheets and paper-based activities that students can use as 'away-from-the-computer activities'.

Images can also provide very useful classroom resources. With a colour printer teachers are now able to reproduce images in various sizes for making games for students and for including in student worksheets or overhead projector transparencies. The ability to reproduce an image from as small as a 3-4cm cube for a large dice to up to A4 in size or to reproduce enough images for six to eight groups to use for a classroom activity is a wonderful teaching asset.

Teachers wishing to allow their students direct access to the Internet for classwork are finding this requires a certain level of management on their part. Students lacking mature search skills or information management techniques can be handicapped in their efforts to actually locate and make the best educational use of the information they find. A solution for teachers is to structure student Internet activities in educationally valid ways. For example, teachers can bookmark relevant sites and provide worksheet outlines for student activities on the Internet or actually create 'webpages' of their own with hypertext links embedded. Your Web browser will open up an html file that is on your own computer and will link to the WWW as long as you are connected. An interesting framework for structuring such investigations is 'Web Quests'. These are inquiry-oriented, group activities structured in such a way that some or all of the information that learners interact with comes from resources on the Internet. For more about Web Quests have a look at <http://edweb.sdsu.edu/courses/ EdTech596/About_WebQuests.html>. This is a framework that works for junior children as well as for adult learners. For a delightful Web Quest about Hatching Chicks, see <http://www.lfelem.lfc.edu/tech/DuBose/webquest/meneses/chicks.html>. There is also an extensive list of Web Quests at DuBose School at <http:// www.lfelem.lfc.edu/tech/DuBose/webquest/wq.html> which shows the range of cross-curricular topics and levels that this framework supports.

From a professional perspective, teachers are on the lookout for materials that will support them in advancing their knowledge in areas of curriculum delivery methods, pedagogy, management, assessment and in many other areas, and will support personal

---

Websites for New Zealand teachers

- **New Zealand Council for Educational Research – http://www.nzcer.org.nz/**
- **New Zealand Principals Federation – http://sunsite.net.nz/orgs/nzpf/**
- **ERO reports – http://www.ero.govt.nz/**
- **Royal Society of New Zealand – http://www.rsnz.govt.nz**
- **TENZ – http://sunsite.net.nz/orgs/tenz/**
- **Teachers@work – http://teachers.work.co.nz/**

Sources of international professional resources

- **British Columbia Education – http://www.bced.gov.bc.ca/irp/**
Good assessment material and other useful information available.

- **Office of Technology Assessment USA**
  http://www.wws.princeton.edu/~ota/ns20/alpha_f.html

- **The Cornell Theory Center Gateway for Educators**
  http://www.tc.cornell.edu/Edu/MathSciGateway/educGateway.html
A very good starting point for finding a range of resources to support professional learning.

- **Pitsco Resources for Teachers – http://www.pitsco.com/p/resource.html**
This is a great resource for teachers looking for links to background information. For Journals and Professional Publications there is http://www.pitsco.com/p/Respages/journ.html

Sources for finding mailing lists

- **tile.net – http://tile.net/lists/**
- **catalist – http://www.lsoft.com/lists/listref.html**
- **Liszt, The Mailing List Directory – http://www.liszt.com/**

Table 3: Resource sites for professional materials

philosophies that underpin everyday practice. There is a considerable amount of relevant material on the Internet. The ERIC (Educational Resources Information Center) Clearinghouses <http://www.accesseric.org:81/sites/barak.html> provide online articles supporting specific curriculum areas, management, assessment, ESL and others. Many professional journals now provide abstracts and some even provide full text articles online. The New Zealand Ministry of Education have publications including curriculum documents, statistical reports and policy documents available online <http://www.minedu.govt.nz/>. Table 3 on page 63 lists some other websites that provide useful background professional information for teachers.

Mailing lists are useful for accessing resources and background information in particular areas. Several directories with public access mailing lists and information on how to subscribe to them are mentioned in Table 3.

Internet Resources for Teachers of English

Using the communications and informational resources of the Internet as an integral part of the delivery of the English curriculum is valid with all students from age five upwards. The effective use of Internet resources in classrooms is a fresh way for teachers to deliver curriculum in oral, written and visual language strands; as well, it can develop essential skills in communication using text, visual and audio skills, information accessing and processing, problem solving, social and co-operative skills, and work and study habits. The Internet also provides opportunities for the classroom teacher to encourage students to present work to a much expanded and frequently global audience.

Using communications resources for curriculum delivery in English

One of the primary objectives of the English curriculum is to develop the student's ability to communicate in a range of areas. Participation in a communications project allows students to consider the purpose of the communication and who they are writing for (Carrucan *et al.*, 1996).

Most communications exchanges are largely text-based e-mail exchanges. More than any other, this medium presents opportunities for sharing information with another similarly aged group or for presenting written work for another audience, whether students are involved in keypal exchanges or in a large group or whole-class project. There are a growing number of opportunities where students in different geographic locations can 'meet' in real-time and 'talk' using either text screen or audio links. The Kidlink organisation provides an educational forum for young authors, using Internet Relay Chat to come together once a month for the 'Kidwriter Project' <http://www.kidlink.org/KIDPROJ/ Kidwriters/>. The project is well moderated by John Ost and a number of young online helpers. Children are encouraged to post their writing through the Kidwriters listserv. Information about how to join the mailing list is available on the project website. Students' writing and poetry is archived on the website.

Figure 1 is a sample literature project from 'Kidlink', which encourages participants to read and discuss literature and to share literature themes and ideas, using e-mail and the Web.

Real-time collaborations with other groups serve to broaden the scope of English curriculum objectives. The Kidlink organisation provides an educational forum for young authors, using Internet Relay Chat to come together in an online fairy tale project. Many of the Kidlink project moderators encourage IRC 'meetings' as a way

```
DURATION: One term, 11 January - 26 March

AIMS
  To encourage children to identify what makes a book appeal to them and
be able to share this enthusiasm with members of their own classes and
students worldwide, using e-mail and the World Wide Web. To promote
feedback and exchange of opinion by e-mail and encourage the children to
extend their reading and experiment with new authors and genres.

OBJECTIVES
  1. To learn to analyse and discuss characteristics of a book.
  2. To write a creative and persuasive response to encourage others.
  3. To read e-mail messages and respond to other people's comments.
  4. To read new authors and books recommended by their peers around the
world.

TEACHING POINTS      .
  The aim is that the reviews should be the creative response of the child
to the book they've read, rather than an imitation of adult reviewers.
Work with the children by discussing what makes a good review and what to
think about as they are reading. Encourage them to work in small groups
or pairs, composing a review in order to give themselves confidence to
attempt one on their own. Below is a framework of suggestions rather than
a rigid structure for each review.

FOR STORY AND PICTURE BOOKS
  Hint at interesting aspects of the plot without revealing all. Why did
you select this book? What was your favourite part and why? Are the
characters and places described believably or in such a way as to capture
your imagination and attention? Does the action move along quickly? Are
the words used imaginative, challenging or easy to read? What do you
think of the illustrations (if any)? Were there any parts which surprised
you? Has it changed the way you think about a problem or view a character?
Where does the story take place? How important is this? Would you like to
read any more books by the same author or in the same series? What would
you tell your best friend about this book if you wanted to persuade them
to read it?

REVIEW RESPONSE
  Each review must contain the book's full title, author and ISBN, the
child's creative response and persuasive message, together with a
recommendation as to what age group or type of person would enjoy it.
Children would be encouraged to try some of the recommendations and
comment informally to the reviewer by e-mail.

HOW TO JOIN THIS PROJECT: See http://www.kidlink.org/KIDPROJ/Books/
```

Figure 1: A sample literature project from 'Kidlink'

Table 4

of keeping project participants in touch and to help establish and maintain a sense of community.

The Global SchoolNet Foundation promotes CU-SeeMe or video conferencing across the Internet as support for a number of their projects. As with IRC, students from different geographic locations can meet in real-time and talk with the aid of a video screen monitoring the view at each location using a quick cam video camera, audio capability via a microphone and a text screen as in IRC.

Given the limited amount of data that phone lines in New Zealand can carry, the CU-SeeMe links with other countries are limited by the speed at which we can see or hear a link group. Successful local CU-SeeME links indicate students need to bring a wide variety of sophisticated communication skills to video sessions. These include good speaking and listening skills, and the ability to read and write, to analyse and interpret ideas and information quickly and effectively, and to respond immediately and appropriately to maintain effective communication.

There are useful professional communications lists for teachers of English that assist in facilitating the exchange of ideas. (See Table 4.)

The World Wide Web is also a valuable resource for the English teacher. There are sites which are valuable for the study of literature, others which offer considerable resources for student writing and oral expression, and others which promote reading and the publishing of student work. (See Table 5.)

Table 5 (opposite): Resources for teachers of English

Reading

• **Sunshine Books – http://www.galaxykids.co.nz/**
A not-to-be-missed site for the junior reading teacher.

• **Online Children's Stories http://www.acs.ucalgary.ca/~dkbrown/stories.html**
There are story collections here as well as folklore, poetry and other literature resources for children.

• **International Kids Space – http://www.kids-space.org/**
This is a site designed for 5-10 year olds. It is a delightfully creative site and is visually attractive for children. The print is large and colourful and links are colourful icons. There are pictures, stories, concerts, and the availability of space for children to respond to written texts and view and present information in a different way.

• **Internet Public Library – http://www.ipl.org/**
The site operates as a virtual public library and is designed to appeal to children between the ages of 4 and 14. Children can travel around the library with J.J. the Librarian and Bookie the Worm. As well as contests where children can submit their stories and poems there are stories to read or listen to in the Story Hour section, places to submit story reviews, and biographical information on children's authors.

Online magazines (E-zines) and children's publications

• **Cyberkids – http://www.cyberkids.com/**
Of particular interest to English teachers is the reading room at http://www.cyberkids.com/ReadingRoom/ReadingRoom.html There is a high quality of written work and art material presented from the 8-12+ year old contributors. The stories could be used as an online reading resource and as material for remedial reading teachers working with older children. Printouts of stories could be taken home for practice reading without student embarrassment or the worry of lost books.

• **Cyberteens – http://www.cyberteens.com/ctmain.html**
In the words of the organisers of this site 'our goal is to create and promote youth worldwide, and give teens a voice and an interactive place to express their creativity. Young people all over the world make Cyberteens a sharing, caring space.' The site functions similarly to Cyberkids and is in fact an off shoot of the Cyberkids initiative. A very worthwhile magazine and support site for the 13+ year olds.

• **Kid Pub- http://www.kidpub.org/kidpub/**
This site contains a number of published children's stories which would be useful to teachers as models of good writing, and for reading activities. Easy method to publish stories.

• **Midlink Magazine – http://longwood.cs.ucf.edu/~MidLink/**
MidLink Magazine is an electronic magazine created by kids, for kids aged 10 to 15. This site was set up by a primary teacher of gifted children as a collaborative project where classes around the world could share ideas about a bi-monthly theme.

• **ISN Kidnews – http://www.kidnews.com/**
This is an online newspaper for children containing news, features, profiles, creative writing, reviews, etc. It is worth a look. There are parts of this site for adults, too.

Table 5 continued

Interactive word games for primary students

• Quai! English Games
These are a series of 12 online interactive games using Flashcards, Matching Games and Concentration Games that provide drill and practice activities for students using contractions, parts of speech, irregular verbs, prefixes, rhyming words and so on. Students need to be online to play these games. Years 3-4+

• FunBrain.com
This site provides a set of interactive word and spelling games for younger students. You do need to be online for all these activities except for Word detective.
the misspelt word. Students need to be online for this activity.

Literature

• Kids Corner – Web Surfin Reading Fun http://kids.ot.com:80/surfin/reading.html
This site contains links to children's stories that are now out of the copyright period and able to be printed in full on the WWW. They include Conan Doyle, *Arabian Nights*, Jules Verne and many more.

• Tales of Wonder – http://darsie.ucdavis.edu/tales/
This is an archive of folk and fairy tales. The stories in this collection represent a small sampling of the rich storytelling art that is the common heritage of humanity. Stories from many parts of the world are included here. Useful for finding that folk tale from a particular region that can't be located in the library. Also in text form, these stories could generate some creative writing or could be cut up for reading jigsaw-type activities for students.

• Shopfront for New Zealand Books – http://nzbooks.com/shopfront.html
Although this is an online bookstore, news items of interest to lovers of New Zealand literature are posted here, such as events and upcoming book awards. There is a useful search engine listing an extensive range of New Zealand authors for both children and adults. Once you have located an author or book title, a short thumb-nail sketch is given about each story and author, book covers are depicted and other titles written by an author are also listed.

Poetry

• PIZZAZ!... People Interested in Zippy and ZAny Zcribbling – http://darkwing.uoregon.edu/~leslieob/pizzaz.html
These are lessons/guides in how to write poems in a number of styles. Some good ideas for poetry writing with your class.

• The Project Bartley Archive – http://www.columbia.edu/acis/bartleby/index.html
Contains the full text of works by a number of well-known poets.

Table 5 continued

Drama

- **Children's Theatre Page – http://members.aol.com/theatreuk/main.htm**
Provides examples of drama games, ideas for improvisations.

- **British Theatre Mining Company – http://britishtheatre.miningco.com**
The schools and youth theatre section may have some links that are of interest for the drama teacher at http://britishtheatre.miningco.com/msub6.htm

- **Theatre Lesson Plan Exchange – http://home.earthlink.net/~shalyndria/index.html**
Some interesting lesson plans listed here which include Assertiveness, Conflict Resolution, Empathy, Handling Stress, Managing Feelings, Personal Responsibility, Self-Awareness for junior to adult learners.

- **Classroom Lesson Plans – http://www.geocities.com/Broadway/Alley/3765/lessons.html**
An interesting site full of teaching ideas created by a drama teacher.

Resources for the Teaching of Maori

Maori language resources for teachers are growing. There is the Kimikupu Hou Lexical Database <http://www.nzcer.org.nz/kimikupu/index.htm> created by NZCER, where the English to Maori and Maori to English translation are provided. Stories are provided by the Weka Web network <http://hobbes.unitecnology.ac.nz/weka/resources/maori.html>. Online quizzes and challenges about maori culture are available from Maori Organisations of New Zealand – <http://www.maori.org.nz/ >. (See Table 6 on the next page.)

Table 6: Resources for the teaching of Maori

Language database

• **Kimikupu Hou Lexical Database – http://www.nzcer.org.nz/kimikupu/index.htm**
Kimikupu Hou is a searchable database of new and technical Maori vocabulary.

• **University of Otago – Department of Maori Studies http://www.otago.ac.nz/Web_menus/Dept_Homepages/Maori_Studies/Maori_Studies.html**
There are some useful links here to other Maori Studies Departments at tertiary institutions around New Zealand as well as the resources on site here.

Maori organisations with educational materials online

• **Maori Organisations of New Zealand – http://www.maori.org.nz/**
The education section of this site contains some online resources for Maori language activities ,including crosswords and multi-choice questions.

• **Toi Rakatahi – Ngai Tahu Children's Site – http://toirakatahi.ngaitahu.iwi.nz/**

Maori stories and legends

• **Maori Resources and Issues: Weka Web – http://hobbes.unitecnology.ac.nz/weka/resources/maori.html**
There are legends and other good Maori language links here.

The Treaty

• **Treaty of Waitangi – The text in English http://nz.com/NZ/Maori/Texts/WaitangiTreatyEnglish.html**

• **Treaty of Waitangi – The text in Maori (with audio) http://nz.com/NZ/Maori/Texts/WaitangiTreatyMaori.html**

Maori language software

• **Reddfish Intergalactic Online – http://www.reddfish.co.nz/**
Software for Te Reo Maori – games, educational software, fonts, and other tools are available from this company.

Resources for Teachers of Mathematics
Communications resources for Maths teachers

Teachers can involve their students in a variety of collaborative projects which cover a wide range of topics and process skills in mathematics. Global data-gathering activities are a favourite. In previous data-gathering projects information has been gathered on weather, temperature and precipitation, and comparative prices of grocery items around the world (current project to be found at <http://www.landmarkproject.com/ggl.html>), and solstice and equinox sunrise and sunset data have been collected among other projects. A good source of maths projects is Education Place<http://www.eduplace.com/projects/ mathproj.html>.

Mathmagic <http://forum.swarthmore.edu/mathmagic/> is another ongoing project where groups of students solve problems and post their solutions using e-mail. There are four e-mail lists which operate the challenges for junior primary, middle and senior primary, lower secondary and upper secondary. Teachers subscribe to the open levels to find out about the challenges and register their teams in the closed listservs to take part in the competitions. A fifth list is operated for teachers only.

Informational resources for Maths teachers

For teachers and students there are a number of mathematics sites that will encourage the development of confidence and competence in information technology in mathematical contexts. For teachers the Maths Forum <http://forum.swarth more.edu> provides a professional interactive network for maths teachers and contains indexed lists of Internet mathematics sites, as well as lesson plans, interactive activities, and opportunities for discussion and teacher collaboration. This is a comprehensive and extremely well-organised resource and is inclusive of professionals working at all educational levels. A similarly conceived professional network a little closer to home is the TAME network for Australian Mathematics teachers at <http:// www.edfac.unimelb.edu.au/ DSME/TAME/>.

Students and teachers can ask for help about any fascinating maths problems from Ask Dr Math, <http://forum.swarthmore.edu/dr.math/>. Previously asked questions are archived into four sections: primary, intermediate, high school and tertiary. Some interesting questions and answers are identified with stars to indicate they are good jumping off points for interesting investigations into maths topics. Figure 2 on the next page is an example of a Dr Math request and reply.

Interactive activity sites for Maths

There are a number of interactive sites that encourage students to experiment and play around with mathematical concepts. Java programming allows for objects to be manipulated on the screen and particular choices to be made. Examples cover almost all strands of the mathematics curriculum. One site which provides very interesting interactive activities complete with lesson plans and well-grounded curriculum objectives is Project Interactivate at <http://www.shodor.org/interactivate/>. These are units of work for intermediate and junior secondary students and are designed to provide authentic learning situations. It is most interesting to be able to play around with the standard deviation of a normal curve and to watch what happens to the curve when the standard deviation draws away from 1 in either direction.

Table 7 on page 73 lists some interactive activity websites for Mathematics teachers.

```
Date: 09/10/98 at 15:05:20
From: ajg@surfshop.net (Alisha)
Subject: Counting in the teens

I take Algebra 2, and one of the questions we need to know the answer
to is why, when you count, you go ten eleven twelve thirteen instead
of ten eleventeen twelveteen thirteen. I have looked everywhere for
an answer. Could you please help? Thanks.
```

```
Date: 09/11/98 at 12:08:01
From: Doctor Peterson
Subject: Re: Counting in the teens

Hi, Alisha,
There's a fascinating discussion of this question (and some others
like it) in the math-history-list: http://forum.swarthmore.edu/epigone/
math-history-list/queldglixgy Look especially at the messages by
John Conway; he discusses this also in his book _The Book of Numbers_.
Here's his answer on eleven and twelve:

There seems to be a natural tendency in language for the first few
terms of a sequence to be treated specially. Thus in English, 'eleven'
is really 'one left (over)', and 'twelve' is 'two left', so that the
implied 'after ten' is omitted. But from thirteen on it seems that we
should explicitly mention the 'ten', since we're getting so far away
from it that we might otherwise forget it!
So the 'e' in eleven means 'one', and the 'tw' in twelve means 'two'!
   - Doctor Peterson, The Math Forum
     http://forum.swarthmore.edu/dr.math/
```

Figure 2: Ask Dr Math – counting in the teens

Also popular are sites that provide a problem of the week that will challenge students. A good example for younger children is Brain Teasers promoted at the Houghton Mifflin site Education Place – <http://www.eduplace.com/math/brain/index.html>. A Brain teaser is published at three levels, each week with solutions the following week for Years 4-5, years 6-7 and years 8+.

There are sites that provide a range of lesson plans and teaching resources. (See Table 8 for some of the best of these websites.)

Table 9 on page 74 is a list of maths resources that link with mathematics in the New Zealand curriculum strands.

Interactive Puzzles and Games – http://www.cut-the-knot.com/
There is a list of 94 interactive onscreen games here with background info on the mathematics and history of each. Great site for recreational maths activities for about Year 7+.

A+ Interactive Maths Site – http://www.aplusmath.com/
There are interactive games and drill and practice maths activities available at this great site. These include flash card activities.

Quai! Mathematics Games – http://www.quia.com/math.htm
This provides online interactive drill and practice games – Flashcards, Matching Games and Concentration practice activities for simple addition to more complex fraction to decimal equivalents. For primary students.

Arith-M-Attack – http://www.dep.anl.gov/aattack.htm
This is a 60-second speed test using a basic operations of your choice or a random choice option. An advantage of this programme is the option to download a copy to your hard drive for extended use.

(Note – one of the problems for many teachers with a limited number of computers in their classrooms and with costs associated with Internet use is that for many of these interactive games the students need to be online for the duration of the activity.)

Table 7: Interactive Maths Activity Sites

- **Explorer**
http://server2.greatlakes.k12.mi.us/GLCbrowse/Mathematics/index.html
The resources at this site link well with Mathematics in the New Zealand Curriculum strands and mathematical processes. (This is actually one of the few Internet sites which provide some useful measurement activities for metric users, and also some nice integrated curriculum units.) The activities are presented in Adobe Acrobat Reader file format but it is worth the effort of downloading this freely available software from the Internet.

- **Ask Eric mathematics**
http://ericir.syr.edu/Virtual/Lessons/Mathematics/index.html
This is a huge resource of lesson plans classified into learning strands and process skills.

- **Big Sky lesson plans**
gopher://bvsd.k12.co.us/11/Educational_Resources/Lesson_Plans/Big%20Sky/math
This site is one you have to spend time browsing. Lessons are still in an older pre-WWW gopher format interface and are not well classified or organised for easy access. There are, however, some worthwhile ideas for primary teachers in particular. These resources, graded for all levels from junior primary upwards, contain descriptions of maths games, problem-solving activities and teaching ideas.

Table 8: Maths lesson plan websites

Links to other sites with resources in number

• **Mathematics Archives**
http://archives.math.utk.edu/topics/arithmetic.html
Topics in Arithmetic provides a whole series of links to computation sites that include interactive sites, lesson plans and more.

• **Number Math Forum A-Z Index**
http://forum.swarthmore.edu/~steve/steve/mathtopics.html
An annotated collection of sites that lead directly to maths work relating to number. See also
  • Arithmetic
  • Number Theory
  • Number Analysis

Puzzles and challenges for number

• **SMARD database-http://smard.cqu.edu.au/Database/index.html**
A resource of lesson plans and puzzles and challenges submitted by teachers. There is a junior and senior database. The junior database covers the same curriculum strands as MINZC. Ideas and problems are downloaded to your hard-drive as Word files. (Acceptable on Word 98 for either Mac or PC).

Topics in number

• **Today's Date – http://acorn.educ.nottingham.ac.uk/cgi-bin/daynum**
Some information about the numbers relating to the current day and month. For instance, all sorts of mathematical info is given about the number 25. A great project starter for middle/upper primary children investigating numbers.

• **The abacus – http://www.ee.ryerson.ca:8080/~elf/abacus/**
Everything you ever wanted to know about the abacus ... the history, different types, even a link to the abacus museum.

• **Egyptian Maths – http://eyelid.ukonline.co.uk/ancient/numbers.htm**
A description of the Egyptian numerical system, with some practice problems. A great project starter for upper primary children which could be used with Mayan Maths information **http://hanksville.phast.umass.edu/yucatan/mayamath.html**.

• **Magic squares, magic stars and other patterns – http://www.geocities.com/ CapeCanaveral/Launchpad/4057/**
Fun maths work with number patterns. Upper primary.

Table 9: Maths resources for teachers – number

Links site for resources in geometry

• **The Maths Forum Internet Resource Collection**
http://forum.swarthmore.edu/~steve/steve/mathtopics.html
Check out:
>   Trigonometry Math Forum A-Z Index
>   Computational Geometry
>   Differential Geometry

Lesson plans

• There are more units available at **Computational Methods in Elementary Geometry page http://www.geom.umn.edu/~demo5337/**

• **The Geometry Center – http://www.geom.umn.edu/**
Software and units of work can be found here. The following sets of lessons utilise Internet websites to support the teaching ideas and unit plans:
>   Introduction to symmetry
>   Classification of patterns
>   The golden ratio

• **Art & Geometry – http://www.pacificnet.net/~mandel/Math.html**
A series of lesson plans.

Topics in geometry

• **EggMath – http://chickscope.beckman.uiuc.edu/explore/eggmath/**
This unit of work, which would work well with a technology unit on packaging eggs, consists of work on symmetry, surfaces, ellipses and ovals, as well as spherical geometry, tangents, slopes and exponential growth. Great integrated unit for upper primary and lower secondary.

• **Project Interactivate**
Some good units of work available on geometry topics.

Table 10: Maths resources for teachers – geometry and measurement

Links site for resources in probability and statistics

• The Maths Forum Internet Resource Collection
http://forum.swarthmore.edu/~steve/steve/mathtopics.html
Check out links to Probability, Statistics and Algebra

• **Maths Archives, Topics in Mathematics – Algebra**
http://archives.math.utk.edu/topics/algebra.html
This listing is largely for secondary teachers.

Topics in algebra, probability and statistics

• **Project Interactivate – http://www.shodor.org/interactivate/index.html**
Some good units of work available on algebra and probability and statistics topics for upper primary and lower secondary classes.

• **Newspaper Maths – http://www.teachingonline.org/maths1.html**
A teaching unit from starters and strategies.

Interactive games

• **Interactive Mathematics puzzles and games**
http://www.cut-the-knot.com/probability.html
Probability and chance scroll down the page and there are some nine interactive onscreen games here with background information on the mathematics and history of each. Great site for recreational maths activities for about Year 7+ See also Interactive mathematics – **http://www.cut-the-knot.com/algebra.html** for algebra plans.

Table 11: Algebra, probability and statistics

Resources for Teachers of Social Studies
Using communications resources for social studies

Many of the interactive projects that are available to students and their teachers on the Internet through such organisations as Kidlink and the Global SchoolNet Foundation fit snugly with the intended aims of social studies education in New Zealand. Projects aim to develop understanding of people, their actions, and their activities by global exchanges and information sharing through international contacts. These projects develop knowledge and understanding of others as part of their learning contexts. Even those without a specific social studies context often fit the aims of the social studies curriculum.

It is difficult for students who have no experience of other cultures and lifestyles to understand or identify what makes them uniquely New Zealanders. Many global projects require the participating schools to say something about themselves. These thumbnail biographies generate inquiry into the uniqueness of such things as the language students use, or the events or situations that they may be describing. For instance, when young children are asked to describe a game of rugby or cricket, or what they mean by kia ora, they begin to clarify their own beliefs and values, and understand their unique place in the world a little better.

Collaborative projects can range from such activities as sharing intercultural recipes and ideas about food, as in an intercultural cookbook, to studying families, understanding past cultures (as in the Maya Quest project) or gathering a database on multicultural holidays and the reasons for celebrating them.

Some interactive collaborative projects are based around the idea of being a virtual tourist. Where on the Globe is Roger <http://www.gsn.org/roger/index.html> is one such project promoted by the Global SchoolNet Foundation. Roger Williams travels the world in his van 'Bubba' and sends back reports of his travels and visits to schools along the way to the registered project participants. This project like many others run by the Global School house are relatively long-term projects. Roger has travelled much since my class joined him in 1994 during his travels through outback Australia and used his e-mailed reports as part of their reading programme.

Telefield trips are very popular. Projects run by NZ Telecom Education Foundation – such as Expedition Icebound in 1995, Seakeepers in 1996, Explorers and Adventurers in 1997, and Wonders of the World in 1998 (Descriptions of these projects are to be found at <http://www.telecom.co.nz/tef/>) are telefield trips providing opportunities for children to directly contact the participants or content experts and ask or listen to other children asking questions via audio conferences. Many of these projects are cross-curricular in nature and include opprtunities for social studies, science and language activities.

Other interactive projects are based on the idea of thinking globally and acting locally. One such project was helping children in the Lebanon. This was a project organised by a group of 13 to 16-year-old students and their teacher, who held a 24-hour messagathon, actively gathering responses by e-mail or Chat. Sponsors donated a dollar for every country that sent a response and the proceeds went to Lebanese children in need. Other social action projects have covered issues of nuclear waste, global warming, and acid rain, providing a rare global viewpoint for students. For a range of the types of projects currently available see I*EARN Youth Action Projects at <http://www.igc.apc.org/iearn/action.html>. See also the newsgroup news:iearn.teachers for current action projects and discussion.

Popular interactive activities are online games and challenges. There are several examples of these to be found in the following places Thinkquest – <http://www.gsn.org/project/index.html> and Geogame http://www.gsn.org and Hunt for Famous Explorers <http://www.kidlink.org/KIDPROJ/Explorers98/ >.

Figure 3 is an example of the 'Hunt for the Famous Explorer Challenge'.

Hunt For Famous Explorers Game
Played between 20 April – 1 June, 1998

To Play

Choose an explorer anywhere in the world. Students, research facts concerning the explorer and compose nine interesting clues and send them along with your the name of your explorer to the Explorer Moderators. Three clues per week will be posted by the Explorer Moderators to the Kidproject board over a three week period. All registered schools may ask one question per week which requires a 'yes' or 'no' answer to each school. At the end of the three weeks the school which guessed the most explorers will be declared the winner!

Follow-Up Activity

Once the answers are posted to the KIDPROJ forum e-mail discussion may begin about:

What did that clue mean?
What resources did you use to do research?
What did you learn about geography?
What did you learn about history?
What neat Web pages did you find?
Is there a Web page for your explorer that helped to compose clues?

Figure 3: Hunt for famous explorers

There is an economics game for New Zealand school children called Share Market Clash where teams compete in an online buying and selling shares simulation. This game is found at <http://www.schoolsnet.ac.nz/share/index.html>. There is also an interesting site called Good News Bears <http://www.i2s.com/gnb/index2.html> which provides extensive resources for teachers and students learning about the stock market.

Online interactive activities are also available. See the UN CyberSchoolbus site for an interactive Flag Tag Game at <http://www.un.org/cgi-bin/pubs/flagtag.pl>. Flags can be randomly chosen or purposefully selected. Thumbnail information about each country is also available.

Starters and Strategies Magazine is also online at <http://www.teachingonline.org> and the site contains many valuable activities for language and social studies for primary children in particular.

Teachers wishing to see what kinds of educational projects have previously been available can consult Judi Harris's Network-Based Educational Activity Structures which can be found at <http://www.gsn.org/Web/_lib/_harris/Harris-A.htm>. (See Table 12: for lists of current educational projects.)

- **Global SchoolNet Foundation – http://www.gsn.org/project/index.html.**

- **Kidlink – http://www.kidlink.org/**

- **Education Place – http://www.eduplace.com/projects/**

- **I*EARN – http://www.igc.apc.org/iearn/projects.html**

Table 12: Sources for good educational projects for Social Studies

Informational resources for social studies teachers

Resources for social studies education have burgeoned on the Internet since my last publication (Trewern,1996). Some major providers of educational resources have entered the field, such as *Encyclopedia Britannica*, Discovery Channel, *National Geographic* and the United Nations, and the quality of the online educational resources they provide is quite outstanding.

Another site is New Zealand Maps <http://bb2.bitz.co.nz/nzmaps/> which uses an interesting graphical method of locating websites about specific localities within New Zealand. It is most useful for locating online information about various places, place names and features around New Zealand.

A must-visit site for the teacher of social studies is the United Nations Cyber School Bus website at <http://www.un.org/Pubs/CyberSchoolBus/>. At this site check out School Kits on the United Nations at <http://www.un.org/Pubs/CyberSchoolBus/ bookstor/kits/english/index.html> for background and resources (some samples online) and kits that can be ordered. There is a Virtual Tour of the UN <http://www.un.org/ Pubs/CyberSchoolBus/around/tour.htm>. As well, check out the following online teaching units:

- Human Rights in Action
<http://www.un.org/Pubs/CyberSchoolBus/humanrights/index.html>

- Cities of Today, Cities of Tomorrow
<http://www.un.org/Pubs/CyberSchoolBus/special/habitat/index.html>

Many governments maintain online resources that are useful in supporting the social organisation strand of the curriculum with particular resources. Many full text treaties are also available. (See Table 13.)

- **New Zealand Government Web Pages** – http://www.govt.nz/

- **Australian Government Homepage** – http://www.fed.gov.au/

- **a2z International Government Links** – **http://a2z.lycos.com/Government/International_Government/**
This Lycos alphabetical listing can connect users with various governments and governing agencies from around the world .

- **The White House** – **http://www.whitehouse.gov/WH/Welcome.html**
For The White House for Kids see http://www.whitehouse.gov/WH/kids/html/kidshome.html

- **The Multilaterals Page** – **http://www.tufts.edu/fletcher/multilaterals.html**
Provides links to a variety of political, economic, human rights and warfare treaties signed world wide.

Table 13: Government webpages

Very popular online resources for social studies are the expeditions which support the culture and heritage strands of the curriculum. Such expeditions are ably supported by *National Geographic*, PBS Online and Nova Online and also Discovery Channel School. Creating a virtual world is a feature of the Internet site Pyramid the Inside Story <http://www.pbs.org/wgbh/nova/pyramid/>. Learners are encouraged to develop a feeling for the people inhabiting this virtual world of the past by identifying with Egyptian bread-makers and their task of feeding the pyramid workers. Students are able to visualise the pyramid by walking their mouse pointer down passages, rooms and caverns, working out spatial relationships and room sizes. It is a vibrant introduction to a teaching unit investigating ancient technologies. The making of flower-pot bread, the science of mummification, and investigating building structures in archaic societies could also be included. (Side investigations could make use of the Ice Mummies of the Inca website at <http://www.pbs.org/wgbh/nova/peru/>, and the Unearthing South America website at <http://school.discovery.com/fall97/programs/unearthing southamerica/> as well as the Mysterious Mummies of China <http://www.pbs.org/wgbh/nova/chinamum/>. Also useful would be the Discovery Channel School theme on Ancient Egypt <http://school.discovery.com/lessonplans/themesancientegypt.html> and a classroom activity on Discovery Channel School called Build a Tomb – <http://discoveryschool.com/fall98/activities/buildatomb/index.html>.

- **Nova Online – http://www.pbs.org/wgbh/nova/onlinelibrary.html**

There are some excellent cross-curricular online projects available from NOVA/PBS Online Adventures. The adventures follow scientists and explorers into the field, reporting on science as it happens and allowing the Internet audience to participate via e-mail. Social studies teachers need to check out the following topics from the above homepage. Each of these are extensive resources. Highly recommended are:

    Ice Mummies
    Lost City of Arabia
    Mysterious Mummies of China
    Pyramids – The Inside Story
    Search for the Lost Cave People
    Secrets of Easter Island
    Secrets of Lost Empires

- **PBS Online – http://www.pbs.org/**

There are some excellent resources located here especially in the world history section.

    Historical – http://www.pbs.org/history/world.html
    In the Footsteps of Alexander the Great
    The Peoples' Century
    The Gold Rush
    The Great War and the Shaping of the 20th Century
    The Face of Russia

- **Discovery Channel School – http://school.discovery.com/schoolhome.html**

This site is packed with resources, including online information and lesson plans about upcoming TV presentations. Unfortunately past events and lessons are not archived.

- **Encyclopedia Britannica – http://www.eb.com/**

This is a subscription site. However, Britannica does maintain a couple of examples of online information for people who wish to browse the type of content available here. An excellent resource. Check out their spotlight features which are available for a limited time to non-subscribers. Current interest topics at the time of writing are Titanic and D-Day landing at Normandy.

- **Planet Think – http://www.planet-think.net/network/default.htm**

The resources here are of a more geographical nature. Journeys are a series of month-long interactive explorations around various countries. These change regularly. At the time of writing these journeys included Venezuela, The Caribbean and Great Britain. Teacher activities are supplied in PDF format for these explorations.

Table 14: Resources for teachers of Social Studies. This table continues on the next page.

- **Xpeditions@nationalgeographic.com**
http://www.nationalgeographic.com/resources/ngo/education/xpeditions/main.html
Access to some 600 *National Geographic* maps (that can be printed) teacher forums, and online projects. A great site for teachers.

The quality of the following online learning modules from Xpeditions is outstanding:

- **Ice Treasures of the Inca**
http://www.nationalgeographic.com/features/96/mummy/
An online exhibition from National Geographic Expeditionary team in Peru and the story of finding an Inca mummy high in the Andes. Also online, a virtual autopsy of the Ice Mummy.

- **Eyes on the Tiger**
http://www.nationalgeographic.com/resources/ngo/education/geoguide/tigers/
A *National Geographic* study module on the world of the wild cats and the issues they face in terms of poaching and environmental management. Comes with lesson plans for school and activities for home and family. These plans require Adobe Acrobat reader but include excellent games and other activities that are organised across a range of age levels (i.e. there are separate plans for lower primary, intermediate and secondary students). See also **Wolves – http://www.nationalgeographic.com/resources/ngo/education/geoguide/wolves/index.html**

- **Nenets Reindeer Herders of Siberia**
http://www.nationalgeographic.com/resources/ngo/education/geoguide/nenets/
A study module on the Siberian Reindeer Herders.

- **Dams**
http://www.nationalgeographic.com/resources/ngo/education/geoguide/dams/
A module about the reasons for building dams, how people build dams, and exploring the good and bad impacts a dam may have on a community.

Teachers intending to have their classes study a past generation such as 'Living at the turn of the century' can supplement the artifacts children bring from home (e.g. family photos and items used in the kitchen and elsewhere), with Internet database images from the Turnbull Library collection. This superb online collection contains thousands of quality images of New Zealanders living and working in, and celebrating and enjoying, the past. (See Table 15.)

A resource also not to be missed by the social studies teacher is the New Zealand Ancient and Modern History at http://www.enzed.com/hist.html. This site has some worthwhile links to a range of New Zealand topics that are very useful, ranging from Polynesian navigation to information of interest to local teachers.

Also useful is a database of famous people available at Biography.com <http://www.biography.com/>. A number of famous New Zealanders are part of the database.

The History/Social Studies Website for K-12 Teachers at <http://www.execpc.com/~dboals/ > is an annotated index site for history topics for teachers prepared to dig out those history sites on the Internet.

- **Timeframes**
http://timeframes.natlib.govt.nz/
The picture archives of the National Library of New Zealand have some images of early
Dunedin and of the early days in New Zealand in general that would be useful.

- **The Library of Congress Prints and Photographs**
http://lcweb2.loc.gov/pp/pphome.html
Is an online catalogue which also contains a wealth of early photographs, some of which
actually relate to early New Zealand.

Table 15: Historical picture resources. Table 16 (below): Current events.

For teachers interested in assessment of historical methods there is the National
Center for History in the Schools – <http://www.sscnet.ucla.edu/nchs/>.

Utilising the World Wide Web for current events is an effective way of meeting
many of the objectives of the strands and processes of the social studies curriculum.
Also most local newspapers have online resources and this is a most useful way of
keeping students in touch with current happenings and local perspectives. Table 16
lists websites which summarise world news items at various levels for students.

- **Current Events in the Social Studies classroom**
http://www.eduplace.com/ss/current/index.html
Every month, the Social Studies Center at Education Place highlights an issue currently in the
news. The themes and ideas discussed in the social studies classroom are combined with
challenges and with links online to further information to help students with the challenges.

News Sources

- **Internet CNN Newsroom**
http://www.nmis.org/NewsInteractive/CNN/Newsroom/contents.html
This site supports video files about latest news events which can be downloaded and activities
are provided for students investigating and following news events. News stories are archived.
A strong US perspective is presented.

- **Yahoo – Reuters International News Summary**
http://dailynews.yahoo.com/tx/wl/summary.html
Text summaries of news stories are outlined with links to previous stories that are relevant
to that particular story. Easy for students to follow any previous leads to a story. A strong
European perspective is presented.

- **Reuters Home Page – http://www.reuters.com/**

- **BBC News – http://news.bbc.co.uk/**
Images and news headlines are linked to more in-depth text and audio stories about events.
Possibly a better site for upper primary students. Strong European perspective is presented.
Comparison of the bias of these news services would make an interesting unit of work for
older students.

Internet Resources for Science Teachers
Communications resources for science teachers

Projects based around a science topic are generally found in the same places as those on social studies and mathematics. There are various types of science projects. Some may be small in scale and involve several classes studying a common topic. Large projects may include a science component in a more integrated curriculum theme. Some projects may operate at the level of limited personal exchanges or sharing of information, while others may involve global data collections or many classes in parallel problem-solving activities. For an overview of current science projects visit the Education Place Project Center at <http://www.eduplace.com/projects/scproj.html>.

NASA also support online projects which can be seen at Sharing NASA <http://quest.arc.nasa.gov/interactive/index.html>. These projects involve online discussions with NASA experts and regular updates of information to project participants. There is also an archive of past projects available from a link on this same page. Projects have involved participants in all major NASA projects, including The Hubble Space Telescope, the Marsfinder Expedition and the Shuttle/Mir Online Research Project.

Telefield trips are as popular for science topics as they are for social studies topics. NZ Telecom Education Foundation at <http://www.telecom.co.nz/tef/> and LEARNZ at <http://learnz.icair.iac.org.nz/98/> have supported cross-curricular projects with a strong science emphasis for New Zealand school children for several years now. There is also Galapagos Quest at <http://africaquest.classroom.com/ gqmarket/gqmarket.asp> which is based on the successful MayaQuest framework. The Thayer Expeditions <http://www.goals.com/thayer/expfrm.htm> are yet another example of telefield trips about science.

An archive of the types and varieties of shared science projects has been put together by Judi Harris and can be found at Networked-Based Educational Activity Structures at <http://www.gsn.org/Web/_lib/_harris/Harris-A.htm>.

Mailing lists for teachers of science are fairly extensive and a mailing list can be found for educators interested in general science and in specialist science subjects. A good place to check up on the available mailing lists is tile.net at <http://tile.net/lists>.

The education links at Royal Society of New Zealand Web pages at <http://www.rsnz.govt.nz/> provide some excellent and up-to-date reports on scientific research for teachers. The magazine published by the society is available online in a full text version and is a valuable newsletter for science educators.

Information resources for science teachers

Science as a subject is generally exceptionally well supported on the Internet. Such non-profit American organisations as the National Science Foundation and NASA have been instrumental in promoting science-through-technology delivery and in supporting a range of educational providers, such as science museums and professional development providers, with stimulating resources for online users. A number of commercial providers, educational TV providers, book publishers and even pharmaceutical companies are also becoming involved in delivery. A very good site for combinations of Internet sites on a particular science topic is KIDS – <http://scout.cs.wisc.edu/scout/KIDS/>. A biweekly report is available online and would be a good starter for science teachers looking for Internet resources on a similar topic. For instance, the topic flight combines a large number of good sites into one page.

Some science centres are heavily involved in the provision of extensive and well-packaged science education and curriculum resources online. The best resources are not that readily found using the search engines. Listed in Table 17 are some of the 'not to be missed' science multimedia presentations that include lessons, teaching ideas and experiments, and activities across the range of science curriculum strands.

Table 17: Science centres with great online teaching units (continued on page 86)

- **Miami Museum of Science http://www.miamisci.org/**
There are some excellent online teaching resources here. Do look at:
    PH Factor
    Hurricane
    Internet Island
    The Atoms Family

- **The Natural History Museum. http://www.nhm.ac.uk/**
The online learning multimedia presentations called casebooks are very good for Year 5 + and are well worth a look.
    Recreating Dinosaurs
    Fact or Fiction
    Cosmic Football
    The Beast of Bodmin Moor

- **Oregon Museum of Science and Industry – http://www.omsi.edu/sln/**
Particularly worthwhile are the resources
    Air Travellers
    Water Works

- **Questacon http://sunsite.anu.edu.au/Questacon/**
There are some good classoom resources available here for teachers of younger children. They are in the form of games, colouring in activities, puzzles etc.

- **The Exploratorium http://www.exploratorium.edu/**
Here you will find online interactive games and puzzles, teaching resources, facts, experiments for the classroom. An area teachers will find useful is The Learning Studio, which is an excellent resource for primary and secondary teachers that includes online information and activities relating to space. Spectra from Space, Auroras, Third from the Sun, Graphing Stratospheric Ozone and The Great Satellite Search are online teaching tutorials written by teachers. These teaching resources require students to use Internet resources to complete the projects. Also the Exploratorium Snackbook activities are useful to secondary teachers looking for starter investigations for sixth form physics projects. There is the Science of Cycling and the Science of Ice Hockey that also should not be missed.

Table 17 continued

• **The Franklin Institute Science Museum – http://sln.fi.edu/**
Check out the following multimedia presentations:
     The Heart – An Online Exploration
     The World of Benjamin Franklin
     An Enquirers Guide to The Universe.
There are a variety of other lesson plans and activities at this site. See Wind our Fierce Friend, Franklin's Forecast, El Nino – Hot Air Over Hot Water and Earth Forces and Living Things and Water in the City.

• **Science Museum of Minnesota http://www.sci.mus.mn.us/**
There are a number of good teaching resources available at this site. Make sure you visit:
     The Thinking Fountain
     Monarch and Migration
     From Windmills to Whirly Gigs
     Worms
     Maya Adventure

• **Museum of Science, Boston – http://www.mos.org/**
There are good resources for teachers including Exploring Leonardo which includes lessons plans and activity ideas for this topic that can be used in the classroom.

• **The Field Museum of Natural History – http://www.fmnh.org./**
This much visited site contains a good resource for younger students about the development of Life Over Time.

• **The Smithsonian – http://www.si.edu/newstart.htm**
This is a very large site. There is a lot of very worthwhile material here but you need time to locate much of it. Search features have been included on the site homepage to help with locating resources.

Table 18 is a list of science resources that link with science in the New Zealand curriculum strands.

- **Ask ERIC Lesson Plans Science: Biological and Life Sciences**
http://ericir.syr.edu/Virtual/Lessons/Science/Biological/index.html
A great collection of lesson plans can be found here for students from junior/primary and secondary.

- **Living Things from the Franklin Science Institute**
http://www.fi.edu/tfi/units/life/
A compilation of many lesson plans and student activities which have 'living things' ideas grouped as individuals, families, neighbourhoods and cycles.

- **Ocean Planet**
http://seawifs.gsfc.nasa.gov/OCEAN_PLANET/HTML/ocean_planet_overview.html
An exhibition from the Smithsonian containing some diverse but interesting material about the Earth's oceans. At this site it is not altogether easy to find things, but it does contain some worthwhile information on marine animals and plants, care of the ocean environments, ocean science information and lots of ocean facts.

Animals

- **SeaWorld/Busch Gardens Animal information database**
http://www.seaworld.org/

- **World Wide Fund for Nature**
WWF: Virtual Wildlife – http://www.panda.org/kids/wildlife/
This is a delightful site with much interesting information and beautiful drawings for children about endangered wildlife around the world.

- **Cincinnati Zoo** – http://www.cincyzoo.org/
A delightful site that would appeal to children. The link to the field guide to animals and plants would be most useful to teachers. This index gives a brief description and picture of each animal or plant.

- **The Interactive Frog Dissection**
http://curry.edschool.Virginia.EDU/go/frog/menu.html
An online tutorial taking students through the stages of dissecting a frog.

- **Monarch and Migration**
http://www.sci.mus.mn.us/sln/monarchs/top.html
Some excellent ideas for a unit on the monarch butterfly with science background, and other cross-curricular activities for primary students. There is an online slide show about a school visit to the Monarch butterfly sanctuaries in Mexico. Also check out the Gallery at the Butterfly Website for a very extensive collection of butterfly images.

- **Worms** – http://www.sci.mus.mn.us/sln/tf/w/worms/worms/worms.html
A science unit for junior primary children from the Museum of Minnesota Science Centre. Anyone having a look at this unit would just have to have a look at Worm World where you need be sure to get yourself equipped with video and sound plugins to see the birth of a baby worm video and to hear young poets read their own wormy poetry. A delightful site that is both educational and imaginative where even the bad worm jokes are fun.

Table 18: Living World websites. This table continues on page 88.

Biology

- **Shuttle/Mir online research experience**
http://quest.arc.nasa.gov/smore/teachers/activities.html
Activities relate to a range of age levels from primary to secondary students and include seed germination, hydroponics, refractive indexes of water and effects of closed systems on living things. The great plant debate http://quest.arc.nasa.gov/smore/events/datashare.html is an interactive activity in which students investigate the conditions that lead to the germination of wheat seeds and observe the early stages of the plant lifecycle. For older students, there are additional options for experimental variables to test.

- **Access Excellence – http://www.gene.com/ae/**
A must-see site for biology and biotechnology teachers and students at secondary level. Check out the information on cells.

- **Your Genes Your Choices**

Exploring the issues raised by genetic research

http://ehrweb.aaas.org/ehr/books/index.html
This full text version of the book describes the Human Genome Project, the science behind it, and the ethical, legal, and social issues that areraised by the project. The content is very useful teaching material for upper secondary students. Issues are raised in the form of actual cases and full descriptions of the science supporting the issues is also provided.

The microscopic living world

- **The Cells Alive – http://www.cellsalive.com/website** has visually well-presented information on parasites, viruses, bacteria and allergies, and infections. There is much information available here for senior-level secondary school science and biology students. The site is also an good launching pad to other links in biology and microbiology. Some excellent microscopic images are available.

- **Also Bugs in the News http://falcon.cc.ukans.edu/~jbrown/bugs.html** is a good text information site to find out about the latest in bugs in health news.

Activities requiring problem-solving and puzzle solutions

- **Forensic Files – http://forensicfiles.bc.sympatico.ca/**
This is an online version of something similar to Carmen Santiago. The purpose is to follow the links through the game and see if you can piece together the clues to help solve an international heist of an endangered species.

- There is also the Mystery Spot section at **Access Excellence – http://www.gene.com/ae/ AE/mspot/** There are three problem-solving activities at this site called Arctica, River of Venom and the Blackout Syndrome. Others have been created by teachers. These are excellent group problem-solving activities for secondary students.

Table 18 continued

Physical and material worlds

For teachers of younger students, the online presentations from the science museums meet many of the objectives from the physical and material world strands very well. The Exploratorium offers some very worthwhile online activities and they are continually expanding what they offer. Discovery Channel School usually provides life sciences and physical sciences online projects to support their televised science series every three months. Table 19 lists other online providers for science projects.

- **PBS Online Science – http://www.pbs.org/science/**
Steven Hawking's Universe
Science Odysseys – People and Discoveries

- **Nova Online – http://www.pbs.org/wgbh/nova/onlinelibrary.html**
There are some interesting physical science presentations here:
> Einstein Revealed
> Avalanche
> Faster Than Sound
> Fastest Car
> Lost at Sea: The Search for Longitude
> Special Effects
> Titanic's Lost Sister
> Top Gun Over Moscow
> Balloon Race Around the World

- **Discovery Channel School**
http://school.discovery.com/schoolhome.html
A commitment by this TV channel to science topics which includes topics that support the timetabled programmes.

- **The Contemporary Physics Education project (CPEP)**
http://www-pdg.lbl.gov/cpep.html
Both online and other media resources available in the physical sciences. See online tutorials for The Particle Adventure – An Interactive Tour of the Inner Workings of the Atom and the Tools for Discovery. Energy Sources and Conversion – A guided tour. Fusion – Physics of a Fundamental Energy Source: An online interactive 'course'.

Table 19: Information resources for Physical and Material World curriculum strands

Resources to support Planet Earth and beyond

The information resources of the Internet are an important way for students to develop many of the understandings in this strand. The resources in this area of the curriculum are extremely extensive and it is impossible in the space of this article to even begin to cover the range available. NASA covers planetary and deep-space astronomy so extensively that it is hard to look beyond much of the up-to-date and useful material that is provided by this organisation. Many NASA sites are also producing lesson plan sets for all ages. If you have access to a colour printer, picture resources from these sites can be used in a variety of interesting ways to support the curriculum. Earth science and natural history is also extensively covered by a range of Internet sites, particularly museum sites.

Table 20 lists some good sites to visit that support the Planet Earth and Beyond section of the curriculum.

Earth Science

- **Volcano World – http://volcano.und.nodak.edu/**
Supported by National Air and Space Administration, this site is a very good educational resource for those interested in volcanoes.

- **Earth Force – http://www.fi.edu/earth/earth.html**
From the Franklin Institute of Science. Information and links about the topic to other resources.

- **USGS Learning Web**
http://www.usgs.gov/education/learnweb/index.html
Presents lesson plans and information about Earth Sciences for both primary and secondary teachers and students. See units on:
    Global change
    Working with maps
    Earth Sciences

- **Nova Online – http://www.pbs.org/wgbh/nova/onlinelibrary.html**
    Hawaii: Born of Fire
    Cracking the Ice Age
    Deadly Shadow of Vesuvius

Weather

Weather resources at some of the previously listed museum sites are very good, especially the hurricane module at the Miami Museum of Science and the weather activities at the Exploratorium.

- **Nova Online – http://www.pbs.org/wgbh/nova/onlinelibrary.html**
    Flood
    Warnings from the Ice

Table 20: Resources to support Planet Earth and Beyond. This table continues on pages 91-3.

Natural History
For primary students

- **Questacon – http://sunsite.anu.edu.au/Questacon/**
There are some good classoom resources on dinosaurs available in the Kidspace section for teachers of younger children. They are in the form of games, colouring-in activities, puzzles, etc.

- **Dinosaurs – http://www.knowledgeadventure.com/features/kids/**
A let's find out encyclopedia with a range of science topics for primary children that includes lots about dinosaurs. The activity centre http://www.kidspace.com/kids/dinosaurs/ This is an activity site for young students – join the dots activities, creatasaurus, colouring books and sticker books are available here.

- **Dinosaurs**
http://www.enchantedlearning.com/subjects/dinosaurs/allabout/
Hypertext book about dinosaurs. It is designed for students of all ages and levels of comprehension.

- **Field Museum of Natural, Boston**
http://www.fmnh.org./exhibits/lot/LOT1.htm
This much visited and very graphical site contains a good resource for primary students about the development of Life Over Time.

- **Tour through time**
http://www.ucmp.berkeley.edu/education/life/tournew.html
A series of virtual tutorials about genetic similarities and differences, presented by the UC Museum of Paleontology for various levels.

For upper primary and secondary students
- **Nova Online – http://www.pbs.org/wgbh/nova/onlinelibrary.html**
    The Curse of T-Rex

- **The Museum of Natural History in London – http://www.nhm.ac.uk/**
The science casebook is a series of very good online learning modules:
    Recreating dinosaurs; The Beast of Bodmin Moor; Cosmic Football

- **The Paleo Ring – http://www.pitt.edu/~mattf/PaleoRing.html**
A collection of websites and pages that are devoted primarily to the promotion of Paleontology, Paleoanthropology, Prehistoric Archaeology, The Evolution of Behavior, and Evolutionary Biology in general. The following sites are part of the linkage of websites:

- **The National Museum of Natural History – Virtual Tour of the Dinosaurs**
http://www.nmnh.si.edu/paleo/dino/tourfram.htm
An excellent overview of dinosaurs from the Smithsonian.

- **Fossil Hominoids – http://www.talkorigins.org/faqs/fossil-hominids.html**
Links to text information about Earth's early humanoids.

- **Paleontology Without Walls**
http://www.ucmp.berkeley.edu/exhibit/exhibits.html
A virtual exhibit from the University of California Museum of Paleontology. Looks at geological time, the development of evolutionary thought, and Phylogeny – the 'family' of life.

Astronomy

Resources for primary students

• **Educational Activities at the Space Telescope Science Institute**
http://oposite.stsci.edu/pubinfo/edugroup/educational-activities.html
This website contains many of the images that Hubble is famous for and of course some excellent lesson plans, online games and activities that are ideal for primary students.
Star Light Star Bright – Stellar Encounters – Which Star is Hottest?
Solar System Trading Cards
Hubble Deep Field Academy
Student Astronaut Challenge
From Galileo to Hubble
Blackholes

• **A Virtual Tour of the Sun – http://www.astro.uva.nl/~michielb/od95/**
This virtual tour shows the user the various parts of the sun. Use of MPEG movies will require a support programme called 'Sparkle'. This is a well-developed presentation.

• **Views of the Solar System http://bang.lanl.gov/solarsys/eng/homepage.htm**
In-depth information about objects in the solar system; suitable for S2-F2.

• **Nine Planets**
http://seds.lpl.arizona.edu/nineplanets/nineplanets/nineplanets.html
Another site that is similar in content to the Views of the solar system website. Useful for S2-F2.

• **Our solar system – http://pds.jpl.nasa.gov/planets/**
The planets and their motion is a set of lesson plans and activities from the NASA Athena site relating to science curriculum topics.

• **Science Education Gateway**
http://cse.ssl.berkeley.edu/segway/spa_sci_list.html
There are some excellent resources here.

• **The Star Child Project – http://legacy.gsfc.nasa.gov/docs/StarChild/**
Yet another not-to-be missed website that includes planetary and space information, great activities for younger astronomers and a huge array of resources for the classroom that are too extensive to list here. There are also some excellent resources for secondary students and teachers.

Astronomy
Resources for secondary students

- **Exploration in Education – http://www.stsci.edu/exined/exined-home.html**
This site features a series of electronic picture books using material from NASA space images and using hypercard stacks. You need to download the hypercard player (if you don't already have it – it is available from the site itself) and uncompress it in order to use the picture books. You also need to download the picture books themselves but it does allow students to then use the material offline. These picture books are exceptional in their presentation and are well worth the effort of downloading the material. For example Windows on Orion (3.1mb) is a fascinating and in-depth tour of the Orion constellation, with exceptional images and examples of star lifecycles. It is an ideal resource for secondary students. See also:
> Gems of Hubble
> The Red Planet
> Comparing Earth
> Apollo 11 at Twenty-Five

and there are many more.

- **Use with the Life Cycle of Stars**
http://imagine.gsfc.nasa.gov/docs/teachers/lifecycles/LC_title.html (for Grades 9-12 or F4-7)
An information and activity book (in text only) that provides information about the birth and death of stars and the observable space products of star lifecycle stages.

- **The Martian Sun Times**
http://www.ucls.uchicago.edu/MartianSunTimes/
A series of six investigations about Mars which includes seasonal changes, weather on Mars, and life on Mars.

- **Nova Online – http://www.pbs.org/wgbh/nova/onlinelibrary.html**
> Hunt for Alien Worlds
> Doomsday Asteriod
> Terror in Space (about various disasters that have occurred in space
> exploration programmes)

Internet Resources For Teachers of Technology
Communications resources for technology teachers
There have been very few interactive and collaborative online projects that meet technology curriculum objectives aside from information sharing and communication. One type that can be found is the technological challenge, where participants are required to be involved in parallel problem-solving activities such as a bridge building project or a bottle rocket building project. One example is the Pringles Potato Chip Challenge <http://geocities.com/CapeCanaveral/Hall/3499/index.html>. The objective is for a team of students to design and test a container for shipping a single 'Pringles' potato chip, via the Postal Service. The goal is to engineer the packaging with the smallest volume and smallest mass that will protect the chip so that it arrives at its destination undamaged.

Projects in design technology are also often available. A project about space flight <http://www.concentric.net/~Jberger5/#partc> offers opportunities to share experimental work and data collected on glider flight, access to expert space technologists and professional materials on space flight.

For New Zealand teachers interested in information technology the NZCompEd mailing list <majordomo@massey.ac.nz> is very worthwhile. To subscribe leave the subject line blank and write in the first line of the message space:

subscribe NZCompEd

To mail to the list use the following address:

nzcomped@massey.ac.nz

Information resources for technology teachers

For technological areas, the information resources of the Internet contain some gems but they are not always obvious and easy to find. Some of the resources listed under physical science areas will also yield valuable resources for the teacher of technology. As an example, the Smithsonian multimedia module on flight would provide some good resources for physical sciences and for technology, depending on the curriculum objectives and the ways teachers use the material.

For technology educators TENZ provides background resources for its members at <http://sunsite.net.nz/orgs/tenz/>. TENZ is a professional resource network to promote and support Technology Education in New Zealand.

A museum specifically devoted to technology is the Tech Museum of Innovation – <http://www.thetech.org/>. The online museum provides material and limited teaching resources in communication, innovation, technological exploration and life technology.

Table 21 lists websites suitable for the structures and mechanisms section of the New Zealand technology curriculum.

- **Mr G's Applied Technology**
http://www.sd68.nanaimo.bc.ca/schools/coal/at/at.htm
Site Check out Mr G's lesson designs which include developing an oil rig base, a pneumatic lift, paper bridges and many others for primary and upper primary levels. Also included are profiles of technology-related occupations. This site is well worth a visit – and more than once.

- **Simple Machines (Primary S2-4 Science and Technology)**
http://www.lerc.nasa.gov/Other_Groups/K-12/Summer_Training/KaeAvenueES/SIMPLE_MACHINES.html
Simple activities that are designed to give years 3-5 children experiences in using simple machines. These include activities on pulleys, levers, inclined planes, screws, wedges, wheels and axles, and machines within machines. This may be excellent support material for students needing information for technology projects.

Table 21: Structures and Mechanisms – continued on the next page.

- **Marvellous Machines**
http://www.galaxy.net:80/~k12/machines/index.shtml
Experiments and activities to try, using springs, levers, gears, pulleys and inclined planes. See also Spotlight – Simple Machines – for more facts, examples, and activities to try and Simple Machines – Grade 4 Science.

- **Leonardo – http://www.mos.org/sln/Leonardo/**
Some very good activities about machines for students. The Inventors toolbox has examples of simple machines. Check out Gadget Anatomy for a test on recognising simple machines used everyday.

- There is also **Mechanisms and Simple Machines – http://www.cs.cmu.edu/People/rapidproto/mechanisms/chpt2.html#toc**
Textbook explanations of how things work, for older students.

- Also about machines is the **Inventions section at the Museum of Minnesota Science centre – http://www.sci.mus.mn.us/sln/invent/**
In this online project students as designers are given a series of interesting tasks which include Design a Mini-mini Golf Course, Marble Machines, Contraption Drawings, Imaginary Fund-raiser, Motion Machines, Zoo Keepers, Shoebox Whirligigs, Air-power.

- **Rockets on Wheels – http://www.pbs.org/tal/racecars/**
An interesting site which looks at the science and technology behind the racing car industry.

Problem-solving activities

- **Design Exploration – The Three Little Pigs**
http://www.sedl.org/scimath/compass/v02n03/pigs.html
Early elementary students gain experience with construction techniques for strength and stability based on the well-known story.

- **Power Boat Design**
http://www.sedl.org/scimath/compass/v02n03/boat.html
A Design Exploration for Upper Level Students. This activity, Power Boat Design, is excerpted from a unit presented in Technology Science Mathematics (TSM) Connection Activities, a curriculum of integrated design projects for Form 1 and up, published by Glencoe/McGraw Hill.

- **Get off the Deserted Island**
http://www.cs.bsu.edu/homepages/kirkwood/getoff.htm
In groups of four, design and build a system that will catch the attention of a passing ship, because you are castaways from a sunken ship. You have certain materials to use, but use them wisely and creatively! The water is full of sharks and coral reefs! Please keep this in mind when you are creating a system of communication to the passing ship!

- **Island Hopper**
http://www.cs.bsu.edu/homepages/kirkwood/Islandhopper.htm
Another group problem activity in communications technology (2-day challenge).

- **Bats and Echolocation**
http://www.cs.bsu.edu/homepages/kirkwood/aabats.htm
Groups design a tool to help them move blindfolded around a room (Juniors).

- **Chemistry Polymer Project (Secondary – Technology and Science)**
http://www.lerc.nasa.gov/Other_Groups/K-12/Summer_Training/Magnificat/Polymer_Project.html
Students will learn about polymers, their history, their uses and their recycling. Students also have the opportunity to produce some polymers (slime and glue) in the laboratory. The project covers about two weeks of class time. Included are lesson plans and experiments and other Internet links.

- **Plastics Resource – http://www.plasticsresource.com/**
Click on 'Polymers are Everywhere' for a tutorial on polymers presented by the National Geographic Society.

- **National Plastics Center and Museum**
http://npcm.plastics.com/slimystuff3-98.html
There are some interesting experiments presented here.

- **The Science of Hockey – http://www.exploratorium.edu/hockey/**
This online series of lessons from the Exploratorium looks at ice hockey ... what high tech materials the players are using, how much stress is on the stick and so on.

- **The Science of Cycling – http://www.exploratorium.edu/cycling/**
What is the Science of Cycling? Why do road bikes have thin tyres, while mountain bikes have fat tyres? What is a gear ratio? And how do gears help make the bicycle so efficient? What are the best materials for frames? What are the best designs?

Table 22: Materials technology

- **Access Excellence – http://www.gene.com/ae/**
A professional network for biology and biotechnology teachers.

- **National Centre for Biotechnology Education – http://134.225.167.114/**
A centre at Reading University in the UK for teachers interested in biotechnology. Some good units of work available here. PDF reader required to access some of the teaching resources.

There are many explorations for students that would form the basis of ideas for secondary teachers. Only some of them are listed here:

Clarification of apple juice – cloudy juice becomes clear with a cocktail of enzymes
Prove it! Bread dough, and the factors that influence how it rises
Design a washing powder – in this investigation, pupils make and evaluate their own washing powders, by adding enzymes to 'non-biological' products.
Yoghurt with a difference – yoghurt fermentation with two different substrates
Yoghurt with another difference – why antibiotics foul up fermentation

Table 23: Biotechnology

- **The Graphics Den – http://www.actden.com/grap_den/index.htm**
There is some excellent material included here about the basics of digital image manipulation. Students are taken through a step-by-step tutorial in the use of graphics packages incorporating a delightful set of activities that are designed to ensure success. The graphics application program recommended is Paint Shop Pro, a low-cost shareware application ideal for graphics manipulation in schools. Check out the following modules:

> The Graffiti Wall
> The Little Shop of Horrors – Creating montages (Great stuff!)
> Pop Art – Designing a drink can label
> In Living Colour – Turning black and white images into colour.
> Speed Freak – Turning clear images into blurred images.
> The Shadow
> The Vanishing Act – Creating transparent images for Web pages

- A teaching module called **Internet Island** is available at the **Miami Museum of Science – http://www.miamisci.org/**
This is an online teaching tutorial for children.

- **The Net: User Guidelines and Netiquette**
http://www.fau.edu/netiquette/net/index.html
This very worthwhile site provides users with some guidelines and protocols for Internet communications and use of the World Wide Web.

- **Patrick Crispen's Internet Roadmap**
http://www.nmusd.k12.ca.us/Resources/Roadmap/welcome.html
The Internet Roadmap was one of the first-ever online Internet training tutorials and was very popular. All the training modules are online and available for new users to work their way through.

Table 24: Information and Communications Technology

Production and process technology

- **Offshore Technology – http://www.offshore-technology.com/**
A site of interest to those wanting to find links to offshore gas and oil industries.

Electronics and control technology

- **Technology Education Index – http://www.technologyindex.com/**
Some excellent links to other areas of technology education.

- **The Technology Education Lab – http://www.techedlab.com/main.html**

Table 25: Other Technology Areas

Internet Resources for Arts Teachers

The computer is increasingly becoming another medium for artistic expression as more interesting software programs, with more advanced features for creating and editing images and sound files, become easier to use. Extra peripherals such as scanners, digital cameras, midi and keyboard systems give younger artists great freedom for artistic expression. The images students create or edit from their own drawings, scan from art works created using other media or photograph using a digital camera and store on CD-ROM, or sound files they can create and capture, can easily be attached to an e-mail message and sent by the Internet to another user. Classes with international links can and do send images and audio clips of themselves and their schools to support communications with other classes. Activities involving art works by students are growing. The Kidlink organisation holds an annual global art exhibition where participants are encouraged to submit their work in a gallery-type format. The Kidart Coord mailing list supports the communications activities for this virtual exhibition. The Kidlink Gallery of Computer Art can be found at <http://www.kidlink.org/KIDART/index.html>. This site contains information about how to go about submitting works of art and is an archive of past regular pictures, animations, ASCII-drawings, and music files submitted for exhibition.

International Kids Space <http://www.kids-space.org/gallery/> and Cyberkids <http://www.cyberkids.com/> are venues where students can upload illustrations and sound files to go with their regular contributions.

Information resources for arts and music

The World Wide Web can be used to support the arts curriculum in a variety of ways. Many sites provide motivational images and inspiration for ideas. Images can be used as story starters or for building classroom resources. For instance, at the Kidlink site children are encouraged to write about an online picture.

Another use of the Internet is to display the work of new artists looking for commissions or simply to advertise their work. This is an excellent way for art teachers to access and view the work of contemporary artists.

Students can access the galleries of well-known institutions such as the Web Museum Paris <http: http://metalab.unc.edu/wm/> where regularly updated shows are online and so is the permanent collection, which features Western art from renaissance artists such as Michelangelo to modern artists such as David Hockney. This is an excellent site, as there is much information provided about major artists and art trends both in the form of text and downloadable images.

Another useful site for visual arts teacher is ArtsEdnet <http://srtsednet.getty.edu>. The site is designed for professionals and contains excellent background material resources, and resources that advocate the place of visual arts in the school curriculum. Table 26 lists some useful visual arts sites. For a list of good websites for the performing arts, see Table 5.

General sites to start

- **Art on the Web**
http://www.bc.edu/bc_org/avp/cas/fnart/Artweb_frames.html
The links to other sites available from here are extensive and it is a good place to start if you are looking for very specific information such as art of a particular period or type, or a major auction house, or online educational courses on art.

- **Voice of the Shuttle – Art and Art History page**
http://humanitas.ucsb.edu/shuttle/art.html
There are links here to many interesting visual arts sites on the Web.

- **Carol Gerten's Fine Arts Museum – A Virtual Art Museum**
http://www.hol.gr/cjackson/
This is an excellent site providing scanned images of artists' work that can be searched for by time period, artist or nationality. Scanned images are of extremely high quality.

- **@URL – NZ Arts on the Web – http://url.co.nz/arts/nzarts.html**
Links to all arts resources in New Zealand, including many performing arts sites.

Museums

- **The Louvre – http://mistral.culture.fr/louvre/**

- **Web Museum Paris – http: http://metalab.unc.edu/wm/**

- **Vatican Museum – http://www.christusrex.org/www1/vaticano/0-Musei.html**
An excellent site with extensive galleries of images of the museum collections.

- **The Guggenheim Museums – http://www.guggenheim.org/**

- **J. Paul Getty Museum – http://www.getty.edu/museum/**

- **The Victoria and Albert Museum – http://www.vam.ac.uk/**

- **The Krannert Art Museum – http://art.uiuc.edu/kam/**

- **The Metropolitan Museum of Art – http://www.metmuseum.org/htmlfile/newexhib/ E_Current.htm**
Extensive current exhibitions.

- **Auckland Art Gallery**
http://www.akcity.govt.nz/around/places/artgallery/

- **Robert McDougall Art gallery – http://www.mcdougall.org.nz/**

Table 26: Internet resources for the visual arts. This table is continued on page 100.

Arts from other cultures

- **Africa: Art of a continent**
http://www.artnetweb.com/guggenheim/africa/index.html
Also there is the **National Museum of African Art at http://www.si.edu/nmafa/**

- **Jim Breen's Ukiyo-E Galler**
://www.rdt.monash.edu.au/~jwb/ukiyoe/ukiyoe.html
An excellent collection of some of the best of Japan's woodblock print artists including Hiroshige, Utamaro, Sharaku and some excellent links to other websites on this topic.

- **Russian Icons**
http://www.auburn.edu/academic/liberal_arts/foreign/russian/icons/index.html
A selection of images.

- **Aboriginal Art and Culture Centre**
http://www.aboriginalart.com.au/gallery/

Antiquities

- **Looking at the art of Ancient Greece and Rome**
http://artsednet.getty.edu/ArtsEdNet/Resources/Beauty/index.html

- **Trajan's Rome -The Man, The City, The Empire**
http://artsednet.getty.edu/ArtsEdNet/Resources/Trajan/toc.html
This is a cross-curricular art and art history teaching module about this second century Roman Emperor and his times, with images, Internet links and lesson plans for junior high school level.

Visual artists

- **Leonardo Da Vinci – http://metalab.unc.edu/cjackson/vinci/**
A collection of works from Carol Gerten's Fine Arts Museum – A Virtual Art Museum at http://www.hol.gr/cjackson/

- **Paintings of Vermeer – http://www.ccsf.caltech.edu/~roy/vermeer/**
Excellent colour images available, and text discussion of the artist and his environment.

- **Picasso – http://www.club-Internet.fr/picasso/homepage.html**

- **The Salvador Dali Art Gallery**
http://members.xoom.com/daliweb/main.htm A nice site with extensive galleries of the work of Dali as well as information about the man himself.

- **Cezanne – http://www.cezanne.com/fr/index.htm**

- **The sculpture of August Rodin**
http://www.bc.edu/bc_org/avp/cas/fnart/rodin/rodin.html
A virtual gallery of images of the work of this artist available in thumbnail form, which can be viewed in larger format if desired.

- **MC Escher Gallery – http://www.deryni.com/escher.html**
Some images and links to other Escher sites.

Internet Resources for Music Teachers

The range of music options for Internet users is growing rapidly. The resources of the Internet now range from interactive music sites to information about classical composers and the popular music cultures of today. It is possible to download midi files and sheet music, submit compositions, and download software. Musicians can incorporate Internet sound files into music software systems and generate new and exciting sounds and melodies from these files. They can also be added as background for students' own stories and presentations.

The Co-NECT project is one where each school has an electronic music studio with midi synthesisers and computer sequencing software. Using the Internet, students collaborate on studying music composition, sequencing and creating their own sounds, and presenting the results collaboratively. More about this project can be found at <http://co-nect.bbn.com/WorldBand/Pages/WorldBand.html>. Table 27 lists some websites for music teachers.

Orchestras

- **The New Zealand Symphony Orchestra – http://www.nzso.co.nz/**
About the New Zealand Symphony orchestra and an interesting set of links to resources for performing artists. There are also links from this page to a long list of international orchestras.

General resources for educators

- **Music Education Online**
http://www.geocities.com/Athens/2405/links.html
A general site aimed to connect music educators with a variety of music education resources on the Internet.

- **Leeds University Department of Music**
http://www.leeds.ac.uk/music.html

- **K-12 Resources for Music Educators – http://www.isd77.k12.mn.us/resources/**
staffpages/shirk/k12.music.html/newsgroups.html
A very extensive list of links to vocal and instrumental resources for teachers.

- **Music From Around the World**
http://library.advanced.org/11315/world.htm Click on the part of the world map to find out more about the origins of the music indigenous to the area.

Table 27: Music Resources. This table is continued on page 102.

Classical music

- **Classical composer biographies**
http://www.cl.cam.ac.uk/users/mn200/music/composers.html
This site includes information about Mozart, Sibelius, Mendelssohn, Mahler and other classical composers. Links to other sites are also included.

- **Classical Composers Information Archive**
http://spight.physics.unlv.edu/picgalr2.html

- **Smithsonian Musical History**
http://www.si.edu/resource/faq/nmah/music.htm

Popular culture

- **The Rock and Roll Hall of Fame and Museum**
An interesting and extensive set of Lesson plans are available at **http://www.rockhall.com/ educate/lssnplan/index.html** These cross-curricular resources for secondary music students are intended to stimulate student interest and creativity. Well worth a look.

For tunes

- **Ceolas Celtic Music Archive – http://www.ceolas.org/ceolas.html**
An extensive site containing printable tunes, midi files, software and tune indexes as well as information about musical instruments and Celtic music from Ireland Scotland and Wales.

- **Richard Robinson's tunebook**
http://www.leeds.ac.uk/music/Info/RRTuneBk/tunebook.html
A variety of tunes from folk music and other traditional sources largely in print form.

- **Children's songs by D.F.Saphra**
http://www.geocities.com/Athens/Olympus/8075/

For lyrics

- **Searching the International Lyrics Server**
http://www.lyrics.ch/search.html
This is a very extensive database of song lyrics.

Search engine

- **Musicsearch – The Internet's Music-only Search Engine**
http://musicsearch.com/
This is an excellent search engine for music lovers. Includes directory and meta-search functions.

- **Allegro – The Music Education Search Site – http://talentz.com/Allegro.hts**

Internet resources for teachers in the area of health and well-being

Table 28 lists some of useful Internet information resources for teachers that support the health and well-being curriculum in New Zealand.

- **World Health Organization – http://www.who.int/**
This is the WWW Home Page for this organisation.

- **Kidshealth.org – http://KidsHEAlth.org/index2.html**
A general health site about children's health and well-being.

Anatomy

- **Human Anatomy Online – http://www.innerbody.com/indexbody.html**
This is an excellent site for upper primary students and teachers, providing fun as well as interactive and educational views of the human body.

- **The Heart – http://sln.fi.edu/biosci/heart.html**
A Virtual Exploration. Very useful resources are located here, including how to look after your heart, how the heart works, parts of the heart, etc.

- **The Visible Human Project –**
http://www.nlm.nih.gov/research/visible/visible_human.html
A series of scanned cross-sections of the body are available. May be suitable for older students.

Health and fitness

- **Hillary Commission Homepage – http://www.hillarysport.org.nz/**
You can download the latest issue of Kiwisport News or access online projects for kids relating to sporting activities. This is a fun site with activity ideas for teachers and kids.

- **Hotlist – http://sln.fi.edu/tfi/hotlists/health.html**
Good list of health links provided by the Franklin Science Institute.

- **Health Information Resources – http://www.nau.edu/~fronske/coolinks.html**
Another good health links site which covers a wide variety of health and well-being subjects.

Fitness

- **Stretching and Flexibility**
http://www.enteract.com/~bradapp/docs/rec/stretching/stretching_2.html
Physiology of Stretching. Text information may be useful for background material for teachers and older students.

- **Mind Tools – http://www.demon.co.uk/mindtool/spintro.html**
Sports Psychology. Information here may be of interest as teacher background material, and for students.

Table 28: Health and Well-being Resources. *This table is continued on page 104.*

Dental hygiene

- **Colgate-Palmolive Kids World**
http://www.ridesafeinc.com/supportmat.htm A delightful site for younger students. There are interactive games, messages from the tooth fairy, colouring books, facts and links. Very enjoyable site.

- **Kids stuff – http://www.adha.org/kidstuff.htm**
Fun and games for young children plus facts for children and parents.

Food and nutrition

- **Dole 5 a day – http://www.dole5aday.com/school.html**
Have a look at the just-for-kids section and follow the adventures of Amber Orange and Barney Broccoli as well as the section for educators. A great site for a nutrition unit of work.

Sex

- **Just Say Yes http://www.positive.org/cps/Home/index.html**
Straight answers are given here to teen questions about sex.

- **Sexual Assault Information Page**
http://www.cs.utk.edu/~bartley/saInfoPage.html
Information here about abuse, harassment, incest, rape, victimisation, etc.
Safety

- **OUDPS – Kid Safety – http://www.ou.edu/oupd/kidsafe/start.htm**
This is an excellent safety site for younger students. The resources could be used with whole-class sessions to generate ideas and questions about personal safety. There is some excellent work available on:
    Crime Prevention
    Personal Safety
    Internet safety
    Kid Safety
    Fire Safety
    First Aid and Health
    Drugs and Alcohol

- **Ride Safe Bicycle Helmet Program Support Materials**
http://www.ridesafeinc.com/supportmat.htm
A site about safety on the roads.

- **Coppertone online – http://www.coppertone.com/kids/sunsmart.html**
Keep safe in the sun. There are more interactive activities here for children.

Conclusion

This chapter is filled with the exciting and unlimited possibilities that information and communications technologies can offer the practising teacher. A wide variety of feasible activities have the potential to generate high levels of student interest and are relevant to students' learning needs, even with limited equipment or online access. Regardless of how sophisticated the technology may become, teachers are and will remain the 'critical filter' through which all learning opportunities are realised for students. As our children become more technologically conversant with the medium and as more high quality online educational resources become available, there is a growing need for teachers to actively include these supporting media to stimulate, motivate and nurture a productive and effective learning environment.

Acknowledgement

My thanks to Russell Butson for his help in putting together the Mathematics resources for this chapter.

Please note that all sites were checked and found to be operating at the time of writing. The World Wide Web is a dynamic resource and sites can be subject to change for a variety of reasons. If a link does not work try typing the name of the site into the search engine of your choice.

References

Brophy, J., & Alleman, J. (1991). Activities as instructional tools: a framework for analysis and evaluation. *Educational Researcher*, 20(4), 9-23.

Collis, B. (1996). *Tele-learning in a Digital World: The Future of Distance learning*. UK: International Thomson Computer Press.

Carrucan, T., Crewe, T., Matthews, E. and Matthews, S. (1996). *The Internet Manual for Teachers' Access. Skills and Curriculum Strategies*. Macmillan Education, Australia.

Harris, Judi (1995). Network-based educational activity structures. http://lrs.ed.uiuc.edu/activity-structures/harris-Activity-Structures.html.

Harris, Judi (1995, March). Educational telecomputing projects: interpersonal exchanges. *The Computing Teacher* 60-64.

Harris, Judi (1995, April). Educational telecomputing projects: information collections. *The Computing Teacher* 44-48.

Harris, Judi (1995, May). Educational telecomputing activities: problem solving projects. *The Computing Teacher* 59-63.

Rogers, A., Andres, Y., Jacks, M., and Clauset, T. (1990). Keys to successful telecomputing. *The Computing Teacher*, 17, 8, pp. 25-28. http://www.gsn.org/teach/articles/keys.2.success.html

Soler, J. & Trewern, A. (1997). Using computer technology for reflective inquiry in social studies. In *New Horizons for New Zealand Social Studies* (eds) Benson, P. and Openshaw. Massey University, Palmerston North: P. ERDC Press. pp 161-190

Trewern, A. (1996). The Internet: what's in it for me and my students. In *Words have Wings* (ed.) Lai, K.W. Dunedin: University of Otago Press. pp. 35-81.

Trewern, A. (1996). The best museum websites online: an introduction. *Computers in New Zealand Schools*. 8 (3) pp. 3-11

5 Designing and Implementing Computer-Mediated Communication Projects in Schools

Nola Campbell

The telephone lines have been available in some of our communities for more than a century but as we reach the end of the twentieth century we are only beginning to come to terms with how we can make good use of this resource in our classrooms. Pressure on schools to join the computer-mediated global schoolroom has come from business, industry and parents. The Ministry of Education's Interactive Education strategy for New Zealand schools was released in October 1998 and has at last given a clear direction for the school and classroom use of information and communication technologies. What is not clear for some teachers is how the strategy can be translated into classroom practice. This chapter explores the design and implementation of computer-mediated communication (CMC) projects in schools and some possible steps to getting started.

Any journey worth going on is enhanced by looking back to where we have been and remembering what was learned before planning the next trip or stage. Computer-mediated communication in the 1980s taught us some important lessons and initially it is worth reflecting on what we have found out. The need to refer to our earlier experiences is highlighted by the durability of the Water and Air Projects that were initiated in New Zealand in the early 1990s. Both projects are still gaining in strength and global participation. This chapter will examine the implications of participation in projects like these before planning your own CMC adventures.

A Look Back at Early Interest in CMC Projects in the 1980s

The Department of Education commissioned a number of exploratory studies in the mid 1980s in an effort to identify how computers were being used in New Zealand school classrooms and the implications for future development. In the 1987 report *Exploratory Studies in Educational Computing* (Department of Education) a statement was made that:

> The teachers in both electronic communications studies believe that children have little difficulty in understanding and using this technology at an appropriate level. Students are clearly highly motivated to write when electronic publishing is possible. Teachers and students are excited about the opportunities for development of multi-cultural awareness, afforded by international exchange of letters, stories and information of interest to the students. (*Report on the Exploratory Studies in Educational Computing,* 1987, p.8)

There was no mention of links with the curriculum but clear evidence of a growing level of interest. In January 1988, the Department of Education published *Computer Communications in Education* as a result of the discussions of a working party at Hamilton Teachers' College. This photocopiable resource booklet for teachers provided a valuable guide on how to get started, what resources were available and information about some case studies. Any links with the curriculum were not emphasised in this document. It is interesting to note that at this time there was a lot of interest in interactive software, e.g. 'Where in the World is Carmen Sandiego' and 'Gold Dust Island'. Computers and software were beginning to be seen as having the potential to involve different curriculum areas. In CMC projects this did not always occur when computers were used as a means of communicating with people outside of the classroom.

The situation in the United States at the time was similar to New Zealand. The *Computing Teacher* magazine devoted an entire issue in April 1987 to telecommunications. The journal reflected the emphasis on the technical aspects and requirements to get started. However, it did also include some anecdotal accounts of national and international CMC projects. An international classroom link between Australia and the United States described by Butler and Jobe (1987) had focussed on the writing aspect of electronic mail. It was their belief that most students generally wrote only when the teacher told them to. Trying to develop a relationship with a person through electronic mail is dependent on the written word. However, in a classroom electronic mail was not always seen as writing and the activity could take on a totally different and exciting perspective. Ann Erikson (1987) wrote enthusiastically of how her students were making new friends and using the written word to share their ideas in this new way of communicating. Erikson summarised her situation, and I suspect that of many other teachers in the USA at that time, by saying that:

> This is just the beginning; we have only started to explore the uses and effects of telecommunications in the classroom. The possibilities of the future are only limited by our imagination and our resourcefulness. (Erikson, 1987, p.32)

A warning from Fred Goldberg (1989) suggested that there was little evidence to suggest that students using electronic mail moved from introductory conversation to a more focussed and positive exchange of information. Structure must be made clear before and not after communication begins. Levin *et al.* (1989) reinforced the penpal warnings and warned of the superficiality of this activity. Rapid turnaround of information must also occur to realise the benefits of electronic mail, otherwise you might just as well post a letter.

In New Zealand, Geoffrey Richardson (1989) from Kotemaori School described how the children were no longer learning *about* children in other cultures but now had the opportunity to study *with* children from that culture. Together the children communicated to explore the similarities and differences in their cultures. He believed that children's natural curiosity could be enhanced by interaction with others.

By 1989 the last *CEDU* (Computers in Education Development Unit) *Newsletter*, No 16, was describing successful electronic mail projects to stimulate children's writing, such as the progressive stories exchange between Waihou Downs School and Brightwell School in England (*CEDU Newsletter* 1989, p. 5). This was an indication of the changes that were now occurring. Some teachers and children were using computer-mediated communication for a wider range of curriculum-related purposes.

The important issues which were to emerge from this period were, to some extent, accurately documented and predicted in the 1986 report on *The Potential Educational Benefits of Electronic Communications Technologies for New Zealand* (Department of Education, 1986). The warnings were: the importance of teacher training to use the tools; the possible misuse of electronic communications so that it was used simply as a penpal system and the need to establish the cost-effectiveness of the new information technologies in education. These warnings were echoed in overseas literature, and generally reflected a period where schools were busy 'doing computing' or 'doing electronic mail' with some tenuous links with the curriculum. Computer-mediated communication was dominated by the tool in many instances, a solution looking for a problem to solve. However, the attitude toward computer-mediated communication was beginning to change as New Zealand schools entered the 1990s.

A New Decade of Computer-Mediated Communication

One objective of computer-mediated communication is to share information with others who are geographically in a different place. David Chapple (1991) described the importance of what he referred to as a 'bottom up approach' where teachers and students use the technology to solve a problem which they have. Use of computer-mediated communication must be issue-driven, teacher-driven, and learner-driven. Computer-mediated communication must be able to enhance the existing curriculum if it is to be of value to a school. When other existing sources can provide the same information, then electronic tools will be little more than an expensive new toy. The use of computer-mediated communication must not only allow the user to carry out a specific curriculum-related task, but it should enable them to do it better.

David Chapple (1991) described the pitfalls of CMC, citing the impersonal nature of this form of communication and the danger of the medium becoming the message. The computer is the tool for sending messages to another computer, and is not the learning exercise in itself. He stressed the importance of establishing a clear purpose for the contact and the need to set up a situation so that expectations are clear and there is a strong commitment from both parties. Too often contacts have ceased because initial enthusiasm has waned and mail goes unanswered. When corresponding internationally holiday periods appear at different times, so these must also be accounted for in any planning.

Colin Anderson (1991) from Tweedsmuir Intermediate School in Invercargill described the contact his class made with one in Alaska during the Prince William Sound oil spill. He described the importance of initial introductory contact followed by a structured exchange of information. This CMC resource, according to Anderson, provided excellent value for money.

For those students with special educational needs, electronic mail has been utilised in a variety of different situations. The Gifted Network based at Lincoln Heights School in Auckland offered gifted students the opportunity to access different subject areas and a tutor through electronic mail. Therefore students could remain in their own schools but still link into the support and resources of the Special Abilities Unit (Le Sueur, 1991). Friendships made at seminars could be maintained through electronic mail and so overcome the isolation felt by some of these students in their mainstream situation. A research project at Kelston Deaf Education Centre examined 'written conversations' between teachers and students who were attending local schools (Leonard, Hellier, Moore, Thomson, & Wilton, 1991). This interactive teaching strategy using electronic mail aimed not only at giving feedback to students but also at giving writing some purpose. As a result of the study it was found that improvements occurred in the areas of turn-taking, initiating topics, rephrasing and expansion. Opportunities were seen by Leonard *et al.* (1990) for the students who are educationally disadvantaged with particular language and reading delays or with English as a second language. For children who are geographically isolated from support, CMC could well be utilised to break down this barrier. The Maori Education and Language Electronic Network was established to provide a forum for teachers, researchers and those with a special interest in Maori language and education (Ropiha, 1991). A English-Maori and Maori-English dictionary was available, as well as electronic mail facilities in this network.

Hugh Barr (1992) in his article 'Social Studies by Electronic Mail' believed that schools had been slow to take advantage of electronic mail opportunities that had been available to them for some time. He suggested that some teachers appeared too conservative or too afraid to make changes from existing information-gathering methods. Technophobia can easily get in the way when teachers are faced with using unfamiliar and apparently expensive pieces of equipment. Barr warned that a lack of a clear structure or purpose and use of sophisticated pieces of technology would not guarantee sound educational outcomes. Barr's perspective and comments are important because, as a person who has vast experience in the field of Social Studies, he was a relative newcomer to electronic mail. He found that CMC could improve his own knowledge of a topic and in turn that of young children. In an earlier article describing the Newstead and Las Cruces schools exchange, Barr (1991) reinforced the importance of seeing electronic mail not as an exercise in using technology but as part of a social studies unit with clear direction and planning.

Learning from Other Learners

Not only does computer-mediated communication provide access to the global classroom but, as Chapple (1992) described, it more importantly provides the opportunity for learners to learn from other learners. He saw this as being one of the most powerful ideas to be confronted by schools at that time. Traditional sources of knowledge, like the teacher or the library, represent knowledge that reflects an adult perspective and at best is second-hand. A teacher who is prepared to fill the role of the facilitator and is not afraid of change can find computer-mediated communication a powerful classroom tool providing first-hand knowledge in all areas of the curriculum. The new curriculum initiatives that are currently taking place in New Zealand place the teacher in a facilitator role and encourage the enhanced use of computer-mediated communication.

Many computer-mediated communication articles in the literature are anecdotal and describe successful electronic mail projects. Few articles ever lay out clearly what a teacher has to do beyond the very basics of planning, etiquette and the required equipment. A teacher who is interested in a project could well be left wondering what exactly he or she is supposed to do to get it right. This is where teacher support materials and strategies are clearly needed. When writing about 'Teleconferencing in Social Studies', Geoffrey Richardson (1990) provided clear directions with a good example on migration and colonisation of New Zealand. This article described the classroom focus and purpose of the activity without placing heavy emphasis on the tools which were used. This was a refreshing change and hopefully pointed to a more positive direction. Like Barr (1992), Richardson was not approaching CMC from the technical point of view. If electronic mail had been first placed in the hands of Social Studies teachers and not those with a leaning towards the use of computers then some painful learning experiences may have been avoided.

When should you become involved in Telecommunications Projects?

One of the arguments that we frequently hear used to justify the use of computers in our schools is that this activity is one that our students will be using when they leave school. However, the tools children use today in primary schools will not be around by the time they leave a secondary school. What they will need is an understanding of the concept of obtaining information electronically, the need to rely not on traditional sources but to go right to the source. If students want to know about fashions in Atlanta who better to ask than somebody who lives in Atlanta? First-hand information is vastly superior to that which is edited and recycled. This concept of going to the source for information is one which children who are familiar with the process appear to have little problem accepting. It is the adults who sometimes struggle as they step aside and learn to share the journey with their students.

Certainly we have a responsibility to ensure that students in our schools are able to participate in a global world. We can assist them to learn about when, why and how to use these technologies. Furthermore, we want to ensure that some higher-order thinking and problem-solving is taking place in the classroom, including when they are utilising the tools. These magical computer-mediated communication tools do not ensure positive educational outcomes will just happen. Only we, as teachers, can assist this process.

Computer-mediated communication tools in classrooms do not provide a solution looking for a problem to solve. The presence of these tools will not ensure positive learning outcomes any more than the colour scheme in the classroom or the attractive furniture. What is critical is the way in which the tools are used as part of the ongoing planning and programme in the school and classroom. People make good things happen and involvement in purposeful telecommunications projects can provide an authentic real-life situation that engages children in valuing the very act of communication. The only problem to solve is the need to answer an information question or problem. Use of these should not be an isolated event but part of an ongoing acceptance of the value of these valuable classroom tools.

The Highway

As mentioned earlier, any journey worth taking is enhanced by looking back where one has been and remembering what was learned before planning the next trip or stage. New Zealand does have a very rich history of involvement in computer-mediated communication projects and they are not a recent innovation. We learned that it was important to plan for the journey, to know what we could expect, to understand where we were going, who we might meet and all the implications of making the trip. The importance of skills in using the tools is critical, but it should not be the only focus of the activity or journey.

Imagine that one of your students is a gifted racing car driver and successfully winning races on the track. She is highly motivated and supported and has access to all sorts of fancy technologies that enable her to go faster. This skill on the race track does not, however, ensure an easy transition to the open road. She will need to learn navigational skills and be able to drive successfully against opposing traffic, negotiate compulsory stops and give-way signs, and take her turn through the roundabouts.

Moving back to the classroom situation and using the race track analogy demonstrates that teachers do have a choice. You can let your students use the computer to drive quickly round and round proving how adept they are at using the tools, or you can take them on some very exciting journeys on the local, national or international roads of an information highway. You and your students can meet people, share ideas and information and return home to reflect on the experiences you have had. So where can the exciting journeys take us?

The Choices

Judi Harris from the University of Texas at Austin has long been a campaigner for purposeful curriculum-related activities. On her website Sample Curriculum-Based K-12 Educational Telecomputing Projects, Organized by Activity Structures (found at http://lrs.ed.uiuc.edu/Activity-Structures/web-activity-structures.html.) Judi lists a large range of telecomputing projects. She has arranged them under three headings: Interpersonal Exchanges, Information Collections and Problem-Solving Projects. Each of the three key types of exchanges of information contains different types of structured activities. Each type of project has a specific curriculum purpose which is dependent on both the source of information and the type of interaction which is desired. The type of projects are summarised as follows:

Interpersonal Exchanges (contact with people in other places for general or specific discussion)
Keypals
Global Classrooms
Electronic 'Appearances'
Electronic Mentoring
Question-and-Answer Activities
Impersonations

Information Collections (contact with people or resources to collate data)
Information Exchanges
Database Creation
Electronic Publishing

TeleFieldtrips
Pooled Data Analysis

Problem-Solving Projects (contact with people or resources to collate data and communicate ideas)
Information Searches
Electronic Process Writing
Parallel Problem-Solving
Sequential Creations
Virtual Gatherings
Simulations
Social Action Projects

Getting Started

Previewing what is available and perhaps taking part in one or two projects is an excellent way to get started. Remember, however, that this is someone else's recipe for what might happen in your classroom, it is not your plan. Certainly it is good to become familiar with a project and find out what works and does not work for you. There is no sense in reinventing the wheel. Remember New Zealand teachers have been involved in these activities for more than ten years, so getting started on someone else's trip can be an excellent way to learn the layout of the landscape. This is a bit like going on a bus tour.

Sharing a journey on a project that has developed over time can give you a good insight into what is required. The tools and provisions you will need to make have been planned for and you will be able to safely experience the potential. The Water and Air Projects are a good example of the type of trip that has stood the test of time and will provide you with both a good experience and a well-planned itinerary.

The Water and Air Projects: CMC for the 1990s

The Air and Water Projects are Internet-based computer-mediated communication for global interaction in primary education in the 7-13 age group. The concept for the Water Project was originally envisioned by Nola Campbell and Gray Clayton of the University of Waikato in New Zealand. Working collaboratively with Rhonda Christensen and Gerald Knezek from the University of North Texas and Texas Center for Educational Technology in Denton, Texas, initial development focussed on the belief that many earlier electronic mail projects had failed because they were superficial and lacked any definite structure.

The Water Project initially utilised electronic mail to link three classes in New Zealand, two in Britain and three in Texas to examine aspects of water in all three countries. The project was structured carefully with modules and deadlines so that all participants were clear about direction and responsibility. The children were aged between 7 and 10 years of age, and the project operated from February to June. It culminated in an international teleconference that gave students the opportunity to speak with each other, as well as the members of the audience at the National

Educational Conference in Dallas, Texas.

This first Water Project was successful because it had clear goals, structures, and deadlines. It was not of a superficial nature. A video was compiled showing footage from the three countries, with the children involved in water activities that promoted the importance of having a curriculum focus. Responses from the children showed how transparent the technology really was for them. What was important was finding new friends who shared information about their communities; they valued seeing a child's-eye view of how important water was in different parts of the world.

The following year a similar project structure was developed to support the Air Project. Coinciding with Slip-Slop-Slap campaigns in New Zealand, it was quite a discovery for children in Texas to discover the challenges our children were facing in New Zealand, wearing hats and sunscreen.

Since 1992-93, both Water and Air classroom exchanges have been carried out concurrently each year. Air/Water participation has grown from eight classrooms in three nations in 1991–92, to forty-four classrooms in seven nations in 1995-96 (Christensen, Knezek, & Campbell, 1996). Children from Australia, Bermuda, Canada, New Zealand, South Africa, the United Kingdom, and the United States shared information via teacher-moderated electronic mail exchanges on the uses of water and air in their environment. Two curricular guides have been published by the Texas Center for Educational Technology (Christensen, Clayton, Campbell, & Knezek, 1994b, 1994c) and are distributed by the International Society for Technology in Education. A World Wide Web site at http://www.tcet.unt.edu/global/global.htm has been established to support the Project's curricular activities and provide samples of current activities for interested viewers. Bilingual interaction in Spanish and English was added at selected sites in 1996–97. Translation of one of the curricular guides has been initiated to support this activity. In 1996–97, forty-six schools in eight nations took part, with new enhancements that included a WWW Project Home Page, CU-SeeMe videoconferencing, and the Spanish translations of selected curricular materials.

It is interesting to note that the basic framework developed in 1991 has stood the test of time and only minor adjustments in terms of dates and organisation have been necessary to accommodate the needs of the different curricula, teachers and students in both hemispheres. The February to May time period is still the one best suited to collaboration for a project of this duration.

Air and Water Projects – classroom activities

Air and Water Projects are now designed to facilitate the classroom activities of primary students aged between 7 and 13 years in public, private, urban and rural schools. Collaborative planning among the teachers who respond to an Internet-posted call for participation takes place during the Northern Hemisphere's fall and the Southern Hemisphere's spring. This is a very important planning period for the co-ordinators and teachers involved in the project. The actual exchanges among students do not occur until the period between February and May each year.

Each project has an introductory module plus four modules. Each module has a specific topic and suggestions to be used as guidelines. For example, the Water Project content modules are: a) Water in our communities; b) Using water in our past; c) Using water today, and d) Caring for our water. Each teacher is expected to approach these topics using his/her own teaching style and lesson plans. While there are many available suggestions, there are no recipes for success or a specific list of activities for teachers to rigidly follow beyond the agreed timelines.

The interaction

Students receive module summaries from the other participants in their grouping so they can compare the information they gathered to the information sent from the other sites. Students are encouraged to discuss, make comparisons, estimate results, and draw conclusions concerning cause and effect within a time frame that would not have been feasible with regular mail. The students are researching, discovering and sharing information about water and air in their communities. They are reading, writing and working together, looking at aspects of their global environment that they find interesting.

Data has been gathered to demonstrate how student learning has taken place as a result of participation in Air/Water activities (Christensen, Knezek and Campbell, 1994). Attitudes towards the peoples of other nations have changed as a result of participating in Air/Water activities. When children involved in the Air and Water Projects were asked to give highlights of the project, they mentioned reading, writing and learning about their friends in other countries. In addition to gaining content knowledge, the students learned a great deal about other cultures while gaining greater understanding of their own. Things that seem the same are often very different. Those children who speak English often find that in many ways they are different when holidays and vacations, or faucet and tap, mean the same thing in different places. Even television has not had such a strong impact on the spoken and written language which children are using when writing electronically in their classrooms.

Project trends and plans

The Air and Water Projects were selected as one of nineteen US 'Success Stories' receiving commendation by the International Federation of Information Processing Societies in 1995 (Marshall and Taylor, 1995-96). The project's organisers have had to acknowledge international recognition and increasing grassroots interest by teachers. This has forced them to address the issue of how to accommodate requests for ever-greater participation without over-burdening the existing low-budget support infrastructures. For 1996–97 Water and Air Projects, a deliberate attempt was been made to hold the total number of classrooms at about the same number that participated in 1995–96. This trend has certainly continued in an effort to maintain a quality project structure. While interested classrooms continue to participate in Air/Water activities, it is believed that one of the major hidden success factors has been the way in which teachers have been able to use and modify the structure as models to develop their own unique approaches. The Air/Water Home Page containing sample activities and links to related projects, and Adobe Acrobat files containing the curriculum guides, can be accessed through the Texas Center for Educational Technology Home Page at http://www.tcet.unt.edu.

Close examination of the Water and Air Projects 'Call for Participation' for 1999 reveals some important clues about the types of things you might want to look for in any project model you are considering.

Call for participation: Air and Water Projects

Hello!

We are gearing up to begin the 8th year of our curriculum-based global projects. In the past seven years many children ages 7-13 from the U.K., New Zealand, Australia, Israel, Canada, the U.S. and other countries have participated. Many benefits have been observed such as an increase in cultural awareness and geographical awareness. The students are learning the content through a hands-on approach and appear to be having lots of fun.

This is a CALL FOR PARTICIPATION for the Air and Water projects that will begin in February 1999 and end in May 1999. However, teachers may begin communicating earlier.

Participants are required to "register" their class and agree to follow the timeline for transmitting information. It is crucial to the success of the project that everyone send their information on time. It is very disappointing for the children if they do not receive replies. Please do not sign up if you do not think you can commit to a project of this length. It is all volunteer work to arrange the classes. While it is a great deal of fun, it is difficult rearranging for those who drop out. Thanks for the consideration.

Below are tentative timelines and basic outlines for the Air and Water Projects. Please look at the content to determine if it fits your needs. In addition, there is a Web site with more information at http://www.tcet.unt.edu/global/global.htm. In addition, curriculum guides may be downloaded in pdf format at http://www.tcet.unt.edu/curguide.htm.

If you wish to participate, send an e-mail message to rhondac@tenet.edu. Please include:
1. name of the classroom teacher,
2. whether you wish to participate in Air or Water,
3. age of students,
4. number of students,
5. your e-mail address,
6. your phone number and
7. your mailing address
8. fax number
9. do you have access to a C.U. See Me connection? (not necessary for participation)
10. do you have WWW access? And/or your own web page?

DEADLINE FOR REQUEST TO PARTICIPATE IS NOVEMBER 10TH. YOU WILL RECEIVE NOTIFICATION BY NOVEMBER 23RD.

Call for participation: Air and Water Projects. This message continues on pages 117-18.

If you have any questions, send me a message at rhondac@tenet.edu
I look forward to fun and successful projects!!
Rhonda Christensen
98-99 Air and Water Project Coordinator
Dallas, Texas

The schedule takes into account spring break as well as the differences in school years for students in other countries. Teachers are encouraged to be creative in the study. If you need ideas, let me know and I can tell you what kinds of things have been done in the past.

Each project has an introductory module and four modules of study. Below is the timeline for both studies.

February 8th-Feb 26th As a class, write an introductory message to send to other participants. You may want to include things that are of interest to your class such as hobbies, sports, geographical information, favorite foods, social customs, historical info., etc. You might even make a database and send a summary of your class. Be creative!

Feb 26th is the deadline for transmission of introductory letters
March 1st-March 19th Study of 1st module
March 19th is the deadline for transmission of 1st module
March 22nd-April 9th Study of 2nd module
April 9th is the deadline for transmission of 2nd module
April 12th-April 30th Study of 3rd module
April 30th is the deadline for the transmission of 3rd module
May 3rd-May 21st Study of 4th module
May 21st is the deadline for the transmission of 4th module

The Water Project

Module One – Water in Our Communities
The students will explore the nature of water in their area and its source. Some activities may include measuring and graphing daily water fall and comparing it to other classes. Find out about water in your community and share info with other classes

Module Two – Using Water in Our Past
Find out about historical data concerning water in your area. Which lakes are natural and which are manmade? Has the area experienced flooding or drought in the past? Graph water over time (years or months) to see patterns.

Module Three – Using Water Today
Discover how water is used in your area such as recreational uses, etc. Discuss water safety, visit a water treatment plant, etc.

Module Four – Caring For Our Water
Find out about how to conserve water. In the past we have compared taking a shower to taking a bath and measured to find out which is more conservative. Find out about pollution in your area..what causes it and what your class can do to improve it.

```
The Air Project

Module One - Why Do We Need Air?
Students are studying the importance of air Some activities may include
measuring the air temperature and graphing. Then compare to other classes.
Do experiments with a barometer and negative air pressure.

Module Two - What is Happening to Our Air?
Investigate the causes and effects of air pollution Some activities may
include checking the air quality of the air and comparing it day to day.

Module Three - Commercial and Recreational Uses of Air
Some activities may include designing and making an air hockey game using
ping pong balls, or making up a play or skit depicting these uses of air.

Module Four - Clean Up Our Air World Campaign
The students will determine ways in which they can help clean up the air
(carpooling, creating public awareness, etc.)

These are only a few of the many, many wonderful activities that have been
done in the past. Feel free to use some of these and make up your own. It
is fun to share these with classes in other countries.
```

Close examination of the 'Call for Participation' in the Air and Water projects provides some very important clues about projects, particularly when you are working with colleagues in a different hemisphere. A project checklist will help you to consider whether or not this may fit in with what you are planning for your classroom. Try asking yourself the questions on this project checklist.

Project questions checklist
1. Does my class have access to a computer and the Internet so that we can participate fully on a regular basis?
2. How much time does my classroom programme and planning allow for the range of research activities, contributions and interaction that the project requires?
3. Does the communication in the project include interpersonal exchanges, information collections and/or problem-solving projects?
4. Is the structure flexible enough for me to work in and around? (e.g. holiday periods, start and finish times)
5. What skills are my students and I going to need in order to participate in a project like this? (computer and Internet skills, information skills)
6. Is it clear what my obligations are as a participant in the project?
7. Do I know what I can expect from the other participants?
8. Do we have the resources, time and energy for a project like this?

Have We Arrived?

Over the past two decades tremendous growth has occurred in terms of the attitude towards the use of computer-mediated communication. New Zealand is an isolated country geographically, but this isolation can be minimised by the efficient use of computer-mediated communication. Our isolation is seen by many people as a strength and we have much to contribute to the global schoolroom, whether it is discussing our water or simply understanding our global partners. In 1990, Ann Frampton (1990), the Starnet system manager at that time and one of the leading initiators of computer-mediated communication in New Zealand schools, said:

> The application of electronic mail to expand the available audience for children's writing, and for sharing projects and research with children in another part of the world is well accepted these days, but the possibilities do not stop there. (Frampton, 1990, p.45)

The possibilities will only be restricted by our imagination. The World Wide Web developed in 1994 has allowed us to explore further possibilities which Ann Frampton could only dream about at the start of the decade. The 1980s and 1990s have taught us many lessons and the next decade will teach us many more.

Leadership and Direction for CMC in our Schools

In the mid 1980s a number of New Zealand primary and secondary schools were introduced to the use of electronic mail in classrooms. This offered students and their teachers the opportunity to communicate with peers around the world via a telephone line, computer, and modem. The newly established Computers in Education Development Unit (CEDU) promoted the use of the Starnet system, an electronic mail system that was made available to all schools who wanted to join. Teachers who were familiar with using computers at that time were eager to leap on the new 'bandwagon'. While there were some excellent innovative CMC projects at that time, frequently the projects focused on the technology and not on curriculum-related outcomes. The initial enthusiasm waned when expectations were not met. The demise of the CEDU in 1989 meant that direction for the use of CMC was no longer forthcoming on a national basis.

Further opportunities for teacher development using CMC were available on a regional basis. The Education Advisory and Support Services based in teacher training institutions continued to provide information technology support for schools. From 1993 to 1996 the Ministry of Education offered contracts for teacher development in information technology. This gave many teachers in primary and secondary schools the opportunity to experience a taste for what they might do with these new tools. The Telecom Education Foundation has supported workshops for teachers since 1993 in an effort to assist schools to realise the potential of CMC. For many schools these initiatives, along with a 'spray and pray' mode of teacher development, were not always enough to sustain a radical change in teacher practice. For many teachers this was 'just one more thing to do' in what was an already busy schedule. Until a national focus and direction was identified and there was something of real value for the individual teachers, it was unlikely there would be a purposeful and lasting integration of computer-mediated communication in New Zealand school classrooms.

The long-awaited strategy from the Ministry of Education was finally announced in October, 1998. It was envisaged that this new initiative would finally put information and communication technology in a more meaningful context and a renewed interest and enthusiasm for CMC would emerge. Communication on a global and a national basis were key features of the Ministry's strategy.

The Minister of Education, Wyatt Creech, in his Foreword to the strategy document *Innovative Education* described how he saw the challenge for schools and teachers. It is 'our ability to use this information and communication potential in expert and innovative ways so that we can continue to interact on a global level … to support all seven essential learning areas'. New Zealand now has a focus for using CMC, in which projects like Water and Air can assist the innovative practice we have become world leaders in supporting and promoting.

References

Anderson, C. (1991). Some hints on telecommunications projects. *Computers in New Zealand Schools,* 3 (2), 43-44.

Barr, H. (1991). Social studies by electronic mail. *Social Studies Observer,* 24 (1), 10-11.

Barr, H. (1992). Social studies by electronic mail. University of Waikato. Unpublished article.

Butler, G. & Jobe, H.M. (1987). The Australian-American connection. *The Computing Teacher.* (14) 7, 25-26.

Chapple, D. (1992). Gaining entry to the global classroom: the computer as a key. In K. Lai & B. McMillan (eds), *Learning with Computers: Issues & Applications in New Zealand.* Palmerston North: The Dunmore Press.

Chapple, D. (1991). The good, the bad, and the ugly: taking your pick. *Computers in New Zealand Schools.* 3 (1), 42-45.

Christensen, R., Knezek, G., & Campbell, N. (1994a). Model activities for internet-accessible teachers. Paper presented at the Third International Conference on Telecommunications in Education, Albuquerque, New Mexico.

Christensen, R., Clayton, G., Campbell, N., & Knezek, G. (1994b). *Global classrooms: A study of air – a curriculum and technology infusion guide.* Denton, TX: Texas Center for Educational Technology.

Christensen, R., Clayton, G., Campbell, N., & Knezek, G. (1994c). *Global classrooms: A study of water – a curriculum and technology infusion guide.* Denton, TX: Texas Center for Educational Technology.

Christensen, R., Knezek, G., & Campbell, N. (1996). Global interactions among elementary school classrooms: The Air and Water Projects. *T.I.E News,* 7 (4), 17-19.

Computers in Education Development Unit. (Term 3, 1986). *Newsletter* (9). Wellington: C.E.D.U.

Computers in Education Development Unit. (Term 1, 1989). *Newsletter.* (16). Wellington: C.E.D.U.

Department of Education. (1986). *The Potential Educational Benefits of Electronic Communications Technologies for New Zealand.* Wellington: Department of Education.

Department of Education. (1987). *Report on the Exploratory Studies in Educational Computing.* Wellington: Department of Education.

Department of Education (1987). *Computer Communications in Education.* Wellington: Department of Education.

Erikson, A. (1987, July). An ACOT experiment in learning. *The Computing Teacher,* 31-32.

Frampton, A. (1990). World without speech. *Computers in New Zealand Schools.* 2 (3), 41-45.

Goldberg, F. (1989, June). Selecting and implementing a bulletin board system for your district or school. *The Computing Teacher,* 8-10.

Harris, J. (1997). *Sample Curriculum-Based K-12 Educational Telecomputing Projects, Organized by Activity Structures.* Available at <http://lrs.ed.uiuc.edu/Activity-Structures/web-activity-

structures.html>.

Leonard, V., Hellier, A., Thomson, P., Moore, D. (1990). KID teachng. *Computers in New Zealand Schools.* 2 (2), 45-46.

Leonard, V., Hellier, A., Moore, D., Thomson, P., Wilton, K. (1991). Written conversations; an interactive teaching strategy. *Reading Forum NZ.* 3, 6-7.

Levin, J.A., Rogers, A., Waugh, M., & Smith, K. (1989, May). Observations on electronic networks: appropriate activities for learning. *The Computing Teacher*, 17-21.

Le Seur, E. (1991). The gifted network. *Reading Forum NZ.* 3, 16-17.

Marshall, G. & Taylor, H. (1995-96). The success stories project: an international collaboration. *Learning and leading with technology 23* (4), 28-30.

Ministry of Education. (1998). *Interactive Education: An information and communication technologies strategy for schools.* Wellington: Ministry of Education.

Richardson, G. (1989). Telecommunications within the primary school. *Computers in New Zealand Schools.* 1 (1), 46-48.

Richardson, G. (1990). Teleconferencing in social studies. *Computers in New Zealand Schools.* (2) 1, 46-47.

Ropiha, D. (1991). He punawaru-a-tuhi – te wahapu. *Computers In New Zealand Schools.* 3 (3), 47-48.

6　Designing Web-based Learning Environments

Kwok-Wing Lai

Increasingly tertiary institutes, as well as schools, find it essential to use the World Wide Web for teaching, research, and administrative purposes. Hardly any tertiary institutes are without a presence on the Web. For universities and colleges, websites have been used for advertising and publicity as well as for the delivery of undergraduate and graduate courses. Increasingly, websites are also used to support teaching and learning in schools. This chapter intends to raise some questions and provide some resources as to how a school website could be designed. As well, it discusses briefly some issues related to the design of Web-based learning environments for the delivery of courses at a distance.

Setting up School Websites

While there are good pedagogical reasons for using the World Wide Web in teaching and learning, schools should not rush into setting up their own websites simply because the technology is out there and everyone else in town is doing it. Schools should have a clear rationale and purpose in mind and avoid succumbing to the 'Everest Syndrome'. (When Sir Edmund Hillary was asked why he climbed Mount Everest, his reply was simply, 'Because it was there!' – refer Maddux, Johnson & Harlow, 1994). Rather than being used as a piecemeal solution resulting from the enthusiasm of some teachers, a school website should be developed within a comprehensive information technology plan, which should specify the vision, goals, and an action plan for the use of information and communication technologies in the school curriculum, as well as in management. Such a plan should begin by assessing the needs and status of the school's stakeholders, and could include the following questions:

- What are the current skills, knowledge, and attitudes of students, teachers, and administrators in information technology and networking?
- How do teachers currently use information and communication technologies (e.g. wordprocessing and e-mail) in their own professional use and in teaching? How about school administrators?
- To what extent have information and communication technologies been integrated into the school curriculum? For example, to what extent do students use the Internet for their class work?
- What is the current inventory of computer hardware and software and networking equipment available in the school?
- What is the level of support for staff who wish to integrate information technology into the school curriculum?

An Information Technology Plan

It is not the intention of this chapter to detail how such a plan should be developed.

Suffice to say that an information technology plan should clearly state the vision of the school in using and integrating information and communication technologies (ICT) into the existing curriculum as well as in management and administration. Long and short-term goals and objectives, an action or implementation plan, as well as an indication as to how the plan is to be monitored and evaluated, should also be described. There are many information technology plans available on the Internet, most being developed in the USA (for example, see the NCRTEC Tech Plan Guide available at http://www.ties.k12.mn.us/techplan/techplans.html). The following discussion is based partly on a checklist developed by the Vermont Department of Education (http://www.state.vt.us/educ/chklst.html). To develop such a plan, it is important to give as much ownership to the stakeholders as possible. An iterative consultative process should therefore be put in place and the policy team should include the principal, representative from the board of trustees, teachers, parents, students (in high schools) and the community representatives.

A vision

A vision or mission statement is essential in providing a focus for the plan. This statement should describe the expected outcomes of using ICT for students, teachers, and administrators. It should reflect the school's values and beliefs, not just in ICT use but in teaching and learning in general. In the vision statement, the school should also express its commitment to:

- providing equity of access of information technology for all staff and students in the school;
- integrating information and communication technologies into the school curriculum; and
- supporting professional development for all academic and general staff.

The following example is a short vision statement developed by a school district in the United States, which states the expectation of the school:

In the Bellingham School District, the learning community will be technologically literate life-long learners. Learners will be able to interact successfully in a technological environment to achieve their personal, education, and workplace goals. They will skillfully use technology to access, retrieve and use information school-wide, community-wide, nationally, and internationally. (Available at http://www.bham.wednet.edu/tech/techplan.htm#phil).

Goals

The information technology plan should also include goals for the improvement of: (a) student learning; (b) integrating information technology into the school curriculum; (c) administration and management; and (d) professional development for integration of information technology into the school curriculum.

Action plan

There is also a need for a multi-year action plan to prioritise: (a) software and hardware acquisition; (b) development of local-area or wide-area networks; (c) staffing support, both in teaching and technical support in (i) daily operation of instructional and administrative systems and networks; (ii) software and equipment purchase and maintenance; and (iii) integrating information and communication technologies into the curriculum; and (d) professional development for both academic and general staff. Milestones to be met should be clearly stated in the document.

As a minimum, details of the first year of the action plan should be provided for the purchase of software and hardware, development of networking facilities, operations maintenance and upgrades. There should also be an action plan for professional development, and support for integrating information technology into the curriculum.

Financial implications
Financial implications of the plan should be worked out. Potential funding resources should be stated. A detailed breakdown of expenditures of information technology initiatives for the purchase of hardware, software, development of infrastructure, as well as for professional development and staffing, should be included as well.

Monitoring and evaluation
In the information technology plan, strategies for monitoring and evaluation should be clearly stated. Short-term and long-term improvements in teaching, learning and management should also be clearly stated so that an ongoing process of evaluation can be carried out.

Designing a Website
Once it has been decided in the school information technology plan that a website is to be constructed, the design process can begin by asking the following questions:

What are the main purposes of this website, what is its target audience?
A website can be set up with different purposes in mind and to serve different audiences. A site used mainly for advertising is quite different in design from a site intended for instructional purposes. Information included in a school website that targeted the local community would be quite different from a site for an international audience.

A study was conducted in 1998 to investigate the purposes and contents of some major New Zealand school websites (Lai, 1999). School websites registered with the *CWA Education Web* (http://www.cwa.co.nz/eduweb/edu/nzschool.html) were used as the sample of this study. At the time of the study a total of 306 school websites were registered with the *CWA Education Web* and 272 of them were successfully accessed and reviewed. From this study the following main functions of these websites were identified:

• *Links to the outside world*. The most important purpose of these websites was to provide information about the school to the outside world. In the study nearly every school (96 per cent) included some school information in their site. Information such as the school's mission statement, courses and programmes, event calendars, etc. were published and updated through the website. Most schools involved some students in the design and maintenance of their school website. For example, Tawa Primary School in Wellington stated explicitly the rationale of its website, and it is of particular interest to see the role of its students in contributing to its contents:

> We wanted a website to enable our students to publish their work to an ever widening audience. The website is to be a reflection of the school and the work which is continuing to happen here.
> At all times we want to have at least 20 per cent of our children represented on the website. At the last count we had 362 children at Tawa School, and although the numbers change daily, we believe that the 20 per cent target has been met. Count them for yourself! (http://www.tawa.school.nz/OurPage/OurPage.html#One).

The majority of the school sites (72 per cent) also provided specific information targeted at parents. The link between the school and the local community was weaker, as only 31 per cent of the schools have specific links with their local communities. Very few schools used the Web to communicate with their past students (about 9 per cent).

• *Stores curriculum resources.* A website can also be used to archive materials and resources related to its school curriculum and teachers can use the site to share their resources among themselves. Curricular materials can also be prepared for students who can access them from home. For example, Pakuranga College in Auckland (http://pakuranga.school.nz/culm2.html) has provided extensive links to a variety of curriculum areas for its teachers and students to use. In this study about 43 per cent of the schools have provided links to curriculum resources in their sites.

• *Publishes and exhibits students' work.* A school website could be used as a 'place' to publish students' work in a variety of curricular areas targeted at an authentic audience. Publishing students' work was the second most popular function of the school sites in this study. About 45 per cent of the schools surveyed used the Web to publish their students' work. For example, Lyall Bay School (http://homepages.ihug.co.nz/~lyallbay/kids.htm) has published students' art work, stories, and poetry on their website. Elmwood Normal School (http://www.chch.school.nz/elmwood/elmwood.html) also provides a good example of how students' art works can be presented in a gallery setting. Some schools also allow students to have their personal page. Paengaroa School is a good example (http://homepages.enterprise.net/paengaroa/homepg/moriah.html).

What are the resources needed for constructing a website?

To a great extent the purposes and functions of the website will determine the resources required to set it up and maintain it. For example, if the purpose is to provide information for parents to access (e.g. publishing the school newsletter), contents of the site need only be updated infrequently and resources required to maintain it (both human and physical) will not be too demanding. However, if the website is to deliver distance learning courses, a lot more technical and curricular expertise will be required. It is a good idea to visit some popular school websites to see what kind of resources are involved in setting up a good website (check *Web99* and *CWA Education Web* for school addresses). If your school lacks the expertise, perhaps it is time to plan for some professional development activities in this area. Sending your staff to a Web design course or a workshop for a quick upgrade of skills may be needed.

As school websites are now commonly hosted by commercial Internet Service Providers (ISP), in deciding which ISP should host your school website you may need to think about the following questions:

- How much information can be stored in the host's Web server for the school?
- How easy is it for the school to edit, delete, and save its pages? How easily can these pages be uploaded to the ISP's server?
- Does the ISP create backup files for your pages?
- Issues of security. Are these pages protected from unauthorised people?
- Can interactive pages be easily created? Can users easily submit information to the site?

How to write your homepage

Your homepage is the first page visitors will see when they visit your site. It is therefore important to pay more attention to this page. Your homepage should include the following information:

- local information, such as a brief description of your school;
- information of a contact person (e.g. an e-mail address);
- the date when this page was last updated;
- a copyright note for the page.

If you wish to include links to external resources they should be put on the next level. If they are to be solely used by your teachers and students you might wish to create a password-protected page for this purpose. You should make your homepage and its links as current as possible.

Your Web pages (including your homepage) are written in HTML (HyperText Markup Language). Writing HTML files is perhaps the easiest part of the whole process. Nowadays it is not really necessary for you to know a lot about HTML as there is a lot of powerful yet user-friendly editing software available in the market to assist you (e.g. PageMill or Claris Home Page). Even if you know nothing about HTML, don't be intimidated by the technical aspects of Web publishing.

The appendix at the end of this chapter lists some of the resources which will be helpful in writing and designing your pages (also refer Bremer, 1996; Darling, Peterson, & Smith, 1998). Here I want to stress the importance of providing good navigation guides on your site, as everyone has the experience of getting lost when they surf the Internet.

- *Watch the length of the page.* The length of each page should be carefully monitored as it will affect the ease of navigation. As suggested in the guidelines written by the Southern Indiana Education Center (http://www.siec.k12.in.us/~west/online/ kinds.htm), if the user has to scroll more than three screens, the page is definitely too long.

• *Don't bury your information.* Also, you should avoid burying information on the site. It is suggested that users should not have to click more than three times before they can arrive at the information they are looking for (Southern Indiana Education Center, 1998).

• *Provide an overview of the site.* As the single most valuable thing teachers (as well as students) lack is time, an overview of the information or resources available on your site should be given as soon as possible and should be easy to skim through.

• *Don't distract.* The more images and graphics that are used, the greater their potential to distract users from the main focus of the site. If a lot of time is required to download a page, this will also distract. How to focus users' attention and maintain the relevancy of the site becomes an important design issue (Duchastel, 1997). One suggestion is to stick closely to the needs of the intended audience. A Web page designed for students is different from one that is designed for teachers. If you want to include information for teachers on a Web page designed for students, use a link on that student page to the additional resources you want share with other teachers (Southern Indiana Education Center, 1998).

What are the selection criteria for external links and resources?

You should develop a set of selection criteria when you link your site to external resources. The selection criteria should be described clearly on the page where the links are provided. Internet resources can be evaluated in a number of ways, depending on the nature of these resources. There are some good evaluation criteria available on the Internet. For example, the EdOasis website (http://www.EdsOasis.org) has developed an evaluation guide which examines online features (student action and user-interface), curricular design, program design, instructional design, and instructional support materials of Web resources before linking to them (Gray, 1997). Another set of selection criteria worth looking at is developed by Blue Web'n (http://www.kn.pacbell.com/wired/bluewebn/rubric.html). Its selection criteria include an evaluation of the format (user-friendly, aesthetically courteous, aesthetically appealing), content (credible, useful, rich, interdisciplinary) and learning process (higher-order thinking, engaging, multiple intelligences or talents) of the resources.

What ethical issues are involved in publishing student information on your site?

As resources published in your site will be seen or used by people around the world, you need to get parental permission if you wish to publish your students' work on your site. Attention has to be paid to ethical issues such as privacy and copyright (refer to Chapter 9 for a more detailed discussion). You need to be extra careful if you want to include students' photos and other personal information on your site (e.g. names and e-mail addresses). A sample parental consent letter can be found at the Hillside Elementary School site (http://www.gsn.org/web/_lib/_issues/aup/hillside.txt).

Whether students' photos and personal information should be published on the

Web is a controversial issue. Caroline McCullen, the editor of *MidLink Magazine*, has commented on this:

> Maybe I am missing something, but I don't understand why so many teachers rush to publish pictures of their students on the Web ... Why make up a reason (posting pictures and autobiographies, for example) to construct a Web page? Why not publicise the actual work that goes on in the classroom? Then when other students see it, they can create their own response and post it ... they made the leap from using the Net as a resource to actually *becoming* a resource ... I think if we keep our postings educationally sound, we will have far less trouble with parental complaints and we may even reduce the press's persistent fascination with Net Porn. I'm not naive enough to think we don't have to worry about security. We *must* protect the kids (*Midlink Magazine*, 1995, available at http://www.cs.ucf.edu/~MidLink/).

If students are allowed to publish materials on the school website by themselves (e.g. personal homepage), ways of monitoring and evaluating these materials becomes an issue to consider. An Acceptable Use Policy (AUP) has to be designed (see Chapter 9 for further discussion and a sample AUP).

How to publicise your site

There are different ways of publicising your site. For example, you can advertise it in a community newspaper. Or, if you are a New Zealand school, you can put it in the government *Gazette* for free. However, as your target audience will most likely be people who have access to the Internet, the best way to publicise your site is by advertising it on the Internet itself.

There are at least four ways your site can be publicised on the Internet:

1. *External links.* If your site has links to external sites, you could inform these sites and invite them to link back to you. As the sites you link into are most probably popular sites, you can draw some visitors from them.
2. *Search engines*. Most of the search engines will be keen to include your site information. Just visit their site and you will find out how to register with them.
3. *Website registry.* There are websites on the Internet which keep a registry of school websites or online projects. For example, *Web66* allows you to register your site address with their database. The last time I checked its registry (just before Christmas, 1998), I found 45 New Zealand primary and 105 secondary schools registered with its database. To register your site with *Web66* visit http://web66.coled.umn.edu/schools/NZ/NewZealand.html. In New Zealand, the *CWA Education Web* also keeps a registry and over 300 New Zealand schools have registered in its database.
4. *Educational mailing lists.* Your school website can also be announced in educational mailing lists. Addresses of these mailing lists are available at http://www.siec.k12.in.us/~west/online/announce.htm.

How to maintain and upgrade the site

Once a school website has been set up, it needs to be maintained regularly to update its information and check that the links to external resources are still working. One of the frustrations in surfing the Internet is to find broken links and sites that have not been updated for a while. A good website is maintained and upgraded regularly.

Designing Web-based Courses

Increasingly both schools and universities are using the Web to deliver courses at a distance. With the advent of information and communication technologies, distance education has recently become a major topic of interest not only at the tertiary level but also at the school level as well. For example, it is reported by Simonson (1997) that almost every professional organisation's publications and conferences have shown a huge increase in the number of distance education related articles and papers in recent years. Traditionally, the predominant mode of delivery in distance education is linear and print-based. The distance student is often seen as a lone learner with very limited interaction with the teacher and with other students. With advanced communications technologies, the mode of delivery has shifted from this correspondence model, to the telelearning model where a variety of teaching and learning tools are now used to enhance interaction and collaboration (Jegede, 1995, cited in Dillon, 1998).

The present author's own experience has been in designing Web-based courses at the tertiary level, and examples given in the following section will therefore be very much tertiary-oriented (Lai, 1997, 1998). However, it is believed that many issues will also be relevant at the high school level.

Web-assisted or Web-based?

Nowadays teachers use the Web to support their teaching in a variety of ways. If you browse the World Lecture Hall site (http://wwwhost.utexas.edu/world/lecture/) set up by the University of Texas at Austin, you will see a range of Web tools being used to assist the teaching of a variety of courses on the Internet. Most of these courses are what we call Web-assisted courses, where the Web is used mainly to supplement face-to-face teaching. In most of the Web-assisted courses found in the World Lecture Hall, lecture notes, examination scripts and course-related materials are archived on the course Web site, with the intention of providing students with easier access to course-related materials. Flexible access to course materials is a major reason for using the Web to assist course delivery. For example, in a course on the history of Western civilisation, examination questions are e-mailed to each student and they have to be returned in 48 hours. The practice is similar to an open book examination but has the added advantage of the independence of space. Storing materials on the Web is also a flexible arrangement if students are required to read the lecture notes and materials before coming to class.

In some Web-assisted courses, however, electronic mail and discussion lists are also used to supplement face-to-face communication between students and teaching staff. Sometimes students may be required to participate in class discussion first, before sharing their reflections on the meeting by e-mails or in an electronic discussion list (e.g. a LISTSERV newsgroup). However, sometimes computer-mediated conferencing is used as the main delivery mechanism and students are only required to meet face-to-face once or twice, at the beginning or at the end of the course. For example, in a graduate course called 'Children's Literature on-line', featured authors and illustrators who led online class discussions every two weeks (six altogether). Communication with other students and the tutor were assisted by e-mail and a class bulletin board to supplement some face-to-face sessions (http://www.su.edu/academic/conted/ed501.htm).

The overwhelming majority of the courses listed in the World Lecture Hall were Web-assisted courses where teachers used the Web to complement or support face-to-face teaching. However, increasingly, more teachers use the Web as the sole delivery system. In this mode of delivery, students will not be able to complete the course without having regular access to the Web and no face-to-face meeting is required. These courses are what we call Web-based courses. For example, to deliver one of his Web-based courses, the author has set up a Web server and developed a learning environment where tertiary students have to participate in five asynchronous computer-mediated conferences, weekly synchronous chat sessions, and complete weekly exercises and reading assignments, plus four collaborative assessment projects (Lai, 1997). One of the major advantages for students is that they can complete these Web-based courses from anywhere in the world. Increasingly, revolving enrolment is possible in such a system, whereby individual students can enrol whenever a vacancy occurs. A period of time (for example, one year) is given to the student to complete the course. This gives students maximum flexibility.

In many universities and colleges, distance education has become a mainstream activity. Not only are a variety of courses now being offered on the Internet, but degree programmes right up to the doctorate can also be studied online. To get some ideas of the range of online programmes offered, check the list of courses available at the School of Education, University of Otago website (http://education.otago.ac.nz:800/Teled/Virtual_U.html). This resource was prepared for the Seventh International Telecommunications and Multimedia conference by the author and his colleagues in 1998.

At the school level, more and more courses are delivered at a distance by using advanced information and communication technologies (Nyhof, 1997). The Virtual High School (http://vhs.concord.org) funded by the US Department of Education offers a variety of high school courses for both American and international students. This project provides a good model of how Web-based high school courses can be developed and how teachers can be trained to teach them.

Some design principles

The Web has altered the traditional nature of information communication and access (Duchastel, 1997). In using the Internet for course delivery one has to move away from the traditional paradigm of teaching (see Chapter 1 of this book for a more detailed discussion). If a teacher adopts a conduit approach to learning (where knowledge is to be transmitted directly from the teacher to the learner), lecture notes can simply be converted to HTML files and put into the course website for students to access. (Alternatively, lecture notes can be audio- or video-taped and delivered over the Internet.) In this case the potential of the Internet as a medium of communication is largely ignored. In order to use a Web-based learning environment to scaffold and extend students' learning, the following design principles should be considered:

• *Interactivity.* A major consideration of using the Web as a learning environment is no doubt its capability of enhancing interaction between the learners, as well as between the learners and the teacher. Teachers can employ a range of synchronous and asynchronous tools in such a learning environment. For example, instead of having face-to-face discussion in a traditional classroom, students can share their opinions and co-construct knowledge in asynchronous, threaded, and computer-mediated discussion forums. There are sophisticated computer conferencing software packages, which can be integrated seamlessly into the course website. Students logging onto the website can read and post messages related to the course. Students can also communicate synchronously in real-time chat programs. Private communication between the students and the teacher, and between students, will be facilitated by e-mail. In designing a Web-based learning environment one has to maximise its interactivity as much as possible. The designer has to consider whether text-based communication is adequate for this purpose and how the environment can enhance the student's contribution. How much information is prescribed in the course site for students to interact with also needs to be addressed. The activities in such a learning environment have to be engaging, interesting, and stimulating. Meaningful tasks should be designed to encourage students to engage in a reflective process, and come up with overall strategies to deal with those tasks.

• *Collaboration.* It is important to decide whether a Web-based learning environment is mainly used by single learners who are required to complete their work individually or by groups of learners who will complete their work collaboratively. Assignments have to be set in such a way as to encourage collaboration, and support should be given to students in forming online study groups. We should be aware that even adult learners may not have the social and communication skills to work in a collaborative learning environment, particularly in an online setting. Support has to be given to these learners. To facilitate collaborative learning, the learning environment should be developed so that online exercises and assignments can be jointly edited, and private forums (e.g. private chat rooms) are provided.

• *Social and interpersonal interaction.* A key issue that has not been adequately discussed in the literature concerns social and interpersonal interaction in the Web-based learning environment. As the best environment for learning is a social setting, a Web-based course site should be designed to promote social and interpersonal interaction as well. The course website should be served as a virtual meeting place shared by all the students. Very often when we talk about the Web we refer to it as a huge electronic library and too much attention is given to the cognitive dimension of this learning environment. In a study conducted by Lai (1998) it was shown that tertiary students doing a Web-based distance course regularly shared socio-emotional and interpersonal information with each other and social interaction was a significant factor in contributing to knowledge construction in this environment.

• *User control.* The user here refers both to the learner and the teacher. There are different levels of user control in a Web-based learning environment. The user-interface is the entry point for the user to communicate with the learning environment. The course Web site should be designed to reduce the time needed to learn how to use and navigate it, as well as how to search for information and how to communicate with other users. In designing such a user-interface, perhaps we should recall these five criteria developed by Neilson (1989, cited in Abi-Raad, 1997): the system has to be (a) easy to learn; (b) easy to use; (c) easy to remember; (d) pleasant to use; and have few errors. A convention of design and use for the Internet and the Web has not yet been stabilised. We should therefore anticipate navigational problems even if students are proficient Internet users. It is important to guide the learners in such a way that they know what to expect and how to access information. Learner control also relates to the issue of ownership. To instigate a sense of ownership, students should be encouraged to participate in the design of the learning environment by contributing comments and suggestions to the modification of the course structures and objectives. They should be allowed to set their own learning goals. They should also have some personal space such as a virtual office in the website (Lai, 1997). As well, students should have a clear idea about the ownership of conference postings.

• *Structure and management of the learning environment.* A Web-based learning environment should be a flexible learning environment. At the same time, a good management structure should be provided for the learners. For example, in a Web-based learning environment designed by Lai (1997), a weekly schedule with links to readings, learning activities, and some introduction to the learning objectives was provided and regarded by students as one of the most important features that led to the success of their learning. A good management structure for a distance learner also includes clear and explicit information on the assessment tasks, as well as just-in-time feedback on their assignments. For teachers, it also means that the learning environment is easy to manage and that few additional administrative tasks are associated with the operation of such a system.

Designing the course homepage

The course homepage is the first page students will visit and therefore should include all the essential information and links (buttons) that are required to complete the course. One of the course homepages of the School of Education at the University of Otago is given here as an example of what could be included in the user-interface (Lai, 1997). In this course site (see Figure 1), the school metaphor is used (classrooms, noticeboard, helpdesk, filing cabinets, etc.) to provide students with a familiar structure.

In addition, a weekly schedule is shown as buttons at the top of the page. When clicking these buttons, students will see each week's activities, including links to 'what to know', 'what to read', and 'what to see' (Figure 2).

The most important component of the learning environment is the classrooms where thematic discussions take place (Figure 3).

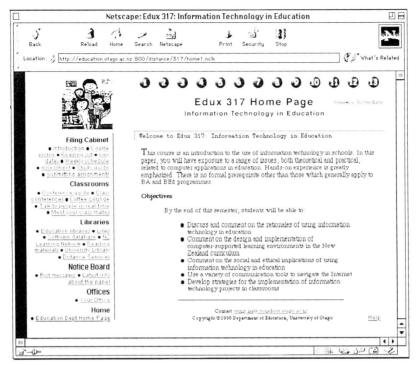

Figure 1

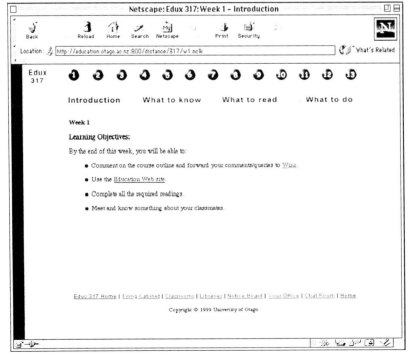

Figure 2

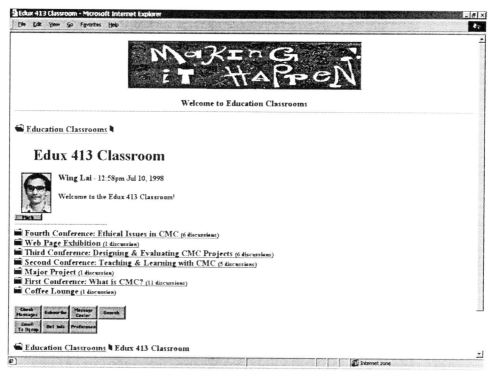

Figure 3

Some Other Issues
Ethical implications

In Web-based learning, learners are very often engaged in computer-mediated conferencing. Ethical issues involving copyright and ownership of the conference postings have to be considered. The following comments from one of the students participating in a discussion forum illustrate the complexity of this:

> The issue of ethics I think is prevalent here. If one is going to use the ideas of others and also combine the idea of others in this on-line document then ethics dictate that permission should be asked. It is just like when one quotes from literature and footnotes are put in to account for copying other people's work.
>
> This reminds me of my experience a couple of weeks ago. I replied privately to a fellow orienteer about a topic and he put my reply over the whole net without my permission. I was annoyed and somewhat uncomfortable. I did nothing about it so he doesn't know how I felt. Therefore it will serve me right if it happens again. However I will probably not answer his queries in the future even if I know the answer.

It is sometimes difficult to determine what is public and what is private information in a Web-based environment. Most of the materials produced by students (including assignments, Web pages, conference postings) will become a permanent part of the teacher's website and may be extended, used, and improved in future classes. Private information may incidentally become public information and it is then difficult to determine who owns the materials (Cox, 1998). It is advisable, therefore, to develop an ownership policy for both teachers and students to follow. The following is an example from a course designer:

> All information produced in this class [Taming the Electronic Frontier], unless specifically marked private, will be shared by the class and, in view of technical limitations for restricting access to electronic information across both time and space, with the world at large. All communications with the instructor will be treated as public unless specifically marked otherwise. (Cox, 1998, available at http://virtualschool.edu/98c/index.html)

Cost effectiveness

Teachers and course designers should be warned that developing and teaching Web-based courses is time-consuming. Time involved in doing this can be categorised as development and operation costs (Montgomerie & Harapnuik, 1997). In developing a Web-based course, time has to be spent in:

• *Setting up a Web server.* If you do not have a server handy to deliver your course, time has to be spent in setting it up. It takes time to purchase the server hardware as well as to select the server software. For a more interactive learning environment, additional software such as conferencing and FTP software have to be integrated into the course website.

• *Course design.* Existing course lecture notes cannot be converted verbatim into Internet-based learning materials. The designer has to decide what kind of interaction in the learning environment can best support collaboration. The designer also has to come up with discussion themes pertinent to the course and yet suitable for discussion online. Learning activities have to be designed in a way that can be carried out individually as well as collaboratively, with support accessible to the learner either online or by other means. The course outline, including the weekly schedule (learning objectives, course contents, course resources, conference themes) and reading materials (reading list, resources on the Internet), has to be assembled (copyright clearance, scanning reading materials). Assessment tasks and methods plus explicit grading criteria have to be prepared. Management issues such as methods of submitting assignments have to be thought through.

• *Designing the course homepage.* The time involved in designing the course homepage will depend on how the learning environment is to be structured. In the online course we just outlined, the high level of interactivity required integrating a conferencing application, an interactive helpdesk, and a searchable database into the course homepage. The libraries provided on the site mean external links to other sites. The weekly schedule means four separate pages for each week linked to the homepage.

• *Writing HTML pages.* You may have some existing course materials that could be converted to HTML pages right away. Time will be involved in the conversion.

Time is also involved in running the course, and has to be spent in:
• moderating conferences;
• monitoring the noticeboard and helpdesk;
• answering individual e-mails;
• answering phone calls and meeting students face-to-face;

- modifying and updating pages; and
- monitoring attendance, collecting assignments, providing feedback.

For a similar class size, my own experience is that it is more time-consuming to teach a Web-based course than a traditional face-to-face class. It is estimated that up to two months' full-time work (for one person) is needed to convert an existing graduate course to a Web-based one. As a lot more attention is given to individual students in an Internet-based learning environment, one may expect an increase of up to 50 per cent of the time needed for the day-to-day running of the course. However, it should be noted that Web-based learning environments have the potential to deliver high quality learning and they also give learners an opportunity to pursue a learning programme that is otherwise not available to them.

Teacher as Moderator

As has been mentioned before (Lai, 1996), in a Web-based learning environment learning should not be seen as confined to four stone walls where the teacher is considered to be the sole knowledge provider. Teachers need to realise that there is a fundamental change in their relationship with the students. They are not there to impart knowledge and skills to students but to provide guidance and support as coach and facilitator. In a Web-based learning environment, it is particularly important for the teacher to take up the role as moderator. In a Web-mediated discussion forum, the moderator is critical in 'defining the membership of the conference, in keeping the discussion on track, and in scheduling the opening and closing of the discussion topics' (Kaye, 1992, p. 6). As well, their role is to provide guidance to students so that they can develop their own discussion threads. Mason (1989) maintains that a conference moderator has three kinds of responsibility: (a) organisational – planning and managing conference activities; (b) social – establishing and maintaining positive relationships among learners; and (c) intellectual – promoting student participation and helping to summarise and connect students' contributions.

The changing relationship can best be represented by the following two communication patterns in a Web-based learning environment. In the first pattern, as can be seen from Figure 4, the students were keen to respond to the teacher's opening question where the teacher's role was mainly to provide answers (in this and the following figures the letter A represents the teacher). Little genuine discussion took place. In the second pattern (Figure 5, refer to Lai, 1997), the teacher was successful in handing back control to the learners and we can see discussion threads were initiated by students independently.

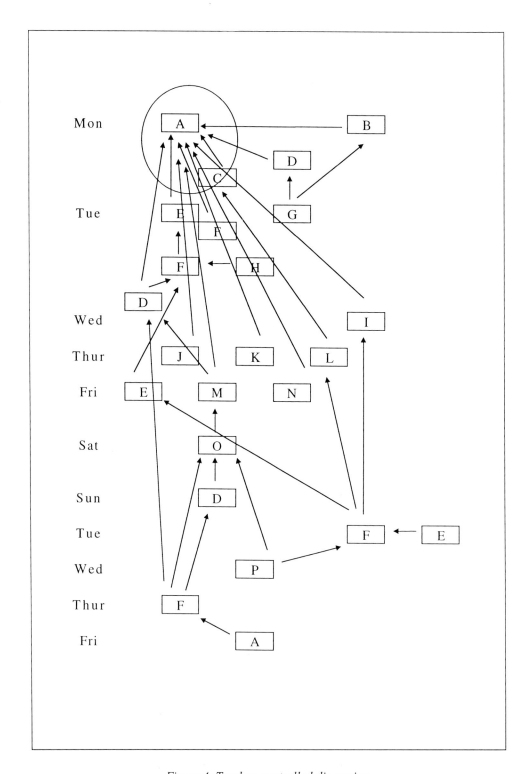

Figure 4: Teacher-controlled discussion

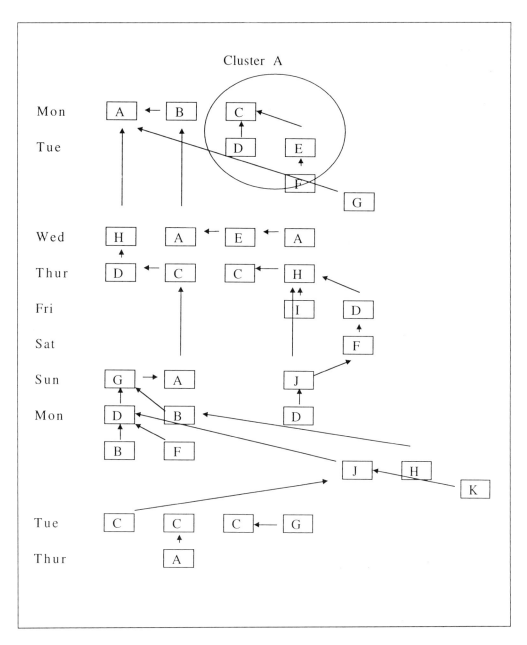

Figure 5: Student-initiated discussion

Learner Profile

Most of the Web-based courses available on the Internet are text-based. If the bandwidth problem is not solved in the near future, only limited audio- or video-conferencing will be employed on a large scale for course delivery. Thus, a certain level of reading and writing is needed for successful participation. But other skills are required to participate successfully in online conferencing, unlike in the traditional classroom system. The following guidelines might be useful for students who are interested in taking Web-based courses:

- *Discipline.* To complete a Web-based course perhaps requires more discipline on the part of the learner than does a course in a traditional setting. The key is to manage one's time wisely by setting aside the period required to complete the readings and assignments on a daily basis.
- *Reading and writing skills.* As at present most of the Web-based courses on the Internet are text-based, the learner has to be a reasonably good reader and a good writer. As well, students are required to have the skills to communicate with other members of the class.
- *Prepared to collaborate yet enjoy working independently.* Although a Web-based learning environment should be interactive and collaborative, students still need to work alone in front of the computer for relatively long periods.
- *A realistic expectation.* The amount of time spent on these courses will not be less than for a traditional class.
- *Willing to seek help.* Students may not be able to reach the teacher or other students for immediate feedback. They should therefore be prepared to seek help whenever it is needed rather than wait until the last minute.
- *Highly motivated.* The key to success in learning is motivation. This is particularly true in an online environment, as additional technical and communication skills are required.

Concluding Remarks

Setting up a school website and designing a Web-based learning environment for course delivery is not a simple venture. It should not be attempted without a clear rationale in mind. This chapter has suggested some key questions that needed to be considered if one ventures into such an endeavour. These questions (and answers) are by no means comprehensive and of course there are different ways Web-based learning environments can be designed and developed. They only provide a starting point where website and course designers can begin to think about the issues. It is hoped that this reflective process will lead to better answers to these questions.

Acknowledgement

The author gratefully acknowledges the assistance of Russell Butson and Anne Elliot in writing up this chapter.

Appendix

Some useful sites in designing and writing Web pages:

HTML - An Interactive Tutorial For Beginners (http://www.davesite.com/webstation/html/)

Computer Education Online: Create A Website (http://www.cybercomm.net/~learn/create.html)

Writing HTML - a tutorial for creating WWW pages (http://www.mcli.dist.maricopa.edu/tut/lessons.html)

Internet Publishing guide from SoftWeb, Victorian Department of Education (http://www.sofweb.vic.edu.au/internet/publish.htm)

The Global School Net (http://ww.gsn.org/) is a good starting point in resource gathering.

References

Abi-Raad, M. (1997). Rethinking approaches to teaching with telecommunication technologies. *Journal of Information Technology for Teacher Education*, 6 (2), 205-214.

Bremer, D. (1996). Weaving a web: Basic HTML editing. In K. W. Lai (ed.) *Words have Wings: Teaching and Learning in Computer Networks* (pp. 159-166). Dunedin: University of Otago Press.

Cox, B. (1998). *Taming the Electronic Frontier*. Available at <http://virtualschool.edu/98c/index.html>.

Darling, L.; Peterson, K.; & Smith, J. (1998). Designing websites for schools. *Computers in New Zealand Schools,* 10 (3), 31-37.

Dillon, P. (1998). Teaching and learning with telematics: An overview of the literature. *Journal of Information Technology for Teacher Education*, 7 (1), 33-50.

Duchastel, P. (1997). A web-based model for university instruction. *Journal of Educational Technology Systems*, 25 (3), 221-228.

Gray. T. (1997). Does virtual teacher support yield real benefits? In In B. Collis & G. Knezek (eds). *Teaching and Learning in the Digital Age: Research into practice with Telecommunications in Educational Settings* (pp. 69-86). ISTE

Kaye, A. (1992). Learning together apart. In A. Kaye (ed.), *Collaborative learning through computer conferencing* (pp. 1-24). NY: Springer-Verlag.

Lai, K. W. (1996). Computer-mediated communication: A new learning context. In K. W. Lai (ed.) *Words have Wings: Teaching and Learning in Computer Networks* (pp. 1-18). Dunedin: University of Otago Press.

Lai, K. W. (1997). Interactivity in Web-based learning: Some observations based on a Web-based course about CMC in education. In B. Collis & G. Knezek (eds). *Teaching and Learning in the Digital Age: Research into practice with Telecommunications in Educational Settings* (pp. 211-230). ISTE.

Lai, K. W. (1998). Social interaction and communication in a web-based tertiary course: some observations. In T. Chan, A. Collins, & J. Lin (eds.) Global Education on the Net: Proceedings of the Sixth International *Conference on Computers in Education.* (Vol. 1, pp. 79-85). Beijing: China Higher Education Press; & Berlin: Springer-Verlag.

Lai, K.W. (1999). A content analysis of school websites. *Computers in New Zealand Schools*, 11 (1).

Maddux, C., Johnson, L., & Harlow, S. (1994). Educational computing: Avoiding the Everest Syndrome in the 21st Century. In J. Willis, B. Robin, & D. Willis (eds), *Technology and Teacher Education Annual* (pp. 371-374). Washington, DC: Association for the Advancement of Computing in Education.

Marantz, B., & England, R. (1993). Can CMC teach teachers training? *Educational Media International,* 30 (2), 74-77.

Mason, R. (1989). An evaluation of CoSy on an Open University course. In R. Mason & A. Kaye (eds) *Mindwave: Communication, compuers and distance education*. Oxford: Pergamon Press.

Montgomeri, T., & Harapnuik, D. (1997). Observations on Web-based course development and delivery. *International Journal of Educational Telecommunications*, 3 (2/3), 181-203.

Nyhof, R. (1997). Teaching seventh form maths with calculus over the Internet. *Computers in New Zealand Schools,* 9 (1),3-7.

Simonson, M. (1997). Distance education: Does anyone really want to learn at a distance. *Contemporary Education*, 68 (2), 104-107.

7 A Rural Educator's Observations on the Use of CMC in the Classroom

Anne Wright

Over 70 per cent of New Zealand's primary schools are small schools with only two to five teachers. About 90 per cent of these schools are classified as rural schools for funding purposes, as they are 15 km from the next school and over 100 km from a town centre with a population of 1,000 or more. Patearoa School, where I teach, is a small, sole-charge school in the Maniototo basin. Historically considered to be part of the Central Otago district, Maniototo remains isolated from any main centre. It is almost the same distance time-wise from Dunedin as it is to Alexandra.

There is a presumption on the part of many urban dwellers that rural isolation means isolation from all contact with the outside world. This is not necessarily so – nowhere in the world is remote from communication. If schools can receive data and voice communication in real time directly from the North Pole, the depths of the Amazon jungle, or the sub-Antarctic regions, surely they cannot be considered to be isolated in the true sense of the word. Nor can they be considered isolated if events remote from them in distance impinge immediately on their capacity to know about and feel for other people; for example, the disastrous floods in Papua New Guinea, the fighting in Kosovo and what was happening at the Commonwealth Games could all be followed avidly on the Internet.

When I returned to my roots – the rural sector – in 1991, I saw technology as a way of building a bridge from a small rural community to this technology-oriented world. My view of a rural school was not as a backwater, but as a real school which could create real twentieth-century experiences for its children. A previous background of IT (information technology) use in classrooms allowed me to envision a context for the use of IT in my first rural school. My background enabled me to see that technology facilitates communication, so that for me computer-mediated communication (CMC) is not narrowly defined as only that computer facilitated communication which is online, but communication which has been in some way enhanced through the use of computers. This definition of enhancing communication through computers may range from something as simple as children using a wordprocessor to produce a legible and attractively presented poster, to a more sophisticated presentation of a computer-aided slide show, right up to full video-conferencing.

For me, as I work IT out in my school, CMC is more than just the interaction of communication through computers. CMC is not just e-mailing other schools, nor is it simply a window on the world participating online, it is a powerful and effective means of communicating with, and within, my community. To understand our journey towards CMC, and to perhaps implement CMC in another setting, it is necessary to know some of the background context and the types of progressions leading up to it.

Background Experience with IT

As a teacher, I had already had some years of experimenting with computers in classrooms when a commercial provider (Learning Enhancement Associates) offered a complete communications package to Central Otago schools in 1991. The package included online communications linked to the Starnet (a national bulletin board system), a computer, a fax machine and a cordless phone. I did not take up the offer, but a nearby school did. I was very envious of what was happening at Naseby, who despite very little support other than from their enthusiastic principal were managing great things in these very early days of computer use in classrooms. Once they had a nationwide hookup for an AGFish day (previously Ministry of Agriculture and Fisheries), inviting local farmers to come in, meet the present Minister of Agriculture and 'talk' online with other groups. This was the first instance of a rural school being online in New Zealand.

Rural Beginnings

Our own first classroom learning experiences at Patearoa began in 1992 with the arrival of a Mac LC. It had 2mb of RAM and a 20mg hard drive, and it was wonderful. My preference at this stage was to integrate computer use with language and visual arts. We received *The Writing Centre* as part of the package. Not long after this we purchased *Kid Pix* because I wanted children to have the choice of using their own illustrations for their language work. In 1993 *Kid Pix* brought out an addition to their paint program called *Slide Show* which allowed pictures made in other programs to be incorporated into a slide show. Slide shows proliferated in my classroom, ranging from stories modelled from junior readers to original songs recorded with accompanying visual pictures. For details of what we have done with *Kid Pix* see Wright (1992, 1993).

Further Professional Development

An exchange visit to Tasmania in 1993 whetted my appetite for further integration of the computer into the classroom. As well, I participated in a conference held in Nelson by the combined rural advisers throughout New Zealand in 1994. At this conference Telecom ran workshops on telecommunications and gave away a free six months' subscription to the very new NZ Online. Not having any real idea of what it involved except that it would allow 'easy' and free computer communication via the phone line with other schools, I duly sent away my free application and received a box containing a modem, several cords and an instruction booklet (which incidentally referred to PCs only). For Apple machines you had to ring the helpdesk once the modem had been calibrated, etc. etc.

During the early part of 1994 the computer was in full use in my classroom, with all the children timetabled to use it for varying periods per week according to their age and ability. Occasionally I would allow older children to use my personal laptop for wordprocessing (it had a greyscale screen only). I had looked at the rather complicated directions for calibrating my modem but in the meantime it had stayed in the box. However, in the first term I attended a two-day professional development course for principals. The subject of technology came up (technology at this stage meant computers) and, having heard a couple of other principals talking about NZ Online, I mentioned I had the 'box' with all the necessary things to get us online. E-mail and modems were still very new to us all and the Internet was not yet available. My inquiries, however, were dismissed with a rather abrupt 'Oh you have to be mechanically minded to install one of those' from a somewhat arrogant male North Otago principal. Having ascertained 'his' e-mail address I returned to my school and some hours later (several hours actually) sent him a very rude message via my e-mail, which I had so determinedly set up to prove a point.

Going 'Online'

NZ Online, then, was our first taste of being online or having a true CMC experience. It was a wonderful concept in the same vein as the New Zealand Learning Network (see Lai & Trewern, 1998) now being operated by the University of Otago and the new online national resource centre being planned under the recently released ICT strategy by the Ministry of Education. It had discussion centres much like bulletin boards for teachers and for communities, where messages could be posted and received, and facilities for receiving personal e-mail. Best of all, it was free for the first six months. The fact that it was free meant that all the options could be explored in detail. I ventured into areas such as 'Penpal' and other types of newsgroup. The groups were very similar to Usenet groups on the Internet but of course were text-based only. We made a lot of use of it initially, setting up penpals within New Zealand and beyond in 'Kidscafe' and posting questions and responses. I never did work out an easy way of negotiating through the traffic on this channel. We were in touch regularly with Oamaru North, a larger urban school, and Taieri Beach, a small school similar to ours. Further away, we sent messages of congratulations on the opening of the tunnel from Britain to France. We wrote answers to questions from a teacher and class in Scotland about New Zealand farming and we found out answers to questions in the maths curriculum from experts.

However, like other areas of communication, it depended on the recipients replying, and it all died a slow death as the children and I became disenchanted when we had no replies for days on end. Sometimes for weeks there would be no new postings on the group discussions. It was still very new to most people. The use of fax machines put paid to the system in the end. Faxing seemed just as quick, and an instant hard copy that could incorporate pictures was at hand.

Taking IT to the Community

A professional development contract for technology in 1994 came at just the right time for me, as I was struggling with ideas for using technology and the slide show aspect at the school's 125th jubilee. During this contract I had the opportunity to use the digital camera and scanner, and immediately I could envisage the use of these for putting pictures of our senior citizens and a record of our school year onto the computer for a display at the jubilee. The whole year had an underlying theme of 'Then and Now' and this fitted in perfectly. We scanned photos ranging from the school camp in

Dunedin at the beginning of the year, to visits from the DB Clydesdales after overnighting in the local village, to Sir Richard Hadlee being bowled out by our youngest new entrant (albeit with Australian overtones). The children took photos of our eight most senior citizens, including 92-year-old Neil Aitken, who could recall horse trams in Dunedin in his childhood, and interviewed them about their school days and earliest memories. For a description of this project, see Wright (1995).

At the school Christmas production I arranged to hire a Magnabyte from the University of Otago. A Magnabyte plugs into a computer and projects the images to a large screen. The hall was packed, as is usual for our end-of-year concert, but at the end of the 45-minute slide show you could have heard a pin drop. The community was absolutely astounded at what the children had accomplished and what had been achieved as a record for posterity. For months afterwards the subsequent video tracked back and forward throughout the community as any and all 'fortunate' visiting relatives were subjected to viewing it again and again. They, the relatives, were then in turn brought triumphantly to school to 'view' the children working with computers. That was our turning point with computers. Since then the community has backed the school in every endeavour, particularly in the field of technology.

The success of the slide show for the jubilee prompted us to hire the video camera on numerous occasions. We took it to school camps and made a record for those who were unable to attend. The camera came with us on every important school outing and recorded image after image. The children became very familiar with its operation and could be safely left to operate it and unload the images onto spare disks later. They were also able to retrieve the images when making the slide show. Children were also familiar with the scanner, but because of time access (each photo took 3–4 minutes to scan) its use was limited in the classroom.

About this time, all the small schools had the first round of visits from the Ministry of Education suggesting Educational Development Initiatives. According to the Ministry, these are developments where schools and communities decide on how best they can use local resources. These options include amalgamation with other small schools and/or closure. Small communities feel very threatened when their local schools receive what has been termed 'the letter'. The Board of Trustees of Patearoa decided, after receiving the first EDI letter, that access to technology (i.e. computers and their potential for online learning) would be their response as an alternative development. For a small rural school at the time, this was truly visionary and resulted in a further computer being purchased. A Macintosh 630 arrived, complete with video in and out, as we needed to offload the jubilee project, which took up 36 megabytes of storage space.

We also looked for ways and means of involving our community in using computers, believing we had a role in this area. Several of our local farmers were debating the purchase of a computer in order to computerise both farm accounts and farm management practices. However, all farming and relevant accounting programs were PC-based and the cost of converting our Macs to use both platforms was too expensive. How were we to obtain a PC? A solution came when we approached a retail chain (Noel Leeming Ltd) to loan us a PC in return for our promoting their generosity to our community with the added bonus of special deals for members of the community buying goods from their stores. Asked to submit a proposal, I duly presented it to them and we were rewarded with an up-to-the-mark Acer, a printer and a handheld colour scanner. Our next problem was to access the current farm program, which was at that time around $1,500 – again beyond our tight budget. A phone call to Lincoln University and yet another proposal later and we had the program installed. Never underestimate what can be done by simply asking, but be prepared to submit a thought-out proposal.

Community classes were offered in how to use a computer, and in the farm management and accounting programs. I felt that this initiative needed to be self-sustaining and not reliant solely on school staff, so a local parent was involved. We had to run several blocks of courses to satisfy the demand. It was felt these farm courses would be run online eventually, as more and more parents were accessing a computer and online services were beginning to be upgraded.

Working with another School

In 1995 we were doing a lot of co-operative projects with another small school at Oturehua, whose principal had had extensive experience with computers. It was a great time for both our schools. I finally had someone else who was conversant with computers in classrooms, and so we planned and executed several joint projects, including combined school camps and musicals. Of course the computers and digital cameras came along. We were experimenting with the video in/out capacity at this stage and were able to capture images from the America's Cup live for use at school. In the middle of this year we were asked to present a workshop at the Principals' Federation National Conference in Dunedin, on the topic of how technology contributed to children's learning and to collegiality in rural schools.

Taking IT Further Afield and into the Internet

In late 1995 the government introduced, through the MRG (Ministerial Reference Group – a select committee made up of school leaders, business leaders, the Ministry and other interested parties), special funding for rural schools. This funding was to enable the schools to introduce innovative programmes which would alleviate the problems of distance, isolation and small populations with concomitant smaller resource bases. It was time to broaden our activities to take in the local cluster. A committee of all principals from the small schools which were part of the Maniototo cluster and three representatives from each age range of the Area school met to consider what resources would be applied for, and what our possible objectives would be. The Internet was becoming more prominent as a must-have resource and schools needed hardware that could run it.

Accordingly a proposal was formulated through Patearoa School (I was becoming an old hand at these) which would give all cluster schools a PowerMac, a modem and online connection, and time online. We did have fond hopes of a dedicated leased line but funding – as always – came nowhere near the total project envisaged. However, early 1996 saw the delivery of a PowerMac 7200, a 28.8k modem and connection to a local Internet Service Provider (Efficient Software) at $360 per annum plus toll call charges for online time. Eventually, of course, the connection and toll call fee was reduced but it did make for major considerations at the time. The Area school, after initial problems, managed to link up through the Otago Polytechnic and offered calculus online to its seventh form students (Nyhof, 1997). The point here is that even given all the favourable conditions and the time being right, introducing CMC into schools is not a simple task. It tends to be fraught with unforeseen problems, which have to be overcome for ongoing success. This takes both commitment and financial considerations.

We now had the possibility of connecting to the Internet with reasonably powerful machines. Included in the package was a QuickCam camera which sat on top of the machine and allowed for video-conferencing using CUSeeMe with other sites. It looked very exciting when I first viewed it in Dunedin, but continuing problems with access to our server and the hardware precluded its use at school for quite some time, as we were also still negotiating a cluster price to connect all schools. However, I had by now introduced the QuickTake digital camera to the other small schools who also caught the fever and eventually as a cluster we purchased a QuickTake 1200 digital camera and a flat-bed scanner. These are still booked monthly and used extensively today.

For our one school that remained with PCs, we had to purchase a separate attachment for both to include in their motherboard. The decision to remain with PCs was made for this particular school because they were a rural community which has a major primary resource industry (a mine) with an exclusive focus on PCs. In addition, the mine gave older hardware to the school as it updated regularly. This is the case with a number of communities – not just in those in the country where the local expertise is PC-oriented. Schools have to follow the trend in their local networks.

Some Ongoing Problems

We still had the problem of connection-time costs, prohibiting all but the shortest time on our school connections. Unfortunately our schools are served by a stand-alone telephone exchange with really old telephone lines. This explains in part our difficulties with connections and the high cost, as we could not connect direct to a main centre. A competitive telephone provider market meant that eventually we were left with a different major provider. So what was an incipient online community in 1996 became once again an off-line community in 1997. Next was the problem of installing software that came with this provider and their proprietary Netscape browser software. What an absolute nightmare! Hours hanging onto a helpdesk after school is not conducive to good relationships. (Others have experienced something similar; see Paton, 1998). By the time I had reconnected six of our seven schools I had quite an extensive vocabulary to describe online connections and their problems.

Seeing Ourselves On Screen, Online!

In mid 1996 we were invited to be a trial school for video conferencing (Trewern, Gaffney, & Hills, 1996). We were intrigued and delighted to see what we could do with this tool. It was amazing to us, to community members and to parents who went to town to see the program in action. We had up to five sites up on our screen where we could see and talk to these other sites simultaneously. It generated great excitement, especially when relatives were present on other sites. Despite many problems with sound and picture quality, I believe this tool will eventually transform some parts of our curriculum. It did point up many potential problems areas which will need addressing. Speech once again became the prime means of communicating with others, although it was helpful to be able to see the person(s) you were talking to. This highlighted several considerations. Children managed best when they knew something about the person they were talking to and improved significantly when this communication occurred over several sessions. At least the level of conversation approached something educationally enhancing.

Many commentators have been amazed at the triviality and shallowness of 'conversations' on the Internet, whether in chat channels or in discussion groups. I am not. I witnessed it first hand during this project. Unless there is a particular purpose or object for the connection, the level of communication remains at best shallow and trivial. This is understandable when we do not know who we are communicating with. Children needed the reference point of the face on the talking window. It was important to them. They at least felt they could glean some nonverbal interchange, which makes many of our conversations intelligible. How much harder it is when there is not only no picture but when we do not know whether the person is who and what they say they are!

Children found it hard to sustain conversations when there were no particular questions to ask. They were quite independent with connecting and disconnecting online and using the program, and eventually managed some independence when they were 'talking' with the children in another class or students from the high school about their combined project. But this independence disappeared the day they were scheduled to speak with McMurdo Base in Antarctica. We were engaged in a study of Antarctica as part of a Telecom Foundations project, and even though questions were prepared, and the children knew quite a lot about Antarctica, the sound of an American accent was enough to strike them dumb. Aware of the cost of this connection, the fact that all the children were watching on our TV monitor and that another high school was participating, and of the length of time the call was scheduled for, I had to get into some serious prompting of answers and further questions. About the only fact the children could remember later was that on that particular day Antarctica was –19 degrees, whereas we were experiencing a truly ferocious bite of winter and were registering –21!

Oral communication skills, which involve speaking clearly and coherently as well as intensive listening, are necessary for the future if this medium becomes universal. Children will need to be able to communicate their ideas quickly, succinctly and positively if they are to gain control over it. This suggests to me that initial projects of this type need to be with other people the children are already familiar with, perhaps neighbouring schools. Once children are conversant with the medium and the process of talking with a person 'onscreen', horizons can be widened. It was, however, despite its limitations, an exciting use of our technology. Unfortunately ongoing problems with telephone line capacity to transmit data other than voice have meant the temporary abandonment of this means of CMC. But the potential for its use means that it will not be left for ever. The possibilities still fill me with excitement and awe. However, fibre optic cable will have to be installed first.

During our 'project on ice' we were able to access the brilliant Antarctic websites at Icair and download lots of suitable material, including plans of Scott Base for our scale model. Our project culminated in making lifesize models of penguins and a cat machine designed by children with a flight deck resembling a jet aeroplane which they could get in and operate. All of this featured in the local press, along with a visit from the Antarctic winter manager for Scott Base (who coincidentally lived at Alexandra, also Central Otago), complete with video and photos. The same year saw us follow the Olympic torch throughout America on the Internet and keep a daily check of medal tables during the Olympic Games. Ready Teddy was our personal hero, as we have so many pony club riders.

North Island Experiences

In August of 1996 the Apple Computer instigated an Apple Bus Tour of North Island schools which were technologically at the forefront. I went along and thoroughly enjoyed visiting several large Auckland schools. I was pleased to know that as a small rural, sole-charge school we were achieving as much and using similar technologies. Nevertheless, I did come away more convinced than ever that computers would only be successful in our small schools if the principals and other staff had access to their own computer and used it for themselves first. All of these leading schools provide laptops that can be taken home by staff, but brought to school each day to provide a pod for class use. The schools also hold regular meetings for staff to assist each other with their computer use in classes and for their own purposes. A commitment is made by each staff member to use the computer at least once per term in their classroom. The staff of these schools are fortunate in that ongoing support is available on site, which explains their successful use of IT. All of these schools had a dedicated budget for teacher development and an organising committee of staff members with an independent IT teacher supervisor.

Online and Elsewhere in the Classroom

In my school, the independent use of the Internet and its resources by children during classtime depends largely on the ability of the children in Year 6 (S4). In 1996 I had some very capable children. Individual projects included using video clips within the perennial slide show. The television series remembering the Second World War was on, and one of the children had a grandfather who was at Casino among other battles. In his slide show he incorporated shots from the TV series, clips from a video depicting scenes from the Second World War (available free of copyright from the National Library), and scanned pictures from books. He also interviewed his grandfather at school straight onto the slide show and took his photo using the QuickCam camera. This was a remarkable achievement of CMC for a ten-year-old who only had the use of these tools at school.

The early Rainforest site allowed for direct communication with teachers and classes in South America. We could learn from them about the problems faced by the inhabitants of the area.

The Internet has no equal for up-to-the-minute, immediate conveyance of breaking news or events. Over time we watched as Ruapehu erupted, followed the progress of the netball and rugby teams, wrote letters to the Iceman when he was again sidelined with injury, sent fan mail to Hanson and various other heart-throb bands, and more recently viewed the latest pictures of the devastation in Papua-New Guinea. The Commonwealth Games provided further impetus to check CNN online news.

A space project in 1997 involved accessing the extensive NASA resources and our own Carter Observatory, and walking through the Virtus VR models of space objects. This program, Virtus VR, came with our multimedia utilities. It is mindblowing. The object of the software is making and creating 3D objects. It is far too advanced for primary children to use as a software application but very exciting for them to access to understand some of the creations used in space (e.g. space shuttles, blast off and splashdown, the Hubble telescope). In addition we had access on CD-Rom to media clips about rocket launches and all manner of space memorabilia. The hardest thing with these is to remember why you are viewing them, as they are just amazing to look at. Internet sites for space include online plans for teachers to use and a vast number of sites where children are given a tour of space and the planets, complete with quick quizzes and other gimmicks. Information was downloaded from various sites for each group's planet passport. We used this program again this year in our Egyptian study as it has a walk-through model of the Great Pyramids. This is virtual reality without the need for headgear. A two-dimensional platform allows for manoeuvring and close-up shots.

The more able Year 6 children in 1997 were able to access images from the Vikings CD-ROM to create their own stack in Hyperstudio. The Vikings have numerous online sites with exposés of old sites and various images of their early voyages. Hyperstudio is a prelude to HyperCard in that the scripts for buttons, and therefore manoeuvrability, are already written and can be accessed from a bullet menu. However, it can create very sophisticated slide show formats, with alternative locations included. Again it is rare for children younger than Year 6 to be able to use this program at anywhere near its potential. However, I have now a growing number of children who have regular access to computers at home, and some as young as Year 2 who regularly use kids' pages on the Internet. Perhaps by the time they are Year 4 or 5 they will be ready to use these more sophisticated programs.

Earlier this year all local schools were involved with the 150 years celebration of the Otago province and the centennial for Ranfurly, the local service centre for the Maniototo. The photo library Timeframes, from the National Library in Wellington, was searched and suitable photos available free were downloaded. The CD-ROM produced for the Otago/Southland celebrations had been given free to all schools and provided further material for study. (For a review of this CD and its availability see Patterson, 1997.) The visit by the Holmes Show and its nationwide viewing capped off an exciting project. Naturally this is all captured on digital film for future school celebrations.

In May of 1998 we were indeed fortunate to be able to take the older Year 3-6 children to Te Papa, the new national interactive museum, and also to visit our ex-pupil Gavan Herlihy at Parliament. Gavan is the local National MP for Otago, and he organised a visit to Prime Minister Jenny Shipley's office for children and parents. Our BOT chairperson was presented with an 89er certificate by the Prime Minister. (An 89er was a special recognition by the government in 1998 who had served on a BOT for nine years. They began their term in 1989 and the certificate is therefore named an 89er certificate.) How was it recorded? Indeed, with our ubiquitous digital camera. Pictures and comments were beamed back to the junior children remaining at school. The resulting photos were printed on the school's inkjet printer and presented alongside other photos and a written record of the trip. Children were divided into groups to draft, write and format a part of the trip each. These records were then circulated among other groups to add extra memories before final printing out. Three copies were made and are still 'doing the rounds' of the community, having been viewed first by all parents. It is an interesting and well-written documentary of our trip mediated by the computer – first through digital images and then through the stages of wordprocessing (with editing, spell-checking and formatting to be considered), and finally printed for consumption by the community. This is CMC not online, but CMC in every other aspect of producing information for communication.

The Potential for CMC

Does CMC alleviate barriers to learning for rural schools? Undoubtedly it can and does, but only after sufficient training in its use has been undertaken. It cannot be considered in isolation from learning and teaching issues. The issues that rural schools have to consider and come to terms with are not new, nor are they issues that pertain solely to rural schools. The same limiting factors to the use of CMC have been formulated time and again through three government-commissioned reports and innumerable research reports. They are:

- time for teachers to experiment and explore (within the school day, not after a full day teaching when energy is low)
- funding for adequate equipment
- teacher development with ongoing local support. (For similar conclusions see Powell, 1998; Elliot 1997)

What rural schools do face perhaps more than their urban counterparts is the lack of professional support for IT, in terms of both teacher support and technical support. Distances are large and travel expensive. Repairs take longer than usual because equipment has to be sent away, although admittedly courier services (where available) have improved the time factor.

The decreasing availability of relief staffing in rural areas makes it difficult for teacher development to be accessed. Teachers work best and progress faster when they are with other professionals they know. The service provider must be credible in terms of classroom practice – many are not. This is the most common request from rural schools – can the provider be a classroom exponent? It means time out of school for the facilitator, and when your school is sole charge this is not always an easy option. In my case I am fortunate in that I have an excellent relief teacher who is also my PR teacher, my school secretary and a community resident. The school hums along whether I am there or not – sometimes a sobering thought – but a relief (forgive the pun) for the BOT and parents. Otherwise what I do would not be possible. But it should be a full-time position, given the number of schools in Central Otago who want access to training in such a way. Suggestions that rural advisers can assist (Elliot, 1997, Powell, 1998) would mean a major reorganisation of this service. School advisory services are at present prioritising school management and have indicated this is the field for their future development. They too have funding and time limitations which do not allow them to be a force for improvement for IT, at least in our part of the country. But I agree there should be provision for rural advisers in the IT area.

A further major constraint in most country areas, particularly for CMC, is the age, reliability and capability of our phone lines (and our computers). It is for this reason that the advent of fibre optic cable is anticipated with increasing impatience. Fibre optic cable can carry aeons of voice data and other data simultaneously. This, for example, would allow full-colour video conferencing. The possibilities of this medium alone are enormous. Imagine real-time connections with children from other cultures in their own communities or participating in laboratories for science experiments or talking with experts in prehistory. For staff and students of any school the prospects are exciting. For teachers in isolated situations, the prospects are all-encompassing.

Ongoing Commitment and Some Advantages

Successful CMC and other IT use requires training and commitment. Bonnie Bracey, in her exposé of the stages teachers go through when using IT, illuminates the amount of training required to reach each stage (for a quick resumé of her stages, see Johnson and Kennedy, 1998). Like learning processes, each stage builds on prior knowledge and experience, and takes time. Time in our market economy means money. Successive governments have dabbled with funding, expecting a huge return for very little. The present round of ITPD is an example. In our case it allowed for $500 per small school (the next round has increased this to $1,000). Rural schools, however, tend to have communities who are committed to IT because they have to be, to retain their school. It is for this reason that many of the movers and shakers in this field have tended to be rural.

An advantage as a result of this commitment has been the provision of more hardware per child than the average classroom. My school, for example, has four computers plus the occasional use for the Year 6 children of my personal laptop. Many rural schools share this advantage (Powell, 1998). Their use, however, does continue to depend on the expertise, dedication and enthusiasm of teaching staff prepared to continue to upskill themselves.

Recent initiatives have been announced by the Ministry of Education in their new Information and Communications Strategy document released in late November 1998 for a further $14 million to be injected for the development of computers in schools. Proposals have been called for from interested schools or school groups to take on a local 'best practice' role combined with teacher development in other schools. At this stage it is too early to determine what sort of impact this initiative will have, but it is a step in the right direction.

What Determines the use of Computers in Small, Rural Classrooms?

First and foremost, the expertise I have gained over the years enables me to see the potential for IT use in the classroom. The teacher must be familiar and confident with the whole range of computer use. This illustrates the importance of teacher training and development. In addition, in a small school the timetable is flexible and can be changed readily. This is less so in larger schools where groups are mixed from various classes for different curriculum areas. Contributions from industry should also be noted. For example, the extra phone lines installed in all local rural schools by Telecom have increased their connectivity to the Internet. Projects sponsored by Telecom have aroused the interests of students, teachers and parents. For example, in the Antarctica project mentioned earlier, an Australian couple (Margie and Don) were enduring a year on the ice in a small hut which they had to erect first. Their weekly faxed diary was awaited with bated breath by the children, who read of their true life-and-death adventures. Children sent their own versions of hut plans to Margie and Don for evaluation, and enjoyed communicating with and receiving a reply from them.

However, it is the needs and abilities of the children who are presently at school which determine whether or not CMC is emphasised. This year, for a variety of reasons, our use in the classroom has been spasmodic. Reasons have included the number of junior children now present – thirteen children in Year 1 and 2, a huge proportion for a sole-charge school with a total roll at present of twenty-four. This year, excluding new entrants, we have had seven new admissions. Our pupil catchment area is changing. The Board have employed a part-time assistant for three days per week to enable a junior programme to run. Our assistant teacher, who works in the main with senior children, is relatively new to computers. The present senior children have extra needs in maths and reading. All of these factors impact on our use of computers. However, most of them are becoming more manageable and IT use will once again be emphasised in the final term. I expect with a very strong Year 5 class (academically speaking) going into Year 6 next year, our use of CMC and IT will increase.

Envisioning the Future

If we cannot envision future worlds, we are already living in the past and, what is worse, condemning children to a future that focuses backwards. Vision arises out of a synthesis of past experience, professional knowledge and expertise that involves recognising and capitalising on present circumstances, and a capacity to project thinking forward to encompass future possibilities.

However, vision by itself is not enough. I believe there is a time within each school which is optimum for introducing CMC, and a progression of events which is more successful than others. In fact, I believe that the introduction of CMC to classrooms and communities that are not ready for it leads to failure. My background of working with computers allowed me to introduce IT into my school successfully first. Once successful classroom practice was established, IT was introduced progressively to the community and out into the local schools cluster. In this climate of support it has flourished. In my circumstances, by good teaching and sheer hard work, I was able to capitalise on a background predisposed by rurality towards sharing, and so create an environment where the time was ripe for future developments. Rural families know each other and have a culture of sharing resources. I was able to push this predisposition of willingness to communicate among rural communities with IT and by judicious selection of projects which would enhance the school's standing.

One of these was our Anzac Day project. Like every other little rural community we have a memorial dedicated to those who gave their lives in the two world wars, and like every other little town the names of soldiers who were local residents at the time are recorded on this memorial. Over the years for a variety of reasons the knowledge of who some of these people were has been lost. As a major project the school became involved in finding out something about each one of these soldiers, including photos – if not of them, at least of their grave – and presented this to the community in a very large and memorable occasion. Descendants came from far and wide to celebrate with us when the project was completed. The information and photos are now enshrined in the local community hall and each year a small remembrance ceremony around Anzac Day is attended by the children and many local community members.

This project, along with the jubilee project and others, has created a huge amount of goodwill for the school. We enjoy many of its rewards in the willingness of community members to come and help during the school day, in their support on open days and other school events, and in their very real financial contributions. Perhaps above all is the willingness of the community to allow the school to progress forward, creating new ideas and new methods.

This is, I believe, the responsibility of principals in small rural schools. The fact that the school is small does not absolve them from the standard responsibilities of being the professional leader for their community and from creating the type of environment that will capitalise on conditions that predispose their communities towards a shared communication. Each rural community is different and the journey they take down the information superhighway will be different, but they all share this wonderful opportunity to work together towards shared visions. Smallness and remoteness are irrelevant.

References

Elliot, A. (1997). Can CMC address barriers to learning in isolated rural primary schools? *Computers in New Zealand Schools.* 9 (2), 11-14.

Johnson, G. & Kennedy, M. (1998). Making IT happen? What will IT take? *Computers in New Zealand Schools.* 10 (2), 3-8.

Lai, K.W. & Trewern, A. (1998). New Zealand learning network: an online community for New Zealand teachers. *Computers in New Zealand Schools.* 10 (2), 33-36.

Nyhof, R. (1997). Teaching seventh form maths with calculus over the Internet. *Computers in New Zealand Schools.* 9 (1), 3-7.

Paton, S. (1998). A small country school midway between Herbert and Hampden. *Computers in New Zealand Schools.* 10 (2), 23-25.

Patterson, R. (1997). History of Otago and Southland on CD-ROM. *Computers in New Zealand Schools.* 9 (2), 31-34.

Powell, T.(1998). Rural teachers' computer encounters: A Different Experience? *Computers in New Zealand Schools.* 10 (2), 17-22.

Trewern, A., Gaffney, M. & Hills, P. (1996). *A Pilot Study of Student's Video-Conferencing Across the Internet with CU-SeeMe.* Dunedin: The Dunedin College of Education.

Wright, K.A. (1993). Kid Pix – A paint programme for kids. *Computers in New Zealand Schools.* 5 (1), 24-26.

Wright, K.A. (1994). Kid Pix companion: The sequel. *Computers in New Zealand Schools.* 6 (3), 40-43.

Wright, K.A. (1995). Creating and maintaining living history. *Computers in New Zealand Schools.* 7 (2), 3-9.

8 Online Professional Interactive Networks: Virtual Professional Learning Communities for Teachers

Ann Trewern

A learning network is a group of like-minded people who utilise Internet telecommunications channels and contextual supports, such as information contained on World Wide Web pages or online databases, to engage in the exchange of ideas and resources in ways that promote learning. The existence of such networks depends on the computer hardware and software that allows for the creation of virtual spaces for resources, services and communication and on groups of people who are prepared to participate in Network activities and who can work and socialise together over the online environment (Harasim, 1996). Computer-mediated learning networks are used at all levels and in all fields of education. Electronic collaborative network learning can take many forms and includes examples of cross-classroom exchanges and group projects, tele-apprenticeships, telepresence, professional interactive, online course delivery, and distance teaching (Riel, 1996). In this chapter we describe some online professional development learning networks that have existed and are currently in operation both within New Zealand and elsewhere, and examine the potential of these networks to influence in many unique ways the teaching and learning communities they serve.

Professional support networks for teachers and educators can be of many varieties and configurations, providing for information, lesson plans, professional support materials, online projects, professional contacts and models of successful practice, with some network structures providing all of these features and others providing more limited combinations. Both within New Zealand and internationally, there are many different kinds of teacher professional support networks. Around the world the delivery of professional services are the responsibility of many categories of providers. They can include ministries of education, faculties of education, multi-national companies sponsoring educational groups and non-traditional suppliers with an interest in maintaining a network for educational purposes, such as museums and galleries (Collis, 1996).

How a network is structured and what it offers teachers depends on the philosophy that underpins the design and purpose of the network. Professional support networks were identified by Watts and Castle (1992) as having three distinct functions:

- **Resource networks** – these exist to provide data and information. teachers@work(NZ) and Starters and Strategies (NZ) are good examples of resource networks.
- **Communications networks usually use e-mail.** Information is posted out in the form of newsletters or updates to subscribers, although subscribers may add news items to be posted out.
- **Dialogic networks** – are involved in interactive discussions and online conferencing.

E-mail mailing-lists and newsgroups promote interactive discussion. So too do some of the group-ware software now available with a WWW user interface. Discussion is archived and is accessible to all participants whenever they access the discussion. (Access Excellence, ASCDWeb and New Zealand Learning Network (NZLNet) are examples of networks designed to encourage professional discussion and further the professional learning of users).

Some networks can have a single function and may provide users with a purely resource network. Others are increasingly working with a combination of these functions so that many networks have at least two of the above functions, such as Oz-teachernet (a resource and communications network) and ArtsEdNet which is a resource and dialogic network for arts educators.

The focus of a network can vary, serving a variety of purposes. Online resources can be focused on teacher-created activities to share with other classes (Kidlink), or on events which bring teachers and their classes together (National School Network (USA), Schools Network (NZ), Global Schoolhouse, National Geographic Kids Network). They can be a directory service for curriculum resources (teachers@work(NZ). S.O.R.T. (UK)). They can be focused on providing teachers with access to better and more up-to-date information within particular curriculum areas (Access Excellence, ArtsEdNet). They can be focused on reforming pedagogical practice (Labnet, TeacherNet) or getting geographically isolated and rural teachers together (RuralNet). They can be focused on broadening the delivery of professional services in curriculum resources – Houghton Mifflin, Starters and Strategies (NZ) professional support materials (ASCD Web) or policy documents (NZ Ministry of Education) or combinations of all or most of these (Sofnet, Community Learning Network (CLN)).

Telecommunications Networks for Professional Learning

For this chapter we will focus on electronic professional interactive networks. We can define electronic professional interactive networks as being designed to specifically meet the professional learning needs of teachers, using the Internet to improve their work-related knowledge and skills. This is achieved by providing a wide range of archived information for teachers' daily work needs and for background materials' and by providing professionals with a range of ways to contact other professionals (Collis, 1996).

These networks are adult orientated. They relate to specific professional work contexts and need to meet the specific goals of working professionals. Online professional interactive networks have the potential to create new ways for teachers to work in a professional capacity. Such a resource can be an encouragement for teachers to begin to consider the concept of self-directed professional learning as a legitimate and important part of professional growth and development. They can contribute to strengthening and transforming learning practices, opportunities, and outcomes for individuals. They can open up new avenues of communication, collaboration and knowledge building for educators by improving access to a range of formal and informal professional learning opportunities. With educational access to Internet technologies expanding, with text, graphical and interactive interfaces becoming more user-friendly and with more developers considering online delivery of courses for adult education and professional learning, networks increasingly offer interesting possibilities for unique forms of both formal and informal learning opportunities for teachers.

Professional interactive networks are designed to support professional growth and development of teachers by linking teachers with colleagues and professionals, expanding teachers' access to just-in-time information, and providing opportunities to carry out joint teaching activities. Some networks even encourage the development of skills of reflective practice and opportunities to promote new teaching approaches. (Di Maurio and Gal,1994). It is a medium that

- is well suited to teachers who are working in isolated settings who can thus maintain contact with other teachers and content experts;
- can provide opportunities for teachers to share teaching ideas and innovations they have tried and to reflect on aspects of practice;
- can be a source of new ideas, foster intellectual stimulation, and can provide a supportive audience for feedback;
- can facilitate peer-to-peer collaboration, enhance proximate community and provide validation for methods of teaching(Di Mauro and Jacobs 1995; Moonen and Voogt, 1997).

Well-structured online learning communities often show a tight inter-relationship between information provision, support for members of the community, opportunity for the community members to contribute, and the development of a dynamic place for members to meet and work. Successful networks often exhibit many of the following components. They

- have a strong sense of place;
- acknowledge the complexities of the classroom and school environment;
- have a well articulated purpose;
- build information archives to suit the purposes and context of the community;
- are participatory and engage in dialogue;
- are collaborative;
- have a strong knowledge base;
- foster and nurture community;
- are developmental in nature;
- are analytic and reflective;
- are sensitive to the ways that teachers think and feel;
- provide opportunity to make meaning of teachers' experiences (Lieberman and Grolnick, 1996; Rhiengold, 1994),

Why Electronically Mediated Networks for Teachers?
Meeting the needs of professional learners

Traditionally teachers have gleaned considerable professional knowledge from peers and mentors, and as a result of informal group interactions. Despite an increasing commitment to directed professional development from national providers and local support services, teachers will continue to develop a significant level of professional knowledge in quite informal ways. Collis (1996) characterises professional learning as being quite distinctive from both formal learning, which is distinguished by 'training' or 'taking a course' and informal learning which is based on an individual's broad interests and may centre around home or hobby activities. Professional learning can be described as a self-directed adult activity where the individual decides on what to read, who he or she communicates with, and what aspects of learning one needs to pay most attention to. It is usually closely linked to job performance. Electronic professional learning networks are uniquely situated to provide the kind of learner control and independence which are key aspects of making learning meaningful for professional activities, and combining learning with context and experience that is relevant to the specific situation of the professional.

Expanding the role of professional subject associations and other professionally orientated groups

Although opportunities for teachers to get together informally are often limited by the physical and structural independence of the classroom, and the social organisation of work and schools (Huberman, 1993), many teachers overcome the constraints of limited time and energy to belong to and support their professional subject associations. Professional subject associations provide an alternative to structured professional development and in-service training. These networks have a tendency to be collegial in nature and to inspire considerable involvement and commitment from teachers. They serve as trusted filters and supply information relevant to the educator's complex work situation (Collis, 1996b). Such professional groups appear to cater well for teachers' learning needs by allowing them to better direct their own professional learning, encouraging them to work with many different people and allowing them to side-step limitations of institutional roles, hierarchies and geographic locations (Lieberman, 1996; Sykes, 1996).

A University of Otago study into teacher preferences for the kinds of professional development delivery they had experienced (Cowan, 1997) indicated that the role of professional subject associations is vitally important to New Zealand secondary teachers. Ninety per cent of the surveyed teachers had participated in activities provided by their respective subject associations – a high proportion when the elective nature of such involvement is considered and when it is compared with other forms of elective professional development. Forty-seven per cent of respondents had participated in in-service courses organised by school support services and only 24 per cent of teachers had been involved in Ministry of Education curriculum contracts. Furthermore, some 75 per cent of teachers who participated in this survey indicated that they wished to continue their participation in such collegial networks, as compared to 37 per cent indicating a wish to continue with support services in-service courses.

Professional associations are a well-established feature of the educational landscape, particularly for upper primary and secondary teachers. Many teachers are completely comfortable about acquiring their professional development needs from peer activities and events promoted by professional associations and are also quite comfortable about ways of working and sharing in these grassroots, collegial and collaborative network environments. Online networks can provide similar opportunities for teachers to pick and choose from a range of professional learning resources, with the added advantage that such resources can be accessed when needed and from any geographical location. As access to Internet technologies expands and grows it seems logical that teacher groups will increasingly make use of telecommunications technologies to expand on these preferred ways of net-working. In fact, many professional associations have not been slow to widen their spheres of influence by moving into online environments. Examples are the ASCD Web and The Royal Society of New Zealand.

Professional support in times of educational change

A community of peers can serve as an important source of support for the profession in times when the 'endemic uncertainties' of teaching become magnified. Community definitions and expectations of schools are currently undergoing considerable change. The nature and definition of teachers' work is being re-organised and re-evaluated within the community at large. Self-managing schools, curriculum reform and changing community values and expectations of teachers are impacting heavily on the work of teachers. The craft of teaching is of necessity required to change and meet the challenges of an increasingly complex and demanding educational environment. For teachers, this frequently represents a departure from any previous experience, established beliefs or present practices. Teachers are being asked to establish learning environments and pedagogical practices for children that they may never have experienced themselves (Little, 1998).

One way of meeting the changes in society head-on, and ensuring conditions for survival, is for teacher groups to become involved in and develop structures which allow members to participate in the dialogue of the professional community that enables the building of new craft. Teacher professional support networks are seen by an increasing number of researchers (Leiberman, 1996; Williams, 1997; Moonen & Voogt, 1997) as a unique and special way for the profession to access the particular expertise and support which is sometimes unavailable within a single work-site or community. These networks can provide support by nurturing new and inexperienced teachers, validating the work of more experienced teachers, providing structures for leaders to create new directions, collecting together the important information of the community and allowing easier access to the wisdom of the community.

Expanding teacher reasons for using technology

Access to information and communication technologies is rapidly expanding and growing. As there is greater public awareness of the role the Internet plays as an educational resource and, as more students become 'Internet savvy', there are greater responsibilities being placed on teachers to become not only more technologically proficient but also 'to understand the culture of technology and ensure their curriculum delivery contains critique of a technology laden world' (Williams, 1997). In order for such a culture to develop, use of the technology must become integral to the way teachers work. This is not a simple process in a work-place culture where teachers may have little or no need for technology to complete daily classroom teaching tasks. Yet, if they are to interpret curriculum in ways which has technology embedded as a core component, then teachers must be given incentives to use the technology in ways in which professional needs are also embedded. Teachers want professional background materials and useful teaching ideas to aid and enhance their repertoire of classroom learning activities and resources. Electronic professional learning networks can provide the incentives; they can be trusted filters of relevant information and they can provide access to content experts and the expertise of practising peers providing opportunities for professional collaboration and enhancement of professional knowledge. If electronic networks can meet these needs for teachers efficiently and appropriately, if they can be used by teachers to support ideas that relate to the context of one's own classroom, then the technology has the potential to become an asset to teachers' daily work.

Alternative ways of speaking out

Learning networks provide communities of practice with a different way to speak out, and take control of learning without the necessary mediation of professional development experts. Virtual communities connect ordinary folk to each other. Lieberman (1996) notes that 'great power exists in the possibility that networking offers members a voice in creating and sustaining a group in which their professional identity and interests are valued'. Many quite experienced teachers often receive limited validation of the work they do with their classes. A supportive online learning environment can be a medium for both experienced and inexperienced teachers to 'talk shop' with colleagues, raise issues, share dilemmas and strategies and resources, discuss teaching approaches and talk about practice in a non-threatening environment (Lechner, 1998) in which status and levels of power become diminished (Kaye, 1992).

Enhancing proximate community

Networks can enhance professional learning and development by providing a community base that is not only larger, but geographically different from one's own local community. Such networks can allow people with similar curriculum interests or who teach similar age groupings to get together in ways that were not really previously possible. They can also provide for just-in-time help, peer support, specialised advice, and new ideas important to individuals in a profession in which inflexibility of instructional timing, lack of time in the working day and isolation are widespread characteristics of professional life. Isolation, inflexibility, and individualistic and busy working-cultures can severely restrict opportunities for professional contact and for professional learning (Flinders,1988). Opportunities for exposure to new ways of doing things and new models or examples of practice can often be limited.

Providing opportunities for professional learning within realistic time-frames

Teachers are always busy. There is little time in the working day which is free of student contact time. Filtered and well authored resources can assist with saving precious time. The ability to contact other knowledgeable professionals can provide a ready group to help solve that problem or point the individual in the right direction to find the necessary contacts. Teachers also confront a lack of flexibility in instructional timing. Deadlines such as assessments, parent interviews, reports and a host of other school commitments have to be met. Teachers often have little of the extensive time required to spend searching the Internet for new teaching ideas or innovative resources. Archived online resourcws allow teachers to assess that lesson idea or professional article at the teacher's convenience. Explicitly designed information and interactive resources can allow participants increased control over the timing of help-seeking, and just-in-time support from knowledgeable colleagues.

Background to Teacher Support Networks in New Zealand

Telecommunications networks designed to support professionals in the task of becoming more 'savvy' with information and communications technologies, and developing a practical understanding of the value such technology can have when integrated within the curriculum, have existed for some time. The specific form and function of these networks have changed significantly as rapid changes in technical capacity, mechanisms of delivery, and advances in user interfaces have impacted on not only how services can be delivered but in what can be achieved and how it can be achieved. Many such networks have been established to explore the field, often with limited funding and of necessity have been short term and experimental in nature.

The Beacon Project in 1992 was a year-long exploratory study undertaken by Learning Enhancement Associates (LEA) in which possible classroom uses of communications technologies were investigated. Embedded within this project were not only many of the attributcs of sound professional development but also some of those that lead to successful networking. Some eighteen Otago schools and the Otago School Advisory Service were provided with telecommunications equipment (with a later option to buy) and a connection to 'New Zealand-on-Line' – an electronic network providing e-mail and access to text-based databases. Pairs of schools were 'buddied' and also buddied with an expert from Telecom, provided with a number of training sessions and encouraged to trial ideas where technology usage was integrated into curriculum activities. The model allowed for collaborative partnerships between teachers, collaborative activity building, opportunity for participants to contribute, ideas to be valued and a strong dose of serendipity (Stanley, 1993, 1996).

The EduNet Project in 1993 was a more broadly conceived educational network that included access to interactive communications technologies as well as access to information databases. Teachers from some twenty Otago schools, principals, curriculum experts and content providers were brought into the project. The focus was on providing access to relevant curriculum and professional materials for teachers and students, professional networking for principals, and an investigation of more in-depth administrative uses and of how such an environment could be customised for New Zealand educational professionals. The project undertaken by LEA was again an exploratory one, investigating delivery systems and projects that would work for teachers, with the idea of ultimately moving towards providing an integrated educational network for New Zealand schools. The model allowed for limited training for teacher-leaders in the project and for some guided exploration of the network features by a series of activity sheets provided for all participants. Procedures for accessing the networks were found to be more difficult than they needed to be and possibly affected the degree of use students and teachers made of them. Those network applications that were most used were electronic mail, and those providing access to information that supported teaching programmes and classroom-based projects (Stanley, 1994,1996).

Schools Network was first developed as a text-based service in 1991 and was intended to be used as a communication service between schools and the Ministry of Education. In 1995 the network was extended to include students in a pilot project trialling the impact of electronic services on student learning. The network utilised its own backbone and telecommunications connections prior to the advent of the World Wide Web and operated in this form until late 1996. This network provided for a greatly expanded role for telecommunications for primary and secondary schools across New Zealand. Incorporated into the dial-up service into the Ministry's server were particular electronic features where certain activities occurred – for instance 'Notice-boards' and 'directories' provided for uploading and downloading of information, real-time chat was provided by a feature called terminal phone, telnet functions to direct access databases, and e-mail access. Access to the World Wide Web could be obtained with special access privileges using a lynx text browser.

Schools Network was evaluated in two phases. By the second evaluation phase some 459 primary and secondary schools had connected (Harris, 1996) and although only half this number had an active user ID this network certainly gathered substantial support. Both information and communication features were built into the network, with teachers using the information directories for searching for lesson-relevant material, searching for professionally significant information and arranging for groups of students to meet online. The technical interface was a problem for users. The need to introduce a graphical user mouse-driven interface rather than use keyboard controls ranked as one of the most pressing improvements required by users in the evaluations. Feedback on the value of this network to teachers revealed that all users, students and teachers found the network to be of tremendous value. The evaluation report noted that links between professionals had the potential to be a significant area for teachers and principals and that the trial needed to be extended and opened to new school users and needed to be free.

SchoolsNet as a distinct and stand-alone network was overtaken by the easier-to-use graphical interface of the WWW and the number of Internet providers willing and able to provide faster links and cheaper commercial services. A modified version of the Schools Network now operates on the WWW and continues to be supported by the Ministry.

Examples of New Zealand Online Professional Interactive Networks

Schools Network – http://www.schoolsnet.ac.nz/

The WWW version of Schools Network aims to provide students with an area that engages them to interact actively with and publish information. The main groups who access the Schools Network are Primary and Intermediate school students, and teachers who are involved in the Learning Enhancements Associates (LEA) Social Studies School Development programme from Wellington, Northland and Auckland regions. While this is a student-orientated network, there is a strong professional development component to the network.

Schools Network publishes examples of good practice in the form of student language work. Teaching units are displayed and a range of interesting student interactive activities are managed, such as 'Writers and Opinion Corner', the 'Sharemarket Clash' (there are various levels of class involvement available, but essentially the activity encourages students to use formulae in spreadsheets and to keep track of buying and selling) and 'Brainteasers' (designed to develop and try out questioning skills.) Although there is an intention to develop some online interaction, there are currently no discussion areas or interactive facilities available for student or professional discourse or collaboration. Users are encouraged to participate but are required to e-mail thoughts, opinions and ideas to the webmaster.

teachers@work – http://teachers.work.co.nz/

This site provides a directory service for teachers looking for relevant Internet resources in specific curriculum areas. Although a feedback form is provided, there are no opportunities for interaction or collaboration for teachers to consider professional issues or to build an online community.

CWA NZ Education Web – http://www.cwa.co.nz/eduweb/index.html

This is a well-designed information and utility network for New Zealand teachers, providing information about educational institutions, some information about the many New Zealand schools that are online and their e-mail addresses, as well as links to useful New Zealand and international Internet sites for educators. Some collaboration is encouraged. Network users can post news messages to the message boards if they are making inquiries or sharing news. However, there are no opportunities for interaction or collaboration for teachers, where it is possible to consider and reflect on professional issues or to build an online community.

Xtra – http://www.xtra.co.nz/home/

Xtra is the New Zealand Telecom online network. The whole site is a broadly conceived service network designed to be a meeting place for all Xtra users and includes information services for a wide variety of users as well as Education. The Education section of this network is supported by the Telecom Education Foundation. The Telecom Education Foundation supports and funds some exceptional telecommunications projects for New Zealand school children which have included Expedition Ice Bound (1995), Sea Keepers (1996), Explorers and Adventurers (1997) and Wonders of the World (1998). These projects have been supported by print materials, and fax and audio conferences, as well as information and resources provided on the website. The network also advertises professional resources created for teachers by the Telecom Education Foundation. While some Internet links to education sites are listed, the network no longer supports the variety of Internet links to resources in specific curriculum areas or to professional materials that it once did. A general chat room is accessible on the Xtra site, but there is no particular provision for this within the education areas nor is there opportunity for teachers to interact and collaborate .

WekaWeb – http://hobbes.unitecnology.ac.nz/weka/home.html

WekaWeb is a nicely designed resource developed and maintained by Unitec. This network provides New Zealand teachers with resources, student activities, school pages and ways of linking with other teachers nationally and internationally. Teachers are encouraged to contribute learning materials to the site, but no discussion areas or interactive facilities are available at the professional level, providing for reflection and analysis of educational issues.

WeNET – http://www.soe.waikato.ac.nz/wenet/

The Waikato Education Network was established in 1994 and is supported and maintained by the Media Centre at the School of Education. The purpose of the network is to support regional primary and secondary schools in accessing Internet resources, and providing resources and information, and to assist the integration of the Internet into teaching and learning. Network members pay $10 per month for membership.

WeNet primarily focuses on professional development. As well as online resources, members can access a variety of workshops, resources and support services.

The New Zealand Learning Network – (NZLNet)
http://education otago.ac.nz:800/nzlnet/home.nclk

The New Zealand Learning Network was established in 1998 and is developed and maintained by the University of Otago School of Education. The purpose of this information, service and discussion network is to provide an online teacher-centred resource that will support and assist New Zealand teachers in the process of integrating the Internet in the classroom. It does this by providing links with colleagues and other professionals locally and nationally, access to Internet information and resources for classroom use, and professional background material relevant to New Zealand teachers.

Interaction online includes computer conferencing areas, online chat room, and news boards for posting of educational news. Online conferencing facilities provide opportunities for teachers to collaborate and build an online community where sharing ideas and resources is part of the network knowledge-building process and for sharing professional knowledge and expertise. The network offers opportunities to plan and share work online, to reflect on aspects of practice and share these reflections with others, and to provide teachers in smaller and more isolated communities with better access to professional support and curriculum content experts. The network also provides opportunities for subject associations or other educational organisations to utilise the discussion spaces and widen their spheres of interest beyond their membership, or for small teaching groups to utilise the spaces for online teaching.

Service facilities provide for a number of avenues of contributions from members. These include hosting of school Web pages, and teacher-organised joint collaborative projects for other classes. Teachers are encouraged to contribute ideas and teaching units to be archived online. News items of educational interest can be posted to a specific news area by participants.

Internet-based accredited courses for postgraduate qualifications or professional development are also available. The network is designed to serve an online community only.

Examples of International Professional Interactive Networks

Throughout the world there are many examples of professional interactive networks. They can be divided according to who is responsible for them, which may include government ministries or central education departments, consortia involving business interests and educational partners, faculties of education, telecommunications providers or non-traditional suppliers (Collis, 1996). In the following section a variety of networks are briefly examined according to who is responsible for the provision of services. There is no attempt to present a complete listing of all available networks; rather a small sample is given to indicate the diverse sample of philosophies, purposes and services provided.

Professional interactive networks provided by consortia of educational partners and business

There are a number of examples of professional interactive learning networks that are provided by a consortia of business and educational partners. There are four examples included below, which are widely diverse in design and composition.

* National Schools Network – http://nsn.bbn.com/ (USA)
* CampusWorld – (United Kingdom)
  http://www.campus.bt.com/CampusWorld/cwnav/cwpublic/campuswd.html
* TeachNet – IMPACT II – The teachers network. – http://www.teachnet.org/ (USA)
* TAPPED IN – http://wwww.tappedin.org/ (USA)

• National Schools Network – http://nsn.bbn.com/

First developed in late 1992, the National Schools Network (USA) has evolved into a large multi-organisational nationwide network comprising state education agencies, schools, and non-profit organisations such as community organisations, museums and science centres. Funded by the National Science Foundation, the network's purpose is to assist these groups in finding ways to organise and deliver their content to schools, make members aware of each other's work, facilitate contact between these groups and organisations, and to provide needed technical assistance to the organisations involved. Also within the network structure is room for businesses and corporations with tools and technology to offer, who have been able to test educational applications of those tools and intellectual resources in schools.

The resource is an example of a sophisticated network with a 'top-down' approach to the organisation of network activities. This is a lively and well supported resource that aims to be motivating enough for users to feel they want to contribute. It also aims to maintain educational validity, technical feasibility, and to be sustainable and scaleable (Hunter, 1997). The primary vision of the network is of a highly distributed knowledge base, where the knowledge that is built by each member organisation on its servers becomes a part of the larger community's resources. Knowledge is also built extensively through the network by collaboration which is supported by a membership database, moderated exchange desks originally conceived to be like Internet newsgroups, a monthly electronic newsletter, case studies of school and community projects, events, telementoring, and professional development workshops. A variety of tools are used for collaborative projects including Ichat, Cybersmith and CU-Seeme video conferencing, but difficulties have been encountered in managing these events as many teachers require considerable professional support in order to utilise the collaborative tools.

- **CampusWorld – (United Kingdom)**
  http://www.campus.bt.com/CampusWorld/cwnav/cwpublic/campuswd.html
  This is one of the few online resources for professionals that contain a strongly professional learning component that is not free to the users. CampusWorld is supported and maintained by British Telecom (BT), whose purpose is to provide their 2,500 user schools safe access to WWW resources, likened to a 'walled garden'. This is a broadly visioned network that includes not only materials and resources for teachers at a professional level but also materials for students. At a subscription cost to users of £10 per month, users are able to access high quality online projects and learning materials commissioned and developed exclusively for the network that are well integrated with the UK curriculum objectives. Also available are resources with closely authored Internet links. Extended expertise is brought to the network in the form of resources provided by other educational institutions and public organisations such as the National Trust. The network also supports collaborative areas such as 'talk-boards' and forums for teacher discussion, as well as contributions from participants which include areas for students to place published material. Because only a very limited amount of material is available for public access, it is difficult to evaluate how this network is actually progressing as a resource for professional learners. An opportunity to access the site during 1997 showed that some exceptional classroom resources were available, which makes this a worthwhile network to include in this chapter.

- **TeachNet – IMPACT II — The teachers network – http://www.teachnet.org/**
  Teachnet was launched in 1996 by a consortia of business and educational partners including the EXXON Education Foundation, AT&T Foundation, and the Chase Manhattan Bank among others. The purpose of this network is to provide electronic support for the work of IMPACT II – the Teacher Network which has a role in encouraging, supporting and disseminating examples of good educational ideas and practice. Where a teacher has a good idea, help is given to the teacher through a small grant to package the innovation, connect the teacher to interested colleagues and recruit all interested teachers into a continuing professional and social network. The electronic

network aids the process of connecting professionals and also provides a resource guide in which educational news items are shared and opportunities to apply for grants, contests, competitions and fellowships are provided. Teacher-created projects are provided. Online bulletin boards provide for interaction and sharing of ideas and work as well as policy-making and teacher leadership. Professional support materials published by IMPACT II can be purchased.

A philosophy of teacher reform pervades TeachNet. This network is innovative. It seeks to utilise the professional experience and intellectual capital of teachers and in remunerating teachers for their knowledge and expertise furthers a sense of professionalism, provides leadership opportunities, encourages the dissemination of good practice, provides professional growth and an alternative voice to teachers (Barker, 1998).

• TAPPED IN – http://wwww.tappedin.org/

Launched in 1995, TAPPED IN provides professional development resources for over 2300 teachers and educators across all levels and promoting best practice and relevant solutions in the teaching of science. The network is supported by SRI International and the National Science Foundation, both non-profit organisations promoting research and development with technological solutions, and is maintained by a co-operative of teacher professional development providers in the San Francisco Bay area. The purposes of the network are to provide educators with the communication tools and support needed to elicit the kinds of cognitive, collaborative and social exchanges that are characteristic of successful collaborative work and to provide for richer and more meaningful levels of interactivity than most professional interactive networks can currently offer. This is largely a communications network providing for both formal and informal collaborative activities, real-time communications and some delayed time or asynchronous activities. Real-time text communication is a feature of the network. The network 'reception desk' is attended from 9 am – 6 pm so that anyone logging into the system will find a person to greet them on arrival. A calendar of upcoming events is available on the website or teachers can get together for informal meetings. This is achieved by the provision of a number of real-time virtual meeting places for teachers, which are assembled to represent as closely as possible the kinds of shared work spaces teachers might utilise within their work environment. These virtual spaces include a whiteboard, ability to share Web page viewing (Web pages can be pushed to the user by the Moo facilitator), notepads and bulletin boards. The synchronous or real-time environment is achieved technically by the use of a multi-user virtual environment (MUVE) or MOO. Asynchronous communications are achieved by e-mail listservs. This is without doubt an interesting model for online professional interactive networks. The Moo groupware technology allows for considerable control by facilitators during the real-time events, which is significantly different from the interaction which occurs in a chat-room structure. Nevertheless, the commitment to providing a manned reception area is considerable and it will be interesting to see just how effectively this technology can ultimately support distributed learning communities with their professional learning needs.

Professional interactive networks provided by education policy-makers/ Ministries or Departments of Education

Three quite outstanding examples of networks provided by central education departments are listed below. These networks are generally service and information oriented, providing pathways to relevant curriculum materials and educational news items. Each of these networks feature some form of interactive participation.

- TEAMS – http://teams.lacoe.edu/ (Los Angeles Office of Education)
- CLN (Community Learning Network) – http://www.cln.org/cln.html (British Columbia Ministry of Education, Canada.)
- Sofweb – http://www.sofweb (Victoria State – Department of Education, Australia)

• TEAMS Distance Learning for K-12 Educators – http://teams.lacoe.edu/

TEAMS is a support network for primary school teachers which is operated as a service of the Los Angeles Office of Education with funding from the Star Schools Project and the US Department of Education. Although online network resources are designed to provide a stand-alone resource, the main purpose of this group is to support a distance learning programme for over 4,000 teachers across twenty states utilising a range of instructional technologies, including public broadcast systems, cable television, and satellite receivers. The network is one facet of the activities of this group.

The network is well designed and functional for teachers looking for easy access to information resources and for areas to discuss educational issues with colleagues. Online resources are well structured, with materials organised in completely familiar and logical ways for teachers, even to the point of providing a classroom area complete with a (graphically represented) school corridor and classroom signs to represent the different curriculum spaces. Not all areas of the curriculum are supported – only maths, science, social studies and English. Although a prime purpose of the network is to provide for professional support for teachers, there does not appear to be any strong encouragement for them to contribute units of classroom work or share those vital resources teachers are always on the lookout for. Nevertheless, this is an excellent example of an online support network.

• CLN – Community learning Network – http://www.cln.org/cln.html

This extensive learning network, initiated in 1994, was designed to provide a leadership role in assisting primary and secondary teachers in British Columbia, Canada, with the process of integrating information and communication technologies into classrooms and the curriculum. This is largely a service network supported and maintained by the Ministry of Education, and includes examples of good practice, Internet links for teachers, policy and classroom support documents and online projects for secondary students through the Global T.H.I.N.K. programme. Materials to support professional training programmes which utilise online delivery are a feature of the network and contain some excellent resources, many of which would have considerable relevance to teachers outside of British Columbia. Such resources have been specifically developed for the network and are tightly written to suit particular training methods and to aid ICT integration. Although this is largely a service network, there are limited opportunities for interaction and active participation provided by newsgroups and listservs. There is however no online opportunity for participation and the archiving of ideas, and nowhere for teachers to contribute their own resources to the network or collectively build resources for sharing. This network links in with the Canada Schools Network, which links all provincial networks across Canada.

• **Sofweb – http://www.sofweb (Victoria State – Department of Education, Australia)**

Sofweb is also an extensive professional learning network supported and maintained by the Department of Education in Victoria, Australia. This highly interactive network provides professional services, classroom and professional information and discussion forums on professional issues, and curriculum and management areas. An area called 'leading practice ideas bank' allows teachers to contribute examples of good practice or good ideas to the network.

The network information resources are extensive and entirely relevant to teachers in Victoria, including useful contacts, Victorian schools online, Internet links for teachers doubly authored under curriculum areas and also under classifications such as newspapers and museums and much more. Educational news items are a feature of the network. These are specific to teachers in Victoria and include information such as school staffing issues and teacher careers material as well as what is happening in education.

This is designed as a 'one stop shop', an ideal launch pad for teachers in Victoria. It is a well structured and well designed network with a clear focus for the very specific group who will be using this network. It is functional for teachers looking for easy access to information resources and for areas to discuss educational issues with colleagues.

Professional interactive networks provided by faculties of education

Electronic professional interactive networks provided by colleges, faculties or schools of education are usually providing network support services for courses and programmes about the Internet or that support Internet integration into curriculum. These are programmes that appear to be more frequently delivered by traditional learning methods. While they can offer some good information resources and examples of shared online resources by teachers, they tend not to promote an active community of practice by interaction or discussion online beyond the professional development group. Two examples of professional interactive learning communities offered by education institutions follow:

• Oz-teachernet – http://rite.ed.qut.edu.au/oz-teachernet/ (Australia)
• WV K-12 RuralNet – http://www.wvu.edu/~ruralnet/index.htm (USA)

• **Oz-teachernet – http://rite.ed.qut.edu.au/oz-teachernet/overview.html**
Queensland University of Technology
Oz-TeacherNet is a general purpose service network providing teachers with online support for using the Internet in curriculum and for professional development. It is supported by the Queensland University of Technology. It is described by the developers as a 'gathering place for information, resources and publications relevant to curriculum projects and the project participants as well as pointers to other projects, archives, e-mail lists for teachers, education departments and teacher professional associations'. The network supports information resources pertinent to Queensland teachers, such as lists of professional associations, Australian-wide Education Departments, and school directories. Direct teacher interaction and participation in providing ideas and discussion of issues is generated by mailing lists in a variety of curriculum and other educational areas, which are archived on the website.

• **WV K-12 RuralNet – http://www.wvu.edu/~ruralnet/index.htm**
The RuralNet Project is a special-purpose professional interactive learning network that is supported by West Virginia University and the National Science Foundation. RuralNet is a limited term, three-year project designed to promote, encourage, and assist primary and secondary teachers to use the Internet in a variety of ways that will enhance and promote problem-based and resource-based teaching and learning into science and mathematics classrooms. The online resource supports face-to-face delivery of workshops and seminars, as well as additional resources such as online courses. Online support is largely achieved by provision of links to online teaching resources created by teachers involved in the project, provision of collaborative projects which have included 'The Great RuralNet Egg Drop', 'Weather Watching' among others, and accredited online courses for Internet integration into the science curriculum.

Overall the network has the feel of being limited to those who are project members. Although the online courses have a strong participatory requirement and online computer conferencing facilities are provided, wider professional involvement beyond the project does not appear to be overly encouraged. However, there is great scope within the network for teachers to contribute learning materials, sharing teaching resources and encouraging the dissemination of good practice.

Another similar and perhaps more broadly based network is the **Minnesota Teacher Network,** which can be found at **http://www.informns.k12.mn.us/uswest/**

Non-traditional suppliers of professional interactive networks
Increasingly non-traditional suppliers are for a number of reasons establishing and monitoring a World Wide Web site for professionals. A general feature of these networks is that expected users tend to be working within a special area of interest in education. Three interesting examples of professional interactive networks are provided here:

Access Excellence – http://www.gene.com/ae/ (for Biology teachers)
teacherzone.com http://www.teacherzone.com/faq/index.html (for school principals)
ArtsEdNet – http://artsednet.getty.edu/ (for arts educators)

• Access Excellence – http://www.gene.com/ae/

Launched in 1993, Access Excellence is a special-interest network for teachers and others with an interest in teaching and learning about biology. The network has been developed by Genentech Inc (a pharmaceutical company) in conjunction with local area science teachers. The network that has grown around this association of a leading biotechnology company and teachers has the look of a professional association, providing many of the materials and possibilities for interaction and collaboration in a particular knowledge domain that would be carried out by such a group. From the beginning the purpose in developing this network was for the professional development needs of biology teachers and was designed for teachers 'to break the isolation' they experience from other science teachers and 'to be able to share their teaching ideas, strategies, activities and best practices with their colleagues'.

This is a network that is well designed and functional for teachers looking for easy access to particular information resources and for collaborative areas to discuss biology and science issues with peers. All online resources are visible from the entry-point page and materials are organised in ways that are familiar and logical for teachers. The network is rich in both useable classroom resources, e.g. lessons, and biological mysteries to solve, as well as professional background content such as issues in biology, ethics information, fact sheets, news updates information about careers and so on. Materials and resources that may use extensive online time such as biological mysteries are also formatted for off-line use, providing an excellent resource for teachers with limited access to computers in the classroom.

Opportunities are available for teachers to contribute online resources, collaborate in discussion areas, and share work. Resources written by teachers can be uploaded to the site and are placed among the impressive list of teaching resources that are available. This is a well-developed resource and an excellent example of how online networks can successfully meet the professional development needs of teachers.

• teacherzone.com – http://www.teacherzone.com/faq/index.html

teacherzone.com is a small network financed by business working in combination with several individual teachers to provide a news and information service for primary school teachers and particularly for principals to provide online support for technology integration in curriculum. Like many professional learning networks, teacherzone.com promotes greater Web use and integration of technology into classroom practice, providing relevant Internet links, news, reviews, professional background materials for teachers and principals in information technology in schools, as well as interactive chat and discussion areas. The network is maintained on a laptop computer wherever it may be and is a good example of what can be achieved with limited resources.

• ArtsEdNet – http://artsednet.getty.edu/ (for arts educators)

ArtsEdNet is a professional service and interactive network developed by the Getty Education Institute for the Arts. The purpose of this network is to support the needs of general classroom teachers using the arts in their curriculum, museum educators, arts educators, and university faculty involved in the arts. The network promotes the exchange of ideas and experiences, professional development opportunities, curriculum resources, background professional readings in arts education, and advocates support for arts education.

There is a clearly articulated purpose for this network. Information archives are tightly structured to suit the purposes and context of the specific community this network is designed to serve. The online curriculum resources, archived listserv discussions, galleries of images, contributions of students' artwork and off-line publications are structured to support and inform teachers of a particular approach to the teaching of art. There is a strongly analytic and reflective knowledge base built into the information resources provided and into the discussions and forums. ArtsEdNet is an excellent resource for art educators.

Professional interactive network services provided by commercial developers of professional and classroom resources

The purposes of these groups of professional learning networks are quite different from anything else that has been evaluated for this chapter. With the ease of access to group-wares and online conferencing softwares that allow for increased interactivity, many educational publishing and broadcasting companies are utilising the interactivity of the Web to enhance the delivery of curriculum materials providing a cohesive, systematic knowledge base on the topic. While these professional networks do not generally have a mission to reform and improve current practice, they are nevertheless providing extensive teacher support in the use of the purchaseable classroom materials that are being produced and in so doing are providing examples of good ideas and practice:

- ASCD Web – http://www.ascd.org/xchange/
- Online Learning Net – http://www.onlinelearning.net and Houghton Mifflin – http://www.eduplace.com/
- Planet Think – The Interactive Learning Network – http://www.planet-think.net/default.htm

ASCD Web – http://www.ascd.org/

ASCDWeb is the electronic outgrowth of a large international professional association committed to professional leadership and development in education, with a membership including teachers, principals, and other educators from over 100 countries. The online network provides substantial opportunities for the professional learner, offering professional development courses online, discussions of educational issues through a wide range of online forums, access to extensive offline professional publications, access to the online store, and information about ASCD conferences and affiliated groups. This is a professional interactive network with a strong existing knowledge base that is building information archives to closely suit the purpose and contexts of the learning community it supports. Both informational resources and participant contributions are provided within an online culture which is analytic and reflective in nature, and sensitively deals with the ways that teachers think and feel.

• **Online Learning Net – http://www.onlinelearning.net and Houghton Mifflin – http://www.eduplace.com/**

This is an interesting partnership between a leading textbook and curriculum materials publisher and a tertiary provider of online courses which is designed to enhance the marketability of published materials and distance courses to busy teachers and business professionals. The Online Learning Net, first developed in 1994, is a professional network maintained by UCLA in combination with other business consortia and offers online courses and certificated programs in Education, Business and Management, Computers and Information Systems, and Writing. Some 4,500 courses are offered through UCLA Extension to over 5,000 students across the USA and worldwide. Courses are asynchronous, interactive, and are limited to twenty-five students per class. That the majority of participants in online learning programmes and in the market for curriculum materials are teachers, has been a major reason for the close cooperation.

Houghton Mifflin is a publishing company specialising in textbooks, instructional technology, assessments, and other materials for the primary, secondary and tertiary education markets. The online network is known as Education Place and provides one of the most extensive sites for online curriculum and interactive resources for the classroom anywhere on the Internet. Resources are available for children, parents and teachers. There are lesson plans, online discussion forums, games and activities and Houghton Mifflin publications for purchase. It is one of the best sites available on the Internet for a comprehensive collection of interactive classroom projects.

• **Planet Think – The Interactive Learning Network-
http://www.planet-think.net/default.htm**

A growing trend in the professional learning networks area is for publishing and broadcasting companies to incorporate an interactive Internet component into the delivery of educational resources for users. Planet Think is an example of a US educational pay television company that is expanding resources for teachers and parents around its various TV channels. The features of the educational activities of this network include the 'Primary channel' for junior primary children, 'Intermediate and High School Channels' as well as the 'Journeys Channel'. Online classroom resources accompany the TV programmes. Newly developed discussion areas are available for teachers and parents that are quite specific to the resource itself. The network resources, especially the discussion areas, are quite newly established.

The purpose of the network is to provide teachers with a wide range of materials to enable them to structure purposeful and learning opportunities with real world applications for their students. With the use of PDF file formats, nicely designed instructional activities have been created for teachers to download and use with little alteration to support the published or televised materials. Many materials also have restricted access. This is support information for background materials on a topic which can be accessed by both students and teachers. Discussion groups that accompany each Channel are designed to support teachers in the use of the materials.

Conclusion

The Internet can offer teachers a range of opportunities for professional learning and advancement that can circumvent traditional professional development providers and allow individual teachers to begin to take some control of their own learning. Electronic professional interactive learning networks are providing opportunities for teachers to investigate new ways of learning, to pick and choose from a range of professional learning sources that can be accessed at any time or from any place. This chapter explores some examples of the professional learning networks that are currently available and the range of tools, communication channels and contextual supports needed to encourage the kinds of reflective, collaborative and social interactions that are characteristic of successful communities of practice. Whether such networks can indeed provide for rich and meaningful interaction and learning for teachers or whether they only peripherally reflect the concept of a professional community will require considerable research into this area.

Note

Labnet was a professional support network for science teachers in the US which began in 1993 located at **http://labnet.terc.edu/labnet/index.html**. The Labnet research team has produced a series comprehensive guides about the philosophies and practices underpinning professional interactive networks. The network has not been cited in this paper as it closed its virtual doors in February 1998 with the death of its mentor Richard Ruopp.

Appendix

Addresses of websites mentioned in this paper

Kidlink – http://www.kidlink.org/
Global Schoolhouse – http://www.gsn.org/
National Geographic Kids Network – http://www.nationalgeographic.com/
Teachers@work(NZ)- http://teachers.work.co.nz/
Schools Online Resources for Teachers (SORT) – http://www.campus.ort.org/library
Starters and Strategies(NZ) – http://www.teachingonline.org/
The Royal Society of New Zealand. – http://www.rsnz.govt.nz/
New Zealand Ministry of Education – http://www.minedu.govt.nz/

References

Collis, B. (1996a). Telecommunications for teacher support and professional development. *Computers in New Zealand Schools*, 8 (1), 31-39.

Collis, B. (1996b). *Tele-learning in a Digital World. The Future of Distance learning*: UK: International Thomson Computer Press.

Cowan, B. (1997) *Teaching the Teachers: Professional Development for Secondary Teachers in Otago and Southland.* Research Report. Education Department, University of Otago.

Di Maurio, V., & Gal, S. (1994). The use of telecommunications for reflective discourse of science teacher leaders. Available at <http://hub.terc.edu/terc/LabNet/Articles/Reflective/reflective.html>.

Di Maurio, V., & Jacobs, G. (1995a). *Filling the gaps: Active teacher participation on a telecommunications network.* (Draft.) San Francisco: AERA Annual Meeting.

Di Mauro, V., & Jacobs, G. (1995b). Collaborative electronic network building. *Journal of Computers in Math and Science Teaching.* Available at <http://hub.terc.edu/terc/LabNet/Articles/>.

Flinders, D. J. (1988). Teacher isolation and the new reform. *Journal of Curriculum and Supervision.,* 4 (1), 17-29.

Harasim, L., Hiltz, S., Teles, L., & Turoff, M. (1995). *Learning Networks – A Field Guide to Teaching and Learning Online.* Cambridge, Massachusetts: MIT Press.

Harris, D. (1997). Information and Communication Technology in the New Zealand Educational Context. Available at <http://www.minedu.govt.nz/Schools/ITinSchools/>.

Harris, D. (1996). *Schools Network Evaluation – Phase Two.* Wellington: New Zealand Council for Educational Research.

Huberman, M. (1993). Model of the independent artisan in teacher's professional relations. In J. W. Little & M. W. Mclaughlin (eds), *Teacher's Work. Individuals, Colleagues, and Contexts.* (pp. 11-50). NY: Teachers College Press.

Hunter, B. (1997). Fostering collaborative knowledge building: lessons learned fromthe National School Network testbed. In B. Collis & G. Knezek (eds), *Teaching and Learning in the Digital Age* (pp. 99-117): Texas Center for Educational Technology (TCET) and International Society Technology in Education (ISTE). Available at <http://nsn.bbn.com/dissemination/docs/Hunter_TelEd97.html>.

Kaye, A. (1992). Learning together apart. In A. Kaye (ed.), *Collaborative Learning through Computer Conferencing* (pp. 1-24). New York: Springer-Verlag.

Lechner, S. (1998). Teachers of the n-gen need reflective online communities (and so do the teachers of teachers). *Journal of Online Learning.* Available at <http://technology.msstate.edu/jol/newfirst.html>

Lieberman, A. (1995). Practices that support teacher development – transforming conceptions of professional learning. *Phi Delta Kappan,* 76 (April), 591-596.

Lieberman, A., & Grolnick, M. (1996). Networks and reform in American education. *Teachers College Record,* 98(1), 7-45.

Little, J. W. (1994). *Teachers' Professional Development in a Climate of Educational Reform.* Available at <http://www.ed.gov/pubs/EdReformStudies/SysReforms/little1.html>.

Moonen, B., & Voogt, J. (1997). Using networks to support the professional development of teachers. In B. Collis & G. Knezek (eds), *Teaching and Learning in the Digital Age* (pp. 11-24): Texas Center for Educational Technology (TCET) and International Society for Technology in Education (ISTE).

Riel, M. (1996). The Internet: a land to settle rather than an ocean to surf and a new 'place' for school reform through community development. *Telecommunications in Education News (A Special Interest Group Publication of the International Society for Technology in Education),* 7 (2), 10-15. Also available at <http://www.gsn.org/teach/articles/netasplace.html>.

Rheingold, H. (1994). A slice of my virtual community. In L. Harasim (ed.), *Global Networks* (pp. 57-80). Cambridge, Massachusets: MIT Press.

Stanley, D. (1996). From Starnet, to Edunet, to Schools Network: a history of computer mediated communications in New Zealand schools. In K. W. Lai (ed.), *Words Have Wings* (pp. 99-117). Dunedin: University of Otago Press.

Stanley, D. (1994). The Edunet Project. *Computers In New Zealand Schools,* 6 (1), 30-32

Stanley, D. (1993). The integrated educational network project. *Computers in New Zealand Schools.,* 5 (2), 17-19.

Sykes, G. (1996). Reform of and as professional development. *Phi Delta Kappan.,* 77 (March), 465-467.

Watts, G. & Castle. S. (1992). Electronic Networking and the Construction of Professional Knowledge. Phi Delta Kappan (73 (9), 684-688.

Williams, M. (1997). Professional associations: supporting teacher communities. *Computers in New Zealand Schools,* 9 (3), 42-47.

9 Internet Use in Schools: Legal and Ethical Issues

Anne Elliot

Every week we hear about the Internet and its increasing impact on our lives, at home as well as at work. Some years ago there was substantial scepticism amongst parents, teachers and school trustees about the educational benefit of Internet access in schools. However, as the Internet has won popularity and use in business as well as at home, its potential has become better understood. The Ministry of Education's *Information and Communications Technology (ICT) Strategy for Schools* (1998) is an example of the educational benefits now assumed to be associated with children's access to the Internet. In addition, information has become a desired commodity and the Internet makes an entire world of information available via computer directly into the classroom and school library.

So, what information is available on the Internet? The Internet mirrors society in that it reflects the worst and the best society has to offer, and gives children and young people access to the same information as adults. It is not a utopia of sanitised information waiting to be discovered, but a rich environment representing the breadth and variety found in real life. Some consider this richness the very asset of the Internet but the unprecedented availability of material has brought with it new issues and responsibilities for schools. These are both legal and ethical, and involve the custodial role of schools.

When schools first decide to get connected to the Internet it is not always clear exactly how the Internet will be used and for what educational purpose. Often schools have just one staff member familiar with the Internet, and deciding how its use can be integrated into classroom programmes can be a mystery. The problems teachers and schools can run into are not always apparent. This chapter will discuss some of the issues schools should be aware of and suggest ways teachers and schools can make Internet use appropriate for students. These issues include censorship, privacy and copyright issues as well as hacking, spam, e-mail bombs and other antics associated with the Internet.

Internet and Censorship Issues

Reports in the news media regularly draw to our attention the availability on the Internet of everything from the factual to the fictitious, the sensationalised and the distorted; from homework tips to pornography and 'net nasties' such as autopsy photos.

This sudden, unhindered access to material which was previously more difficult or impossible to obtain has led to much debate about censorship of the Internet, especially in the USA where the constitution guarantees freedom of speech with its First Amendment. This right is fiercely defended whenever restrictions on what can be said are attempted, no matter what is under scrutiny. The USA has also experienced a backlash to family values and *Time* magazine played right into the more traditional

(c) 1998 Time Inc. New Media.
All rights reserved.

element's hands when it published a damning article entitled 'Cyberporn' in July 1995. The news media went into a frenzy, both in the USA and abroad. The worst fears had been confirmed: the Internet was fraught with pornographic material which would threaten the moral standards of society and be harmful to children. The article was cited in the Senate by Senator Grassley (Meek, 1995) in support of Internet pornography censorship legislation, but was later found to be completely inaccurate and based on flawed research undertaken by an engineering undergraduate, Martin Rimm. However, such sensationalised media reports caused the American Congress in that same year to agree to Internet censorship through the Communications Decency Act, included in the Telecommunications Reform Bill. Within forty-eight hours of President Clinton signing the Bill, thousands of World Wide Web pages went black in protest and to show the far-reaching impact of the new law. This was the single largest demonstration from the Internet community in history. The many submissions and protests in the form of over 20,000 e-mails and telephone calls resulted in the Bill being challenged in court where it was found to be unconstitutional.

 During this time, the Blue Ribbon Campaign by Electronic Frontier Foundation <http://www.eff.org/br/>, a campaign for online freedom of expression, was launched. Many websites now carry the Blue Ribbon logo to raise awareness of online censorship and freedom of speech issues, both locally and globally.

In October 1998 in the USA, Internet censorship was again on the agenda. Congress passed a new law seen as a 'sequel' to the unconstitutional Communications Decency Act mentioned above. This new Bill, the Child Online Protection Act, would establish criminal penalties for any commercial distribution of material deemed 'harmful to minors'. Immediately, the American Civil Liberties Union, the Electronic Frontier Foundation, and the Electronic Privacy Information Center joined forces in filing a lawsuit against the Bill. They succeeded in being granted a temporary restraining order causing its enforcement to be delayed until the constitutionality could be resolved in court.

In New Zealand, the discredited 1995 *Time* magazine article caused the media to escalate its reporting on 'Net nasties', creating a sensationalised and wholly negative picture of the Internet. Concerns about upholding community standards in the face of the perceived invasion of Internet pornography surfaced and resulted in MP Trevor Rogers putting up a Private Member's Bill, the Technology and Crimes Reform Bill, to Parliament. With it, censorship of the Internet in New Zealand was to be imposed, mainly to control access to pornographic material. The Bill was going to require Internet Service Providers (ISP) to be responsible for the material their clients accessed. This unworkable scheme was later amended to leave the responsibility with families who were to be required to use a filtering software (discussed later in this chapter) on their computer in order to screen Internet material considered unsuitable for children. The Bill was hotly debated for several years but it has so far not been implemented. It is reported to be still in the files of a Parliamentary Select Committee (Watson and Shuker 1998). Its original text is available at <http://iconz.co.nz/nsnz/tcrb.html>.

In response to this threat to their industry and the bad press about the Internet, the Network Society of New Zealand was formed in late 1994 (http://iconz.co.nz/nsnz/). Since then Internet service providers have introduced their own voluntary standards and have, for example, removed access to some of the approximately 32,000 newsgroups, and also require prospective clients to sign comprehensive user agreements when joining up.

The Minister for Information Technology, Maurice Williamson, said at the launch of the Department of Internal Affairs' online safety brochure, February 1998, that

> passing new sets of laws won't stop this problem [of Internet pornography]. Censorship and policing agencies do not have the technology and probably never will have, to decipher objectionable material as it travels the net. (http://www.executive.govt.nz/minister/williamson/pp/safety/index.htm).

He suggests that governments can create global strategic alliances with other countries to enable the prosecution of those operating pornographic sites in the country where such material is hosted. This is currently not possible, leaving local enforcement authorities only able to prosecute those who attempt to make available material from within New Zealand.

In New Zealand, the Internet appears to have 'come of age'. In his article 'The Illusion of Truth', Vaughan-Nichols (1997) suggests that news reporting about the Internet is changing:

> The Internet isn't the news, it's what the Internet can and can't do that's the real news. Instead of the same old stories about online stalkers, we now see positive stories about what the Internet offers business and individual users. The Net, and news about it, has entered the mainstream. (http://www.internetworld.com/print/monthly/1997/04/truth.shtml).

This is not because the Internet has changed, but because business has discovered the opportunities offered by e-commerce, short for electronic commerce. The business community, therefore, has a vested interest in embracing the Internet. This was illustrated by the following item from the Privacy Commissioner's newsletter:

A Boston Consulting Group study estimates that an additional $US6 billion increase in internet commerce could be gained by the year 2000 if consumers' privacy concerns were addressed. (Issue No. 21, January 1998, <http://www.privacy.org.nz/privword/newpw9.html>).

Navigating the murkier waters

In spite of client 'acceptable use' agreements and the removal of some of the worst offending newsgroups by ISPs (Watson & Shuker, 1998), the Internet still gives ready access to material which it is illegal to view in New Zealand. Illegal material is defined as 'objectionable' in Section 3 of the Films, Videos and Publications Classification Act 1993 (see Appendix A) if it depicts or promotes 'sex, horror, crime, cruelty, or violence in such a manner that it is injurious to the public good'. It includes:

- exploitation of children or young persons for sexual purposes;
- sexual conduct with or upon the body of a dead person (necrophilia);
- bestiality (sex with animals);
- acts of torture;
- promotes or encourages criminal acts or acts of terrorism.

This part of the Act, then, refers not only to material of a pornographic nature, but to a wider variety of material, all of which is readily available on the Internet. It can be accidentally stumbled upon when search words unexpectedly have multiple meanings. For example, a site with the following description could accidentally be found while searching for information about 'sleep':

> This site is devoted exclusively to the 'sleepy' fan! We'll be doing stories featuring hypnosis, chloroformings, druggings, blunt trauma and more featuring some of the most beautiful girls to ever go 'sleepy.' (Link information withheld)

This quotation features on a necrophilia site, albeit a simulated one according to the previews (necrophilia is the sexual attraction for, or sexual intercourse with, dead bodies, see Section 2c of the Act mentioned earlier).

It should be noted that it is normally necessary to take out a subscription to access the more graphic material. This requires a credit card and certain personal information such as an e-mail address to be provided. A password is then e-mailed to new subscribers and only then is access available. However, most sites provide previews to entice customers and the previews alone can be very explicit. These previews frequently have a front page where it is requested that you enter only if you are over eighteen.

'Policing' the Internet

The Censorship Compliance Unit, established in 1996, is charged with ensuring the unavailability of objectionable material in New Zealand. The Unit's activities are regularly reported in the news media. The *Sunday Star-Times*, for example, carried the following news item on 1 October 1998:

> Big Porn Raid in North
> A primary school teacher ... is under investigation after the seizure of hundreds of images

of Internet child pornography. Detectives and Internal Affairs staff last week searched two ... addresses and took away computers and disks alleged to contain hundreds of images ... Two men are likely to be charged under the Films, Videos, and Publications Act (p. A4).

The Chief Executive of the Department of Internal Affairs, Roger Blakeley, said in a speech to the NZIPA Conference: Governance in Cyberspace in April 1997:

> Internal Affairs has been quite active in terms of censorship on the internet recently, and we have quite a few prosecutions pending ... a search warrant can be issued, but simply possessing these materials is not enough to allow a warrant. By entering into public chat groups such as pre & teensexpics, our inspectors are able to find people who are supplying objectionable materials. With evidence of this they are able to obtain a search warrant which allows them to get the name and address from the internet service provider. Once they have this information they are then able to obtain a search warrant to search the person's home. (http://inform.dia.govt.nz/internal_affairs/press/speech/governance.htm).

As the Internet cannot readily be intercepted at New Zealand's gateway to Cyberspace, schools are faced with the challenge of making surfing the Internet legal. In addition to this challenge, legal material is classified into restricted and unrestricted categories according to the age and maturity of the audience, as we see used in the classification of film and video:

'Objectionable'	Illegal to view or possess
Restricted	18 – retricted to persons 18 years and over 16 – restricted to persons 16 years and over R – specified restrictions
Unrestricted	G – suitable for general audience PG – parental guidance recommended for younger viewers M – suitable for mature audiences 16 years of age and over

Teachers and schools may wish to bear this classification in mind when they consider the implications of Internet access for children.

What schools can do

Schools have many options for making Internet access an acceptable and legal experience for children, but first they should become informed about the issues by becoming familiar with the Internet. Second, teachers should become acquainted with the Act and how it relates to the Internet. Only then can an informed opinion be expressed about what steps, if any, a school should take in limiting children's Internet access.

Familiarisation with the Internet for teachers could include:

• *Using search engines* Searches using any or a combination of commonly used words associated with sexual activity will provide scores of sites unsuitable for children.

However, as will be discovered, access to these sites is not straightforward. Most sites of this nature have warnings about their content before it can be accessed. An age verification process, called 'Adult Check', gives visitors an opportunity to leave if they are under eighteen. This often deters younger children and can also cause sufficient delay to be noticed by teachers. Such sites usually provide previews of what they offer but require personal information in the form of name, e-mail address and credit card details to proceed. However, the previews can themselves be explicit.

• *Newsgroups*. Sites can also be explored by checking newsgroups, for example those prefixed by alt.sex.

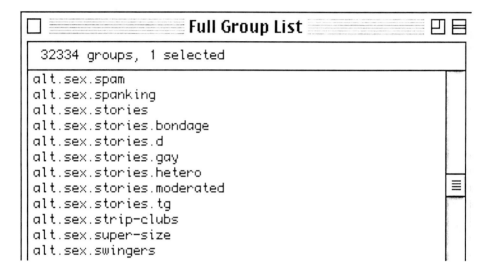

Uniform Resource Locators (URL) to sites are regularly posted in these messages and sites can be accessed by copying these into the URL line of the Internet browser.

Newsgroups often have downloadable binary files which can be converted into pictures.

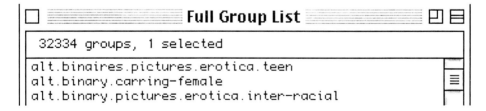

This is one of the places where objectionable material, such as paedophilia, is said to be found.

• *Chat groups* are areas of the Net where students can be propositioned, frightened by inappropriate conversations and asked to divulge personal information. It is common for chat participants to take on persona other than their own, for example by changing their age and gender, which can create a false sense of security in online conversations. Teachers should familiarise themselves with the variety of chat groups available.

Managing Internet Access with Students
Educational solutions

• *Acceptable use policies*. Student policies for Internet use are usually referred to as Acceptable Use Policies (AUP) and state what a student may and may not do with computers at school. They seek to protect students, schools and teachers from legal liability and moral responsibility, and state the standard of behaviour expected. Some schools require students, and sometimes also parents, to sign actual agreements. Others have Safe Surfing permits or computer or Internet licences which are issued when students have demonstrated certain knowledge. AUPs can also establish the consequences of inappropriate use.

There are many examples of acceptable use policies and guidelines for what they may include available on the Internet, for example at the Victorian Department of Education's website, SOFWeb. This also has links to schools' actual policies at <http:/ /www.sofweb.vic.edu.au/INTERNET/takecare.htm#codeprac>. The resources section at the end of this chapter lists other Internet sites with have examples of AUPs and discussion of what they could include.

Developing an acceptable use policy can be a useful way for a school to focus on the educational use the Internet will be put to and the issues involved in this. It may also highlight the need for a staff Internet policy which could, for example, state the purpose of Internet provision in the school, indicate staff responsibilities and rights as employees, procedures for dealing with breaches of copyright and privacy, and 'netiquette'. An example of a school policy is the Bellingham Public Schools policy developed by Jamie McKenzie. It is available at <http://www.bham.wednet.edu/ 2313inet.htm>.

• *Promotion of safe sites*. A school can promote sites which are known to be safe areas for children to access. Such sites can be bookmarked in the browser so that children can visit or search independently. There are many sites entirely devoted to making children's online experiences safe, fun and educational. They include:

Launch Site <http://www.launchsite.org/english/index.html>
This site has a number of different clubs, projects and opportunities for children to 'meet'. Children from many countries participate. The activities include posting stories and poetry online, participating in 'neverending stories' by e-mail, chats about animals, hearing a fruit bat's chatter, receiving e-mail newsletters, going on field trips via the Internet and helping to make an online calendar of festivals and celebrations.

SafeKids.com <http://www.safekid.com/links.html> and
SafeTeen.com <http://www.safeteens.com/teenlinks.html>
Has search engines available to children and numerous links to safe sites, for

example to Museums and Art sites, newspapers and magazines, zoos and animals, encyclopedias and sports.

Yahooligans.com <http://www.yahooligans.com>

A huge indexed site with categories focusing on children's interests, for example 'Around the World', 'Science and Oddities' and 'Art Soup' as well as online activities, sports trivia, homework helpers, current events, and games. An entire database of sites can be searched and there are links to clubs and what is 'cool'.

The KIDS Report <http://scout.cs.wisc.edu/scout/KIDS/index.html>

Produced twice monthly by students from one of the twelve participating classrooms, it is located at the Department of Computer Sciences at the University of Wisconsin-Madison. The students involved are responsible for all aspects of the report, including its title and the site evaluation criteria.

The National Museum of Natural History's Virtual Dinosaur Tour <http://www.nmnh.si.edu/paleo/dino/tourfram.htm>

Located at the Smithsonian Institute, it is guaranteed to fascinate children – and adults! It features excellent photographs of dinosaurs, interactive anatomy lessons, time lines, a 'Top 10 Misconceptions about Dinosaurs' page, and lets children examine and compare animals in the time periods in which they lived.

Internet access, supervision and placement of computers

First, Internet access requires a password to be entered at the beginning of a session and teachers can ensure this is not given out to children. A password can also be changed frequently to keep it confidential.

Second, children could be permitted to use the Internet only when an adult is present or access could be made available only in, for example, the library where supervision may be available.

Third, computers can be placed in such a way that teachers can see the monitor from most places in a classroom or library. They will then know what sites children are accessing. Similarly, when students know that teachers can see the monitor, they will go only where it is appropriate to go.

Technical solutions
'Surfing' off-line

Schools can save Web pages as well as whole sites for children to use off-line. Individual text pages can be saved by using the 'Save as' command and then choose to save as 'Source'. Such pages can later be opened in a browser but the graphics will be missing. Where graphics and links to other pages are involved, special software that works along side the browser can be used to save the entire page, graphics and all, as well as any linking pages. WebBuddy and WebWhacker are examples of such software.

WebBuddy is available for both Macintosh and WindowsPC. A 15-day trial version can be downloaded from DataViz at <http://www.dataviz.com/webbuddy>. This site it also has a list of ideas for using WebBuddy, submitted via e-mail by teachers (http://www.dataviz.com/Products/WebBuddy/eduwaystousewb.html). WebBuddy is particularly useful in that it has a floating palate where a simple click on a button will begin the downloading process while the user carries on visiting other sites. It also allows bookmarking of sites and the sorting of files into useful topics.

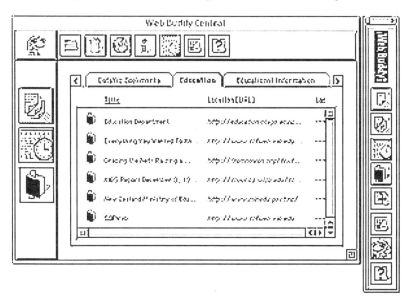

WebWhacker is also available for both Macintosh and WindowsPC. An evaluation copy can be downloaded from Blue Squirrel at <http://www.bluesquirrel.com/download.all.html>. The evaluation copy expires after fifteen 'whacks' or thirty days after installation, whichever occurs first.

Using this kind of software for off-line browsing brings with it other advantages, for example in savings on online costs, speedy access to downloaded pages, ability to involve parents and others in locating and downloading information needed for a particular topic, and being able to transport pages and sites by disk to a classroom computer not connected to the Internet.

Using RASCi-rated sites

Teachers can check if a site they would like to use is rated by the Recreational Software Advisory Council of the Internet (RASCi).

RASCi is an independent, non-profitmaking organisation which rates sites against set levels of sex, nudity, violence, offensive language (vulgar or hate-motivated). If a site is found to fall within certain standards, the RASCi logo can be displayed on the site's pages. An example of a New Zealand educational site which displays the RASCi

logo is the *CWA Education* website (http://www.cwa.co.nz/eduweb/index.html). The RASCi standards can be checked at <http://www.rsac.org/homepage.asp>.

Filtering software

Filtering software, sometimes called blocking software, are programs which interact with other programs installed on a computer and which can be set to monitor, screen and block access to any material whether the computer is connected to the Internet or not. There are currently four major filter programs available, listed here in alphabetical order: CyberPatrol, CYBERSitter, NetNanny and SurfWatch. Each works slightly differently but all have a number of possible settings which can be chosen to suit the environment in which the computer is used. The settings are controlled by password access and can be set to screen information on websites, in newsgroups, chat channels, etc. The filtering software works in the background and is 'invisible' to the user.

The settings include:
* preventing personal information, e.g. address and phone numbers, from being given out on the Internet;
* masking inappropriate words, phrases or language;
* preventing certain specified sites from being accessed;
* keeping an event log which records all sites visited by the user.

The software companies provide updates to the list of 'bad' sites at various intervals and these can be downloaded from the companies' Internet sites.

The filter software mentioned can be found at the following Internet addresses:

Cyber Patrol

http://www.cyberpatrol.com/
Available for Windows 3.1, 95, 98, NT and Macintosh.
7-day demo of full program possible.

CyberPatrol can be downloaded in New Zealand from Xtra's site at <http://www.xtra.co.nz/software/cyber_patrol/> and is provided free to schools who subscribe to Xtra. An online tour featuring screen images and explanations of how this filter software works is also available.

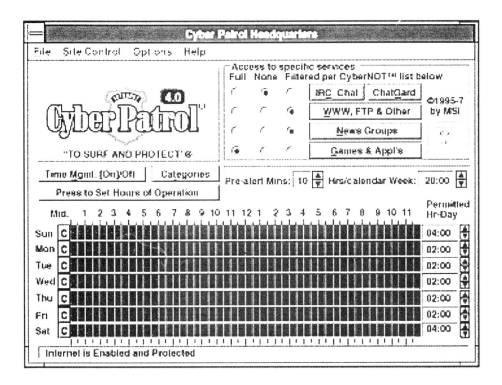

CYBERSitter

http://www.cybersitter.com
Available for Windows 98, 95 or NT 4.0
Trial version available.

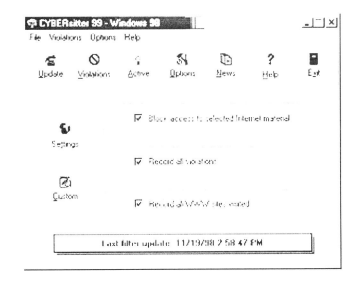

NetNanny

http://www.netnanny.com/
Available for Windows 95, 98 and 3.X.
Also a 30-day trial version.

SurfWatch

http://www.surfwatch.net/home/
Available for Windows95, 98 and Macintosh.
Also 15-day trial version.

Internet Explorer

The Web browser Internet Explorer, version 3.0 and 4.0, has a built-in filter. It uses a ratings standard based on the RASCi rating system mentioned earlier. This filter can limit access to certain types of content such as nudity, sex, or violence, and can be set to allow access to a degree that is acceptable.

The filter is controlled by password access and this can also be turned completely off. This knowledge would have benefited an unsuspecting parent who for a long time was unable to work out why the browser appeared to have its own ideas of where he was to go!

RASCi provides extensive online instructions for setting Internet Explorer up to work with the RASCi rating system. Go to <http://www.rsac.org/homepage.asp> and click on the link 'Parents – How to use RASCi'.

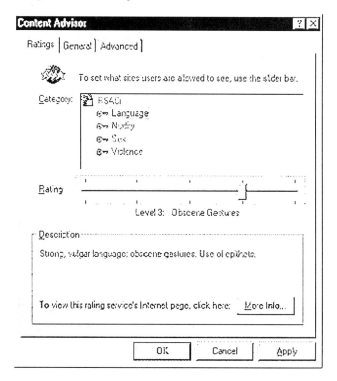

Problems with filter software

Although filters can be set to block objectionable material, they cannot guarantee prevention of access to all. Furthermore, they will also block access to sites which contain no objectionable material. For example, in blocking the word 'sex' they will also block the home page of the punk rock band, the Sex Pistols as well as information about 'Sussex'. Filter software blocking access to specific sites needs to updated every month.

A number of sites provide an overview and assessment of filtering software, for example,

Cyberangels <http://www.cyberangels.org/filtering.html>

Explains in some detail what filtering software is and how it works.

**A Parent's Guide to the Internet
<http://www.familyguidebook.com/updates.html#filter>**

Provides a very comprehensive summary of the pros and cons of filtering software.

**The Internet Filter Assessment Project (TIFAP)
<http://www.bluehighways.com/tifap/**

This was undertaken by a group of American librarians during 1997. A summary of their findings can be found at this site.

A slide show, 'Shining A Light on Filters in Libraries' by one of the librarian researchers, Karen G. Schneider, provides a librarian's overview of tools for managing Internet access. It can be viewed online or downloaded for later use with the PowerPoint97 viewer, also able to be accessed from that page. It provides excellent suggestions of, for example, user education and positioning of computers.
<http://www.bluehighways.com/filters/filtersc/>

**Filtering the Internet in K-12 Schools and Libraries
<http://www.libertynet.org/lion/filtering.html>**

This site contains numerous references to information about filtering issues.

Copyright and Plagiarism

All creative work is automatically protected by copyright. A copyright notice is not required and merely publishing a work without a notice is not a relinquishment of copyright. The owner of a copyright has the exclusive right to their work but can grant other people permission to use it. Copyright can be relinquished by a statement to that effect and otherwise expires fifty years after the creator's death.

Previously, information available to children in schools was mainly in the form of printed material. More recently, CD-ROM encyclopedias have been a ready source of information for children. Such electronic media has made it easy to 'cut-and-paste' information and claim it as one's own. The Internet adds to this possibility.

The New Zealand Copyright Act 1994 prevents literary and artistic work being made 'available to the public by means of an electronic retrieval system' (for example a computer) by being copied when such a work is copyright (Section 10 of the Act, see <http://www.knowledge-basket.co.nz/gpprint/acts/public/text/1994/se/143se10.html>).

An example of a website where children may find material that interests them but where the copyright is clearly indicated is the National Institute of Water and Atmospheric Research (NIWA) at <http://www.rses.vuw.ac.nz/meteorology/metgroup.html>:

Copyright © 1998 NIWA. All rights reserved.
Please address all queries and comments to WebMaster@niwa.cri.nz.

Children are permitted to quote from the site in their work at school, but they cannot use the material in any publicly published work, for example on a website, without permission. This could be sought by e-mailing the Web master. Permission is often granted, specifying the limit of the permitted use. This kind of action can serve as a model of appropriate behaviour. The danger for schools is that if unauthorised use of copyright material finds its way online, or is otherwise made available to the public, schools may face legal action.

What schools can do

Teachers can talk to children about the notion of intellectual property rights and show them how to respect the ideas of others by acknowledging the use of other people's work in their references.

Classroom Connect (http://www.classroom.com/resource/citingnetresources.asp) and SOFTWeb (http://www.sofweb.vic.edu.au/internet/research.htm#reference) have information about doing research on the Internet and referencing electronic resources.

Jamie McKenzie, an American education technology consultant mentioned earlier, has written an amusing article about how 'to cut off the virulent new strain of plagiarism before it becomes an academic plague' (McKenzie 1998a). His suggestions include changing the tasks children have often been set, namely 'go and find out something about ...', to setting tasks where students become producers rather than mere consumers.

Copyright on software

Section 80 of the Copyright 1994 Act relates to copyright of computer programs (see Appendix B). The Act states that it is illegal to make a copy of a program except as a back-up for one's personal use.

The Internet offers many computer programs which schools may find useful. Such programs are called shareware programs and are not paid for at the time of downloading but are offered for a try-out period. Users are then expected to pay a small fee to continue using that software. Registration and payment can usually be done via e-mail using a credit card. An 'activation key' is then returned. As upgrades become available, registered users can download these free.

Example of a shareware splash screen encouraging users to registered the software.

License Agreement
This Software, GIFConverter, is licensed, not sold, and may only be used under the terms outlined below.

License
Under this license, you may use the Software under the following conditions:

• This software may be used for up to 15 days for evaluation purposes. After 15 days, you must either (1) register this Software under the terms noted in the Shareware Notification, or (2) destroy all copies of this Software in your possession.

• You may use the Software on a single CPU at one time that is not used as a server. Each CPU on which GIFConverter is installed requires a separate copy and license. You may use a single copy of GIFConverter on up to two computers provided that such use is not concurrent and is by the same user.

• The Software may not be placed on a served disk unless enough licenses have been purchased to cover the number of CPUs connected to the served disk.

• You may make one copy of the Software for backup purposes.

Example of shareware licence agreement. Note: CPU (Central Processing Unit) refers to a computer's hard disk.

What schools can do

Schools using shareware should ensure that all software, including shareware, is used according to the licence agreements. This entails paying the required fee at the end of the trial period. Having a reminder pop up on the computer screen at every start-up does not send the right signal to children. Modelling appropriate software use reinforces the legal and ethical position taken by a school in other computer use.

Netiquette

In spite of the short life of the Internet, an Internet etiquette of appropriate online behaviour has developed. Referred to as 'netiquette', it indicates conventions used to convey to others the equivalent to Earthly etiquette, such as politely nodding and smiling. It also refers to showing good manners by behaving in responsible ways which are not annoying or inconvenient to others, for example not WRITING IN CAPITAL LETTERS which indicates shouting.

Resources about netiquette can be found at Clear Net (http://www.clear.net.nz/ netscape/services/netiquette.html) as well as Life on the Internet (http:// www.screen.com/start/guide/netiquette.html) which is particularly useful and includes 'core' rules, commonly used e-mail acronyms and smileys, and business netiquette.

Schools Publishing on the Web

The aim of the Privacy Act 1993 is to promote and protect individual privacy and is designed to give people a measure of control over personal information held by agencies. Many schools are now not only accessing information on the Internet but increasingly also publishing their own information there. At the beginning of 1999 more than 300 schools in New Zealand have a website.

When schools publish on the Internet, issues of safety as well as privacy arise. Personal information about either students or staff, such as addresses and telephone numbers, should never be published.

Where schools publish students' work, only the children's first names should be used. SOFWeb, mentioned earlier, recommends that schools get signed permission from parents before publishing children's work online, and they have provided a model release form at <http://www.sofweb.vic.edu.au/internet/model.htm>.

When using photographs of teachers or children, choose those where identification of individuals is not possible. In addition, obtain permission from the children's parents before using photographs that feature their children.

Websites usually include an e-mail link to the 'Web master', the person with responsibility for the site and its pages. Where children are permitted to include e-mail links, that mail should always be to a school mailbox and all such mail should be checked first by teachers.

What schools can do

Schools should check what children plan to publish on the Internet before it is put there. Recently, an American student published a website about what he thought of a particular teacher which was not complimentary. Although this page was created and put on the Internet from home, it demonstrates the ease with which what should be private can be broadcast to the world.

Some schools require an adult to proofread students' work before it can be published on the Internet. These requirements can be included in an AUP detailing the steps involved in putting work online.

Hacking and Other Internet Antics

More unusual uses of the Internet include hacking, spamming and mail bombs, planting viruses and sending hate mail. These are all ways of using the Internet that serve no educational purpose and are either illegal or very bad manners. Most ISPs require clients, including schools, to sign user agreements which protect other users as well as networks from these behaviours. Possible computer-related misconduct is, therefore, a real issue for schools.

An example of such misconduct is hacking. An exhaustive definition of hacker is found at Dictionary.com (http://www.dictionary.com) and includes the following:

- A person who enjoys exploring the details of programmable systems and how to stretch their capabilities.
- One who programs enthusiastically (even obsessively) or who enjoys programming rather than just theorising about programming.
- One who enjoys the intellectual challenge of creatively overcoming or circumventing limitations.
- (Deprecated) A malicious meddler who tries to discover sensitive information by poking around.
- The term 'hacker' also tends to connote membership in the global community defined by the Net. It also implies that the person described is seen to subscribe to some version of the hacker ethic.
(http://www.dictionary.com/cgi-bin/dict.pl?db=*&term=hacker)

'Hacker ethic' varies. Some hackers engage in activities which are both illegal and unethical, for example gaining free Internet access at other people's expense. Others promote the free flow of information and consider their illegal actions ethical because they 'help' people. In October 1998, for example, an American hacker gained access to the website of China's state-controlled Chinese Society for Human Rights. Chinese authorities regularly prevent access to the websites of foreign human rights groups and China's 'cyberpolice' used a firewall to filter out websites critical of Chinese policies and those which document human rights abuses by the communist government. (*Wired News*, 26 October 1998). This was too much for one hacker who hacked into the site, added links to Amnesty International as well as an American site for human rights in China, and then sent the following message to the Chinese system operator:

Dear WebMaster/Admin – YOUR SECURITY IS A TOTAL JOKE! We had rooted your box in an all time record. It took us less than 2 minutes! Don't play with fire when you know you are going to get burned!!

(http://www.antionline.com/archives/pages/chinarights/)

In November 1998, a 15-year-old New Zealand hacker entered and deleted 4,500 websites hosted on a New Zealand ISP's server in California. Many customers had back-up copies which allowed their sites to be reinstated but others were not so fortunate. One commercial customer who lost his pages and had no back-up is reported to have said that 'you learn from your mistakes' (*Otago Daily Times*, 28.11.98). This is exactly the point many hackers hope to demonstrate: security and the management of information is often more insecure than people realise. However, most Internet users would not agree that hacking is ethical or 'helpful'.

Having young, 'venturesome' computer users in a school can cause not only frustration, but cost time and money and have legal implications for a school and its staff.

What schools can do

An AUP will usually cover the consequences of behaving in ways which are illegal, annoying or infringing on the rights of others (see Appendix C for a sample AUP). Most of the more extreme antics students may engage in can be avoided if schools are aware of the potential problems, protect themselves with user agreements which spell out what acceptable computer use is, create a school computer culture which is respectful of the rights of others, provide interesting and engaging learning experiences and believe students to be capable of making the right choices.

Conclusion

While running with the Internet and deciding on the parameters for its use may seem a daunting task, the Internet has a great deal to offer children. This potential can be realised when a school is clear on its educational goals in offering Internet access, when teachers are supported in coming to grips with this new medium, and when they have the opportunity to learn how to use the Internet to itsbest advantage in their classroom programmes.

Some Legal and Ethical Resources for Schools

Acts of Parliament

All Acts, including the Films, Videos and Publications Act 1993, Privacy Act 1993, and the Copyright Act 1994, are available online at
<http://www.knowledge-basket.co.nz/gpprint/acts/actlists.html>

Censorship Office

This is part of the Department of Internal Affairs website
<http://censorship.dia.govt.nz>
The Guide to Online Safety pamphlet is also available here.
Censorship Office, Department of Internal Affairs, PO Box 805, Wellington. Tel: 04-495 5317 or 04-495 5303. Fax: 04-494 0656. E-mail: censorship@dia.govt.nz

Office of the NZ Privacy Commissioner

<http://www.privacy.org.nz/top.html>

From Now On – The Educational Technology Journal
- an excellent on-line journal about IT and IT use in schools <http://fromnowon.org>

Internet Online Summit: Focus on Children
<http://www.kidsonline.org/>
<http://www.research.att.com/projects/tech4kids/>

School Internet acceptable use policies
Oatland School, Australia, Information Technology – Acceptable Use Policy
<http://mag-nify.educ.monash.edu.au/news/97News/oatacc.htm>
<http://mag-nify.educ.monash.edu.au/news/97News/oatacpol.htm>

Legal and Educational Analysis
By Nancy Willard, an American IT Consultant
<http://www.erehwon.com/k12aup/legal_analysis.html>

School of Education, University of Waikato
<http://www.tmc.waikato.ac.nz/wenet/members/information/aup.html>

Eight Australian examples of AUPs from Technology in Schools
Programme at University of Melbourne.
<http://www.unimelb.edu.au/tisp/wwebs/policies/index.html>

Loreto College Policy
Another Australian policy example.
<http://www.uq.net.au/~zzloreto/use.htm>

Internet Licence Training
A 1996 site by Garry O'Shanassy & Jeff Lovegrove of Doveton North Primary School, Melbourne. Eighteen different steps towards safe and appropriate Internet use culminating in a Full Licence.
<http://mag-nify.educ.monash.edu.au/FrontPageSchools/lindex.htm>

Oatlands Primary School Protocol
An Australian Primary school's draft Internet Protocol.
<http://mag-nify.educ.monash.edu.au/news/97News/oatpar.htm>

Student Declaration
<http://mag-nify.educ.monash.edu.au/news/97News/oatstud.htm>

The Virtual Science and Technology Centre
A Project of the Classrooms of the Future Team, Department of Education, Victoria, Australia.
<http://mag-nify.educ.monash.edu.au/news/97News/internet.htm>

Riverdale School

An American school's Acceptable Use policy for Computer Networks.
<http://www.riverdale.k12.or.us/policy/policy.html>

AUPs from various North American schools

<http://www.aupaction.com/auponweb.html>

Computer jargon dictionary. Definitions for terms such as 'hacker' and 'spam'

<http://www.netmeg.net/jargon/terms.html>

Spam

Sources of information (and opinions) about spam include:
<http://www.research.att.com/!lorrie/pubs/spam/>
An article, *Spam!*, is available there in html or pdf format
<http://spam.abuse.net/>
<http://www.cauce.org/>
<http://www.junke-mail.org/>

Appendix A

Films, Videos and Publications Classification Act 1993, Sections 2 and 3
Section 2 defines 'publication' as follows:
(a) Any film, book, sound recording, picture, newspaper, photograph, photographic negative, photographic plate, or photographic slide;
(b) Any print or writing;
(c) Any paper or other thing –
  (i)   That has printed or impressed upon it, or otherwise shown upon it, any word, statement, sign, or
        representation; or
  (ii) On which is recorded or stored any information that, by the use of any computer or other electronic device, is capable of being reproduced or shown as any word, statement, sign, or representation.'

Section 3 is reproduced in abbreviated form:
(1) A publication is objectionable if it describes, depicts, expresses, or otherwise deals with matters such as sex, horror, crime, cruelty, or violence in such a manner that it is likely to be injurious to the public good.
(2) A publication is objectionable if it promotes
  (a) The exploitation of children or young persons for sexual purposes;
  (b) The use of violence or coercion to compel any person to participate in, or submit to, sexual conduct;
  (c) Sexual conduct with or upon the body of a dead person;
  (d) The use of urine or excrement in association with degrading or dehumanising conduct or sexual conduct;
  (e) Bestiality;
  (f) Acts of torture or the infliction of extreme violence or extreme cruelty.
(3) A publication is objectionable to the degree to which it
  (a) Describes, depicts

(i)   Acts of torture, the infliction of serious physical harm, or acts of significant cruelty;

(ii) Sexual violence or sexual coercion, or violence or coercion in association with sexual conduct;

(iii) Other sexual or physical conduct of a degrading or dehumanising or demeaning nature;

(iv) Sexual conduct with or by children, or young persons;

(v) Physical conduct in which sexual satisfaction is derived from inflicting or suffering cruelty or pain;

(b) Exploits the nudity of children, or young persons;

(c) Degrades or dehumanises or demeans any person;

(d) Promotes or encourages criminal acts or acts of terrorism;

(e) Represents (whether directly or by implication) that members of any particular class of the public are inherently inferior to other members of the public by reason of any characteristic of members of that class, being a characteristic that is a prohibited ground of discrimination specified in section 21 (1) of the Human Rights Act 1993.

Available at <http://www.iconz.co.nz/n̈snz/fvpca93.html>

Appendix B
Copyright Act 1994, Section 80

Copyright Act 1994 143

Commenced: 1 January 1995

III: Acts Permitted in relation to Copyright Works Computer Programs, Sound Recordings, and Films 80. Back-up copy of computer program

80. Back-up copy of computer program –

(1) Subject to subsection (3) of this section, copyright in a computer program is not infringed by the making of a copy of the computer program if –

  (a) The copy is made by or on behalf of the lawful user of the copy of the program (in this section referred to as the "original copy") from which the first-mentioned copy is made; and

  (b) The copy is made solely for the purpose of being used by or on behalf of the lawful user of the original copy –

    (i) Instead of the original copy in order to preserve the original copy for use if the copy is lost, destroyed, or rendered unusable; or

    (ii) If the original copy is lost, destroyed, or rendered unusable.

(2) If the original copy is lost, destroyed, or rendered unusable, the copy made pursuant to subsection (1) of this section shall be deemed for the purposes of this section to be the original copy.

(3) Subsection (1) of this section does not apply to the making of a copy of a computer program—

  (a) From an infringing copy of the computer program; or

  (b) Contrary to an express direction by or on behalf of the owner of the copyright in the computer program given to the lawful user of the original copy not later than the time when the lawful user of the original copy acquired that original copy.

Available at GP Print <http://www.knowledge-basket.co.nz/gpprint/acts/public/text/1994/se/143se80.html>

Appendix C
Sample Acceptable Use Policies for Computer Use and Internet Access
(provided by Pakuranga College <http://www.pakuranga.school.nz/IRC/policies.html>)

1) *The use of school computers must support education and research* that is consistent with the Learning Outcomes of the curriculum. Use of another organisation's network or computing resources must comply with the rules appropriate for that network. Transmission of any material in violation of any NZ regulation is prohibited. This includes, but is not limited to: copyrighted material, threatening or obscene material or material protected by trade secret.

2) *Network Etiquette* – Users are expected to abide by the generally accepted rules of network etiquette.

These include (but are not limited to) the following:

- Be polite. Do not get abusive in your messages to others.
- Use appropriate language. Do not swear or use any other inappropriate language. Illegal activities are strictly forbidden.
- Do not reveal personal addresses, phone numbers, or passwords of students, teachers or other staff of the school, including yourself.
- Note that e-mail is not guaranteed to be private. People who operate the system do have access to all mail. Messages relating to or in support of illegal activities may be reported to the authorities.
- Do not use the network in such a way that you would disrupt the use of the network by other users.
- All communications and information accessible via the network should be assumed to be copyright.
- Hate mail, harassment, discriminatory remarks and other antisocial behaviours are prohibited on the network. Therefore, any messages should not contain profanity, obscene comments, sexually explicit material, and expressions of bigotry or hate.
- Student subscriptions to electronic mailing lists are not allowed without permission.

3) *This school specifically denies any responsibility* for the accuracy or quality of information obtained through the Internet. Information (including text, graphics, video, etc.) from Internet sources used in student assignments and reports should be cited in the same way as are references to printed materials.

4) *Security* – Security on any computer system is a high priority, especially when the system involves many users. If you feel you can identify a security problem on the Internet, you must notify a teacher or the principal. Do not demonstrate the problem to other users. Users shall not intentionally seek information on, obtain copies of, or modify files, other data, or passwords belonging to other users, or misrepresent other users on the network. Attempts to gain unauthorised access to system programs or computer equipment will result in cancellation of user privileges. Any user identified as a security risk or having a history of problems with other computer systems may be denied access to school computers.

5) *Vandalism* – Vandalism will result in cancellation of privileges as well as other sanctions cited in the School Rules. Vandalism hardware, data of another user, Internet, or any of the other networks that are connected to the Internet backbone. This includes, but is not limited to, the uploading or creation of computer viruses.

6) *Inappropriate Use* – The teachers and Principal will deem what is inappropriate use. The Principal may request the suspension or termination of computer use of any user who violates these acceptable use practices.

Internet Access Acceptable Use Agreement

To be read and signed by both student and parent/s/guardian.

Student   _____

I understand and will abide by the above Acceptable Use Agreement. I further understand that any violation of the regulations above is unethical and may constitute a criminal offence. Should I commit any violation, my access privileges may be revoked, school disciplinary action may be taken, and/or appropriate legal action may be instituted.

Student name _____

Student signature _____

Date _____

Parent or Guardian

As the parent or guardian of this student, I have read the Acceptable Use Agreement. I understand that this access is designed for educational purposes. I recognise it is impossible for the school to restrict access to all controversial material, and I will not hold the school (or any of its personnel) responsible for material acquired on the network. I hereby give my permission to allow Internet access for my child.

Parent or Guardian name _____

Parent or Guardian signature _____

Date _____

References

ABC News Online, December 2, 1998. *Students using Internet to cheat*. Available at <http://www.yahoo.com.au/headlines/021298/abcnews/912574782-2215452684.html>.

Blakeley, R. (1997). *Governance in Cyberspace*. Speech to the NZIPA, April 1997. Available at <http://inform.dia.govt.nz/internal_affairs/press/speech/governance.htm>.

Department of Internal Affairs (1998). *Guide to Online Safety* (brochure). Available from Censorship Office, PO Box 805, Wellington. Tel: 04-495 5317 0r 04-495 5303, Fax: 04-494 0656 E-mail: censorship@dia.govt.nz Website Address: http://www.dia.govt.nz/.

Fiery, D. (1994). *Secrets of a Super Hacker*. Port Townsend, WA: Loompanics Unlimited.

Jeannine Clark. (1998). *The Evolution of 'Nerd Discipline'*. Education Week on the Web, June 24. Available at <http://www.edweek.org/htbin/fastweb?getdoc+view4+ew1998+1124+15+wAAA+>.

Kallman, E. & Grillo, E. (1996). *Ethical Decision Making and Information Technology: An Introduction with Cases*. 2nd ed. New York: McGraw-Hill.

McKenzie, J. (1998a). From now on. *Educational Technology Journal*, Vol 7, No 8, May. Available at <http://fromnowon.org/may98/cov98may.html>.

McKenzie, J. (1998b). Grazing the Net: raising a generation of free range students. *Phi Delta Kappan*, September 1998. Available at <http://fromnowon.org/text/grazing.html>.

McLoughlin, D. (1997). Net nasties: safety in cyberspace? *North & South*, Feb. 1997.

Meeks, B. (1995). *Muckracker: How Time Failed*. Hotwired. Available at <http://www.hotwired.com/special/pornscare/brock.html>.

Ministry of Education. (1998). *Information and Communications Technology (ICT) Strategy for Schools*. Ministry of Education: Wellington. Available at <http://www.minedu.govt.nz/Schools/ICT/htmls/strat/strateng.html>.

Otago Daily Times, 28 November 1998. Websites being restored. Available at <http://www.odt.co.nz/20Nov1998/startup-800.html>, choose 'General News'.

Privacy Commissioner's *Newsletter*, Issue No. 21, January 1998. Available at <http://www.privacy.org.nz/privword/newpw9.html>.

Sunday Star-Times. (1998). Big porn raid in north. 1 October. A4.

Time magazine (Domestic). (1995). Porn on the Internet. July 3. Volume 146, No. 1. Available at http://cgi.pathfinder.com/time/magazine/archive/toc/950703.toc.html.

Vaughan-Nichols, S.J. (1997). *The Illusion of Truth*. Available at <http://www.internetworld.com/print/monthly/1997/04/truth.shtml>.

Watson, C. and Shuker, R. (1998). *In the Public Good? Censorship in New Zealand* (Chapter 9). Palmerston North: Dunmore Press.

Williamson, M. (1998). *Safety On-Line*. Launch of on-line safety brochure, Pakuranga College, 17 February 1998. Available at <http://www.executive.govt.nz/minister/williamson/pp/safety/index.htm>.

Wired News, 26 October 1998. China: we're only human. Available at <http://www.wired.com/news/news/politics/story/15831.html>.

Wired News, 27 October 1998. Crackers attack China on rights. Available at <http://www.wired.com/news/news/politics/story/15857.html>.

10 Women's Participation in Online Communities of Professional Practice

Linda Selby and Ken Ryba

Gender issues have long been part of the debate about equitable use of computers and technology in education. Within the literature both in New Zealand and overseas, much attention has been given to the study of inequities and strategies which promote the equitable use of computers and other forms of technology in the classroom (Sutton, 1991; Sutton, 1992). More recently, research has indicated that the 'equitable use problem' needs to be addressed through an analysis of the computer cultures and ecological factors that may result in the under-representation of particular groups, particularly women (Selby, 1995). With the advent of the communications era, there is cause for concern that the participation of women on the Internet and other online communication systems is significantly lower than the participation rates of men (Spender, 1995). It is especially worrying that many teachers, the majority of whom are women, are not yet using computer-mediated communications (CMC) for their professional development, personal use and for curriculum-based classroom activities. Given that CMC will continue to become a significant channel for teaching activities, information and professional development, it is essential to understand the conditions that are required to achieve the highest and most effective levels of participation for women and indeed for all professionals.

With the above factors in mind, the purpose of this chapter is to rethink the traditional arguments about women's participation in information technology-related activities and to propose an alternative framework for achieving greater and more meaningful participation of women who are using CMC for personal or professional use. Increasing attention over the past few years has been given to the study of online communications as a context for professional development, peer support, collaborative consultation, and interactive teaching and learning methods. As systems have become less technical, more robust, and more user-friendly there has been a movement away from the technical considerations of the technology towards a focus on the more social and ecological factors that affect the community of practitioners who are using the technology as a means of communicating with one another. A significant part of this investigation has been the study of the creation of communities and how newcomers and tentative participants can be guided into the process of networking with other professionals (Ryba, Selby and Kruger, 1998).

Despite the earlier concerns by Spender (1995) and other researchers, there is growing evidence that technology need not isolate and disenfranchise women. To the contrary, there are a number of innovative new online communities within education that are led by women practitioners who are significantly influencing the direction and development of CMC for teacher use. In Australia, Michelle Williams, Lindy McKeown and the Queensland Society for Information Technology in Education have taken a leading role in promoting the use of CMC for teacher professional development (http://owl.qut.edu.au/qsite/qsite.html). In New Zealand, Nola Campbell at the University of Waikato's School of Education uses CMC to deliver pre-service teacher education. A feature of these new developments is that they focus on the creation of professional communities and the formation of online professional relationships. Unlike earlier communication systems which tended to be dominated by men with technical interests, more recent developments in information and communication technology have provided a context for creating networks where teachers can relate to one another in ways that promote their personal and professional growth.

CMC is ideally suited to provide a context for the development of professional communities that fully include women and men. The view advanced here is that computers and related technologies have been instrumental in creating socially interactive and reflective learning communities. Within these communities, there is active transmission of knowledge between individuals as they are guided from the periphery through to the centre of the learning enterprise. Principles for the creation of equitable and sustainable learning communities apply equally to traditional education settings and to online communities. In this chapter, we advance the 'communities of practice' framework conceptualised by Lave and Wenger (1991) as a means of understanding what needs to be done if women are going to be active participants in online communications.

In order to facilitate a rethinking of gender issues as this relates to the creation of effective computer-mediated communities, this chapter is organised as follows. First, it provides an analysis of research concerning women's under-representation in the field of IT generally. Second, it presents the results of a study of computer learning cultures and the factors that exclude women from participating equally. Third, it provides a discussion on the 'communities of practice' framework. Fourth, it presents two exemplary CMC projects to illustrate the formation of professional communities. Finally, this chapter provides a set of guidelines for the creation of CMC networks in which women are more likely to be active participants.

Analysis of Research concerning Women's Under-representation in IT-Related Fields

Much concern has been expressed by people in industry and in education about the low numbers of women participating in higher education computer science and information technology courses, and the subsequent impact that this has on the industry and society as a whole. Over the last twenty years, women have made significant gains in entry to tertiary level areas of study that have been traditionally regarded as male domains. Equal numbers of women and men are choosing to study in the fields of law, medicine, dentistry, architecture and veterinary science (Selby, 1998). However, the fields of computer science and information technology, like the field of engineering, remain almost entirely the domain of men. While the gender gap in academic achievement and participation in areas such as mathematics has reduced in recent years, in other areas, like computer science, the involvement of women has actually declined (Lovegrove & Hall, 1987; Shashaani, 1994). Women often account for less than one-third of enrolments at tertiary level in computer-related courses and the participation rates continue to decline as the level of education increases (Camp, 1997, Selby, 1998). Moreover, proportionally more women than men drop out, fail courses, or choose to major in another subject. Generally female participation in tertiary level study is on the rise. In contrast, however, the participation of women in computer courses continues to decline. If computer competence were just another occupational or leisure-time preference, the gender gap may not matter. However, this is not the case. There is nothing optional any longer about computing involvement for any of us. The fact is that computers and the electronic media are here to stay and competence and understanding by both women and men is essential.

A recent British study of women and computing concluded that the last decade has produced some slight change in the relative interest and involvement of females as opposed to males, but that it has been in a very limited form (Durnell & Thomson, 1997). Gender equality, in the sense of there being equal numbers of female and male students and no differences between them in terms of attitudes towards and knowledge about the use of computers, appears to be a long way off. Analysis of data from the USA also confirms the findings in New Zealand, Australia and Britain showing that the decline in female participation is positively associated with the levels of educational qualification. These data show a steady decline in female participation in computer science from a high of 50 per cent at school level, through to 36 per cent at undergraduate level and 13 per cent in doctoral programmes (O'Rourke, 1992, Camp, 1997). Such a result is not surprising, but it has a serious implication in that women are virtually eliminated before reaching the highest levels of qualification and achievement. The effect of this decline becomes immediately apparent when one observes the predominance of male computer professionals who hold senior academic, industrial and corporate positions.

Despite the growing amount of data concerning the under-representation of women in computer science and information technology, there has been a lack of research to examine reasons for gender inequity. More recently, however, attention in New Zealand and overseas has been directed at studying social and cultural factors that may account for the exclusion of women from these areas of study.

A Study of Computer Learning Cultures and the Factors that exclude Women from Participating Equally

A recent study, carried out in New Zealand by the authors of this chapter, attempted to discover why women are choosing to study in other fields of endeavour, despite the many initiatives that have been taken by governments and institutions to address this issue. The main aim of this project was to identify day-to-day practices and teaching methods that help to create gender-inclusive learning opportunities, and to provide recommendations on policies and practices that will lead to more women studying in the field. The research documented the views of participants from two tertiary institutions, one a Polytechnic and the other a University (Selby, 1998). Participants were students and staff from both institutions, associated professional women working at the institutions, and secondary school students from a local high school. A range of qualitative and quantitative data analyses and information-gathering procedures were used. This included: (a) a computer experience questionnaire; (b) student interviews, (c) e-mail discussion groups, (d) staff questionnaires, (e) staff interviews, (f) lab environment information, (g) interviews with associated professional women, (h) documentation of high school girls' perceptions of computing as a career; and, (i) course enrolment data from both institutions and other New Zealand universities.

The results showed some important factors that deter women (and some men) from choosing and continuing with study in the computing field. These were:

1. Lack of knowledge about career prospects

High school girls surveyed during the research project showed very little knowledge of what a career in computing involved. They viewed computing as a technical machine-oriented, solitary occupation where people worked all day behind a desk. They had very little understanding of the interesting aspects of a computing career, job opportunities, salaries and conditions or the diverse range of ways that computers are used in the work place. Students in tertiary level first and second-year study were also not as well informed as they could be about the opportunities and the actual work undertaken by professionals working in the industry.

2. The image of computer science and information technology

Interviews and questionnaire data confirmed that there was an 'image problem' in the area. This image takes two forms: (a) 'nerdy' and 'geeky' antisocial image; and, (b) the inaccurate image of computing as a machine-oriented, mathematical, solitary occupation. These images are widespread within society and they discourage women (and men) from wanting to be part of the industry. Young women do not identify with being a 'nerd' – it is essentially a male identity – neither do they want to study in a field where they perceive the young men to be 'nerds'!

3. A perceived lack of confidence amongst women students despite their obvious abilities and successes

Results from questionnaire data and interviews showed that although women are achieving as well if not better than their male counterparts, they do not perceive themselves as competent, confident professionals in the same way that males do. Caution needs to be exercised, however, in coming to the conclusion that women are somehow lacking in confidence. To the contrary, there is evidence from this and other research that males in computer classes tend to over-estimate and over-rate their abilities (Ryba & Selby, 1995). It is possible that women are more realistic in their self-evaluations of skill level. The issue of perceived confidence is an important one because it accounts for the fact that many women students choose not to continue in a particular area like programming. Instead, they switch to another area like multimedia, or they drop out, or they choose to major in another subject.

4. Lack of women lecturers

The small numbers of women in academic positions at universities and polytechnics, particularly in the higher ranks, means that women who might be interested in further study have few role models. The university department that took part in this research project had one woman lecturer and twenty-five male lecturers. The polytechnic department had three women lecturers and eighteen male lecturers. It is interesting to note that in a study of computer science and computer engineering departments in the USA in 1990, one-third of the faculties had no women lecturers at all (Gries & Marsh, D. 1990).

5. Computing as a male domain

One of the findings of this research which is consistent with many other similar studies is that the world of computing is male dominated. This means that many women do not see a place for themselves within the 'masculine culture'. Male role models are very prevalent in every aspect of the industry. At home it is more likely to be the father who is computer literate and who spends time on the computer (Clarke & Chambers, 1989, Clarke, 1990). At school, computers are more likely to be introduced to the students by male members of the teaching staff, and the computer sales people and maintenance experts visiting the school will also most likely be men. When purchasing a computer, the salespeople and 'expert' demonstrators are invariably men, even in educational settings like primary schools where the majority of teachers are female.

6. The learning environment is often not informed by contemporary learning theory

Many concerns were raised by the respondents in the research about issues of teaching and learning. Particular comment was made about the senior students who act as tutorial assistants/demonstrators who often were not trained for the job or aware enough of their role as a teaching assistant. Comments were also made about the need for lecturers to employ innovative new teaching strategies and to be knowledgeable about the conditions required for optimum learning to take place. The students were critical of the way in which programming was taught, for example, and lecturers and managers reported on the difficulties in finding staff who could teach programming well. Poor teaching of programming meant that many students dropped out or chose another option. Students found it most helpful when lecturers related learning to real-life experiences and when lecturers could explain how the study being undertaken was relevant to the workplace environment.

7. The importance of prior computing experience

Research from the USA, UK, Australia, Canada and New Zealand consistently reports that at every level males have more prior experience with computers than females (Klawe & Leveson, 1996). Likewise, this study identified prior computing experience as a factor affecting success in tertiary level study. Males as a group more frequently enroll in secondary school computing classes and often elect to take more advanced computing courses (Sanders, 1995; Schofield, 1995). Males are also much more inclined to participate in self-initiated activities involving computers, including joining computer clubs, playing computer games, undertaking unguided exploration with computers and using computers at home (Taylor & Mounfield, 1994; Shashaani, 1994; Howell, 1993). Not only are boys more likely to have access to a computer at home, but they are likely to receive more encouragement from their parents to use it than girls will. Reported use by boys of the family computer is higher than use by girls, and the use of a friend's computer, which could be a measure of the extent to which teenagers use computing as a social activity, has consistently been reported as higher than girls (Durnell & Thomson, 1997). This is further compounded by the fact that the level of skill of students moving on to tertiary level study is very uneven in New Zealand, because there is not a coherent prescription of study at high school level, and there is a wide variety of experience amongst mature students.

In summary, research on factors affecting participation rates indicates that there are several complex issues accounting for women's under-representation. However, this study has revealed that many of the issues raised by participants were related to the culture of computing and the climate of acceptance which can seriously affect women's confidence and decision to participate. For this reason, it is argued here that more attention needs to be directed at the process of building communities where all members can experience a sense of belonging and progressively move to become centrally located within the community. The communities of practice framework, which is outlined in the following section, provides a means of understanding some of the social and cultural issues that need to be confronted in order to create viable communities both face-to-face and through online communications.

Communities of Practice Framework: An Apprenticeship Model for Learning

Lave (1988) argues that learning takes place as a function of the activity, context and culture in which it occurs. Learning is thus 'situated' within a definite social, cultural and domain context. This contrasts with many classroom-based learning activities in which knowledge is abstract and presented out of context. According to Lave, social interaction is a critical component of situated learning. Learners become involved in a 'community of practice' which embodies certain beliefs and behaviours to be acquired. At the outset, learners begin their journey at the periphery of this community and progress toward the centre as they become more active and engaged within the culture. They move from being a newcomer or novice toward assuming the role of expert or old-timer. Moreover, situated learning is usually not directly taught but is unintentional, occurring through active participation in working together with other people. These ideas are what Lave and Wenger (1991) refer to as the process of 'legitimate peripheral participation'. Such participation is socially interactive in nature, involving an apprenticeship and guided participation between 'newcomers' and 'old-timers' within the educational community.

Anthropological studies of apprenticeships offer alternative ways of understanding the social processes of learning. Lave (1988) draws upon experiences in other cultures – craft apprenticeship in West Africa and apprenticeship among Yucatec Mayan midwives – to illustrate that there are highly valued forms of knowledgeable skill in these cultures for which learning is structured in apprentice-like forms. The perspective of 'guided participation' in communities of practice is highly relevant also to many others forms of socially organised activity that have become accepted within Western society as sites of learning. For example, sports and leisure communities guide their newcomers through a scaffolded sequence of learning steps so that they progress from the periphery to the centre of the activity. Likewise, service and community organisations convey a set of values and beliefs which guide their practices and influence induction of the novice into the expert membership of the organisation.

Peer communities of practice, as described by Lave and Wenger (1991), provide a context for teachers, both newcomers and old-timers, to share the knowledge and practices of the profession and together to gain knowledge and skills in using the Internet and other applications to create better conditions for learning. Adopting the community of practice framework as a basis for creating online communities, Williams (1995a) explains how computer-mediated communications has been used in Queensland to connect teachers and create highly interactive professional communities. Built from a 'teachers-first' perspective, the Queensland projects operate from the belief that the best form of support for teachers is their colleagues. In a community of peers, teachers find help with the everyday problems of using technology in educational environments, as well as a chance to talk about what it means to be an educator in an increasingly complex world. The experiences of teachers in the telecommunications programmes suggest that there is potential for professional communities of teachers to be sustained through this new medium. This has important implications for all professionals, especially women who have not yet had an opportunity to use computer-mediated communications as a context for peer consultation and professional development.

Working within the community of practice framework, Rogoff (1990) advances the concept of the interactive apprenticeship model to explain how the processes of teaching and learning take place within a professional community. Rogoff outlines some common principles of interactive learning that apply to all students whether this be within face-to-face or online learning environments:

1. Apprentices are active in gathering information and practising skills as they participate in skilled activities. Students are active in observing and participating in the activities of those around them and they are motivated to participate more centrally. This is evident, for example, in the Queensland projects where peer support and professional consultation was available online to the teacher in her classroom.
2. The learning of apprentices is structured by practices developed by their predecessors to meet socially valued goals. This aspect of apprenticeship provides a parallel with the importance of recognising that the student's cognitive development involves learning to use the intellectual tools of their society (literacy, mnemonic devices, conventions for representing space, etc.) to handle culturally valued activities and goals. One of the main features of online communities is that they have the potential to be global in nature and much more inclusive than traditional communities which tend to be geographically and socially isolated.
3. Apprentices are assisted in their learning by communication and involvement with

more skilled people – experts and more advanced apprentices – who help determine how to divide the activity into sub-goals that the novice can begin to handle, as well as to provide pointers on how to handle the tools and skills required. This is especially evident with online communities, where peer support is readily available so that novices can be guided through problem-solving and skill development at any level.

4. Apprentices seldom learn alone. In addition to being involved with more skilled practitioners, apprentices often learn in a community of fellow novices (such as fellow graduate students, classmates, siblings). Interaction with and observation of other novices provides challenge, support, collaborative puzzling out of problems, and models of learning in progress. The sense of isolation that classroom teachers can feel within traditional school settings is removed through the creation of socially interactive and reflective online communities. Friendships and collegial partnerships develop despite geographical and professional boundaries.

The main tenets of Lave and Wenger's (1991) communities of practice framework are reflected in the following exemplary projects involving the use of CMC in educational settings.

Two Exemplary CMC Projects

The managers of primary and secondary schools have spent a lot of time, energy and money connecting buildings and computer networks to the Internet. Mostly, the intention has been to use the Internet as a means of providing access for students to the World Wide Web and enable them to download information. However, one of the most promising developments in computer education appears to be those projects that use the Internet as a means of connecting teachers to other teachers. A good example of this is The Global Infolinks (GIL) Project. This series of professional development initiatives throughout Queensland, Australia, has adopted a 'teachers-first' approach in supporting teachers in their use of communications technology. The GIL Project recognised that the best form of support for teachers is their colleagues. In a community of peers, teachers were able to find help for the everyday problems of using technology in educational environments, and were also able to discuss together what it means to be an educator in an increasingly complex world (Williams, 1995b). The key facilitators of this project were women who were committed to the ideas of empowering teachers and students, creating new learning opportunities and establishing and maintaining effective online communities.

This kind of peer support community, which is based on Lave and Wenger's (1991) concept of communities of practice, provides the ideal environment for women to participate in computer-mediated communications, because it provides ways for participants to begin their involvement on the periphery of the community and, as their confidence and skills build, enables them to move toward the centre of the activities. There is an opportunity for newcomers and old-timers to share the knowledge and practices of the profession and together to share experiences and solve problems about issues that are common to them. Many teachers are isolated from colleagues and learning opportunities by the fact that they spend most of their time working alone in classrooms, and many women are not confident users of communications technology. In this Australian example, the Ipswich City Council provided all schools in the area with access to the Internet at the beginning of 1995. The key principles on which the educational module of GIL was founded include:

- making decisions that focused on teachers and how teachers would be involved in the project;
- encouraging teachers to become immersed in the Internet for themselves so they would experience first hand the impact of this new technology on their lives before they would have to think about the use of this technology in classrooms;
- reducing barriers to teacher participation by providing hardware and Internet access for teachers;
- building a community of participating teachers who had a say in shaping the directions of the GIL Project.

This project enabled teachers to be linked to others who shared their interests and frustrations in various aspects of the use of CMC in schools. The teachers were also involved in interesting and meaningful projects with their students, like 'Koala Chris' the travel buddy, and 'Book Rap', which provided a forum online for students to share their interests in books with other students from around the world who were participating in the project. Teachers had an opportunity to take a leadership role by hosting information sessions and sharing experiences with their community of peers.

Through this online collaboration, teachers began to understand how they could move from the periphery of activities to becoming skilled contributors to the professional development of their colleagues in the projects (Blackwell & McKeown, 1994). The analysis of data collected from interviews and e-mail from teachers participating in professional development programmes online showed that there was a definite shift in the teachers' definitions of the Internet and their attitudes toward it. This was evident in the following comment from a special education teacher:

'After only a few short weeks, I know that my Internet access has changed my perceptions of teaching and learning. The biggest change is my understanding that the Internet provides an opportunity for closer links between professionals. I hope that connections between special education teachers and other teachers in this way will result in truly inclusive curriculum and practices. I am convinced that students and teachers alike will benefit from the real-life information exchanges and communication experiences unique to email and the Internet.' (Williams and KcKeown, 1996)

The GIL project has all the hallmarks of a successful venture in which women could become successful users of the technology. Participants were kindly and gently introduced to the technology. They were able to gain support in the technical aspects of getting connected, and they could feel safe and supported in an environment of colleagues who had all at some stage started at the periphery and moved toward the centre of activities. Another key factor was that this all took place in a meaningful and practical context (e.g. online projects for students that added value to students' learning experiences, e-mail discussion groups that meant instant answers were available for problems teachers were experiencing).

The key principles for the creation of sustainable learning communities apply equally to traditional educational settings and to online communities. Contemporary thinking about 'communities of practice' represent an interesting and dynamic way of understanding how to develop more inclusive learning environments.

Global Network for School Psychologists: A Massey University Perspective

The Educational Psychology Training Programme at Massey University in Auckland, New Zealand, has created an online community of professional practice for students and staff who are located throughout the country. In collaboration with the Computer-Mediated Consultation Project at Northeastern University, Boston, participants used the Global Network for School Psychologists for peer support and professional consultation (Kruger, 1998). Graduate students and intern psychologists communicate through class discussions, e-mail, newsgroups, online private chat, community forums and student and supervisor consultations. A feature of the Global Network is that it gives graduate students access to colleagues and professional mentors in New Zealand and overseas. Through networking with others, students find the answers they need from the online community to assist with their academic work and in developing an identity for themselves as professionals. One of the key factors in creating a sustainable community of practice online is that students have an opportunity to meet face-to-face at an early stage in the project. This was accomplished through the provision of several on-campus courses when students and staff met face-to-face several times during the year.

The Global Network is able to provide students with personal support as well as professional consultation. For example, when one capable student announced on the network that she was considering dropping out of the program, messages of support arrived from peers throughout New Zealand. Following consultation with her classmates and many supportive messages, she decided to stay with it. Students frequently exchanged ideas about projects and helped one another with brainstorming and problem solving. This was evident in the sharing of ideas about work folios which all students were required to assemble as part of the programme assessment. Likewise, when there were questions about assignments, a delegation of students would ask the university lecturer to provide further information and clarification of requirements online. Students frequently give each other advice about assessments and interventions for casework. This ready access to peer consultation cannot only help to remove the barriers of living and studying in isolation, but it also provides a range of expertise so that participants can move from the periphery to the centre of the learning enterprise. This was evident with one woman newcomer who contributed so actively to the online community that within a very short space of time she was asked by the CMC Project Director to become the facilitator of the 'students and supervisors' neighbourhood.

The online community of practice became at times a vibrant and active meeting place in which 'newcomers' could be assisted in their learning by communication and involvement with more skilled 'old-timers'. Frequently students began their involvement in the online community by reading messages, not making contributions, and staying on the periphery of the community. However, as they gained sufficient confidence to put something down on line, they began the move from novice to expert. The role of a community of practice should be to nurture newcomers so that they gain confidence to move from legitimate peripheral participation to a central place in the community. Conceived in this way, the online community is not about transmission of knowledge but about the creation of a professional knowledge network.

Guidelines for the Creation of CMC Networks in which Women are more likely to be Active Participants

Analysis of projects such as those described here indicate that there are some important underlying principles for the creation of viable and sustainable communities of practice that can enhance cognition and assist with the development of identity and knowledgeable skills, particularly for women, but also for others. These are as follows:

1. *Active participation.* Teachers and students need to be active in observing and gathering information and practising skills as they engage in their upskilling activities. By being active learners, newcomers will gain confidence and motivation to move from the periphery to the centre of the community activities. This is especially important for women who have not previously been involved in online communications. For example, newcomers to an online community may at first simply observe and read messages, but there needs to be a way to encourage their active involvement. One way this can be facilitated is by using a buddy system so that teachers and students have a point of contact within the community.

2. *Guided learning opportunities.* Participants in a viable online community need to be provided with guided opportunities to enable them to become immersed in the community. Learning could be assisted by communication and involvement with more skilled people who help determine the activities, level of participation and vision regarding the organisation of skills. Effectively this means placing individuals within their zone of proximal development so that their learning can be enhanced through scaffolding provided by a more capable peer (Ryba, Selby and Kruger, 1998). A feature of online communities is that they provide access to a range of potential colleagues who can socially interact and guide the newcomer's learning process in a way that is not usually possible within traditional classroom settings.

3. *Intellectual collective.* Learning through collaboration with others can have synergistic effects, such that the intelligence of the entire community can be raised through shared cognitions and problem-solving. The community forms what could be called an 'intellectual collective', in which there is the potential for all members to advance in their knowledge and skills. The joint online problem-solving activities provide opportunities for newcomers and old-timers alike to further their understanding and professional development.

4. *Identity construction.* Socialisation into a community of practice not only promotes skill development but also assists in the formation of self identity as a capable practitioner. This inclusive process of generating identities is both a result of and motivation for participation (Lave, 1990). This is evident with students and teachers alike, who develop a sense of personal effectiveness through computer-based learning and online projects.

5. *Inclusive communities.* Projects such as those presented here stress the formation of social partnerships in which participants can build bridges from their current understanding to reach new understandings through processes inherent in the communications. The peer communities are inclusive in nature in that they are comprised of a full range of women and men across subject areas and educational levels. The emphasis on 'building communities' and the valuing of diversity amongst members is an aspect that is especially likely to involve women who can take an active role in online activities.

The communities of practice framework provides an encompassing theory for understanding how it is possible to create learning communities that are inclusive in nature, comprising women and men who are a combination of newcomers and experts. The use of the apprenticeship metaphor is relevant for explaining how guided participation enables newcomers, especially women, to develop in their learning through communication and involvement with relatively more skilled old-timers. This guided participation within a community of practice is more likely to ensure the fuller participation of women than any other model we have seen. It is proposed that if this theoretical framework were to form the basis of CMC projects for teaching activities, exchanging information and professional development, then women would very quickly become active participants in online communities.

References

Blackwell, A. & McKeown, L. (1994). Pack your bags with travel buddies. *Classroom,* December. pp 10-13.

Camp, T. (1997). The incredible shrinking pipeline. *Communications of the ACM,* October 40 (10). 103-110.

Camp, T. (1997). Monitoring the status of women in computer science. Available at <http://cs.ua.edu/camp/women.html>.

Clarke, V. (1990). Sex differences in computing participation: Concerns, extent, reasons and strategies. *Australian Journal of Education,* 34, (1), 52-66.

Clarke, V. & Chambers, S. (1989). Gender-based factors in computing enrolments and achievement: Evidence for a study of tertiary students. *Journal of Educational Computing Research,* 5 (4), 409-429.

Durnell, A. & Thomson, K. (1997). Gender and computing: A decade of change? *Computers & Education,* 28 (1), 1-9.

Gries, D. & Marsh, D. (1990). *Women and minorities in science and engineering. Taulbee Survey Report.* National Science Foundation, 10-16.

Howell, K. (1993). The experience of women in undergraduate computer science: What does the research say? *SIGCSE Bulletin.* 25 (2). 1-8.

Klawe, M., & Leveson, N. (1996). Women and computing: Where are we now? *Communications of the ACM.* 38, 29-35.

Kruger, L. (1998). Global Network for School Psychologists. Available at <http://www.dac.neu.edu/cp/consult>.

Lave, J. (1988). *Cognition In Practice: Mind, Mathematics and Culture in Everyday Life.* Cambridge UK: Cambridge University Press.

Lave, J. & Wenger, E. (1991). *Situated Learning: Legitimate Peripheral Participation.* Cambridge: Cambridge University Press.

Lovegrove, G. & Hall, W. (1987). Where have all the girls gone? *University Computing.* 207-210.

O'Rourke, J. (1992). In the CRA Distributed Mentor Project: Mentoring undergraduate females in computer science and computer engineering. Unpublished manuscript, Smith College.

Rogoff, B. (1990). *Apprenticeship in Thinking: Cognitive Development in Social Context.* New York: Oxford University Press, 1990.

Ryba, K., & Selby, L.(1995). *A Study of Tertiary Level Information Technology Courses: How Gender Inclusive is the Curriculum?* (contract research report). Wellington: Ministry of Education, Research and Statistics Division.

Ryba, K., Selby, L. and Kruger, L. (1998). Creating communities of practice in special education. Forthcoming in *Special Services in the Schools* (SSS).

Sanders, J. (1995). Girls and Technology: Villain wanted. In S. Rosser (ed.) *Teaching the Majority* (pp. 147-159). Columbia: Teachers College Press.

Schofield, J. (1995). *Computers and Classroom Culture.* New York: Cambridge University Press.

Selby, L. (1998). *A Critical Analysis of Factors affecting the Participation of Women in Tertiary Level Computer Computer Science and Information Technology Courses.* Unpublished doctoral dissertation. Perth: Curtin University.

Selby, L. (1995). Where have all the young women in computing gone? *Computers in New Zealand Schools,* 7 (3), 25-27.

Shashaani, L. (1994). Gender differences in computer experience and its influence on computer attitudes. *Journal of Educational Computing Research*, 11 (4), 347-367.

Spender, D. (1995). *Nattering on the Net: Women, Power and Cyberspace.* Melbourne: Spinifex Press.

Sutton, R. (1991). Equity and computers in schools: a decade of research. *Review of Educational Research,* 61 (4), 473-503.

Sutton, R. (1992). Equity and school computer use: The nature of the problem, the research evidence, and classroom strategies which promote equity. In K.W. Lai (ed.). *Learning with Computers: Issues and Applications in New Zealand* (pp. 67-85). Palmerston North: Dunmore Press.

Taylor, H. & Mounfield, L. (1994). Exploration of the relationship between prior computing experience and gender on success in college computer science. *Journal of Educational Computing Research,* 11 (4), 291-306.

Williams, M. (1995a). *Learning without whose limits? Negotiating an online community for Australian teachers.* Proceedings of the Australian Computers in Education Conference. Perth: ECAWA, volume 2, 125-136.

Williams, M . (1995b). *Case study of a professional development program conducted in distance education mode using communications technologies.* Masters dissertation. Deakin University.

Williams, M.. & McKeown, L. (1996). *Professional development model for implementing Internet projects at your school.* QSITE Conference CD. Brisbane: QSITE.

Notes on Contributors

Mark Brown is a Lecturer in the Department of Learning and Teaching, Massey University. He specialises in linking contemporary cognitive theory to the use of new educational technologies in school. His teaching and research interests also include innovations in teaching and educational change. The teacher's role as an educational leader is also a major theme of Mark's work.
E-mail: M.E.Brown@massey.ac.nz

Nola Campbell is a Senior Lecturer in Information and Communication Technology at the School of Education, University of Waikato. Many years of involvement in the use of computers in education have included a special interest in special education, telecommunications and online learning. Currently Nola is responsible for the professional development of staff teaching online and the development of the online teaching and learning programme at the School of Education.
E-mail: ncampbell@waikato.ac.nz

Anne Elliot is an experienced primary teacher and has been involved in using computers in schools for the last eight years. She has published in *Computers in New Zealand Schools* and is currently designing Internet-based learning websites. She is an avid Internet user and has an interest in the legal and ethical implications of Internet use in schools.
E-mail: anne.elliot@stonebow.otago.ac.nz

Dr Kwok-Wing Lai is a Senior Lecturer in the School of Education, University of Otago. Wing has a keen interest in studying and researching into the use of computer-mediated communication in the school curriculum, as well as on teacher development. He is currently the editor of *Computers in New Zealand Schools.* He has previously edited two books (one of which he co-edited with Dr Bruce McMillan) and co-authored a third one on the use of information and communication technology in the learning process.
E-mail: wing.lai@stonebow.otago.ac.nz

Elizabeth Probert is a trained Teacher Librarian at Pakuranga College in Auckland. Pakuranga College is a large co-ed high school with over 1900 students. She also teaches English, is past Chair of the Auckland School Library Association, a KidsConnect volunteer (AASL), presents workshops in the cross-curricular use of the Internet and co-ordinates the school website which won the New Zealand Multiserve Education Project Award for School Websites in 1998.
E-mail: eprobert@iconz.co.nz

Dr Ken Ryba is the co-ordinator of the Educational Psychology Training Programme at Massey University, Auckland. His research interests include learning process assessment, cognitive education, and the use of computer-mediated communications for peer support and professional consultation.
E-mail: K.A.Ryba@massey.ac.nz

Dr Linda Selby is Head of the Centre for Information Studies at the Auckland College of Education. Her research interests include teacher professional development in the area of information processing and IT, women in computing, and the development of communities of practice both online and face-to-face.
E-mail: l.selby@aceak.ac.nz

Ann Trewern is currently Senior Teaching Fellow in the School of Education, University of Otago, where she works with the web-based post-graduate and professional development programmes in information technology in education. She has spent some two decades teaching primary children and has experience in school management and board of trustees work. More recently she has worked as a facilitator with Ministry of Education and Telecom information technology contracts, and also in museum education. Ann is particularly interested in educational research work involving computer-mediated communications in the classroom and has a research interest in the role of the Internet in enhancing professional learning and for curriculum delivery.
E-mail: ann.trewern@stonebow.otago.ac.nz

Anne Wright is the Principal of a small, rural (26 pupils) sole-charge school in Central Otago. She has been at Patearoa School for the past eight years. Prior to that she was Deputy Principal at a small Catholic school in Dunedin for 10 years. For several years now she has been the IT resource person for the Maniototo cluster. Anne has always had a strong affiliation with small schools, particularly rural schools. She also had a strong interest in computing and first introduced computers into her classroom in 1982. She has been undertaking a PhD study in Education part-time through Otago University for a number of years.
E-mail: kawright@xtra.co.nz

Index

Are you a current subscriber?

Computers in New Zealand Schools is this country's only magazine for teachers, from pre-school to tertiary level, who use computers in the classroom. The journal publishes articles, many by teachers themselves, on all aspects of computers in education, with the emphasis on practical applications. It features new products, software and book reviews, reports on educational research, fresh ideas and critical comment. Computers in New Zealand Schools is published three times a year, in March, July and November.

❏ Yes, please send me a years's subscription to *Computers in New Zealand Schools*

New Zealand subscribers: $35.00 a year incl. GST.
Overseas subscribers: $60.00 NZ (airmail)

Enclosed is my cheque for $....................................
payable to University of Otago (includes GST and p&p)

Or charge my credit card   ❏ Visa   ❏ Mastercard   ❏ American Express

Card No [ ][ ][ ][ ][ ][ ][ ][ ][ ][ ][ ][ ][ ][ ][ ][ ]

Expiry date [ ][ ] month/year

Signature..

Name..

School..

Address..

....

Post to: University of Otago Press, PO Box 56, Dunedin, New Zealand.
Phone (03) 479 8807, Fax (03) 479 8385   GST No. 11-163-831